MW01033817

Go Nation

ASIA: LOCAL STUDIES/GLOBAL THEMES

Jeffrey N. Wasserstrom, Kären Wigen, and Hue-Tam Ho Tai, Editors

1. *Bicycle Citizens: The Political World of the Japanese Housewife,* by Robin M. LeBlanc

2. *The Nanjing Massacre in History and Historiography,* edited by Joshua A. Fogel

3. *The Country of Memory: Remaking the Past in Late Socialist Vietnam,* by Hue-Tam Ho Tai

4. *Chinese Femininities/Chinese Masculinities: A Reader,* edited by Susan Brownell and Jeffrey N. Wasserstrom

5. *Chinese Visions of Family and State, 1915–1953,* by Susan L. Glosser

6. *An Artistic Exile: A Life of Feng Zikai (1898–1975),* by Geremie R. Barmé

7. *Mapping Early Modern Japan: Space, Place, and Culture in the Tokugawa Period, 1603–1868,* by Marcia Yonemoto

8. *Republican Beijing: The City and Its Histories,* by Madeleine Yue Dong

9. *Hygienic Modernity: Meanings of Health and Disease in Treaty-Port China,* by Ruth Rogaski

10. *Marrow of the Nation: A History of Sport and Physical Culture in Republican China,* by Andrew D. Morris

11. *Vicarious Language: Gender and Linguistic Modernity in Japan,* by Miyako Inoue

Go Nation

CHINESE MASCULINITIES AND THE GAME
OF WEIQI IN CHINA

Marc L. Moskowitz

UNIVERSITY OF CALIFORNIA PRESS

BERKELEY   LOS ANGELES   LONDON

University of California Press, one of the most distinguished university presses in the United States, enriches lives around the world by advancing scholarship in the humanities, social sciences, and natural sciences. Its activities are supported by the UC Press Foundation and by philanthropic contributions from individuals and institutions. For more information, visit www.ucpress.edu.

University of California Press
Berkeley and Los Angeles, California

University of California Press, Ltd.
London, England

© 2013 by The Regents of the University of California

Parts of an earlier draft of chapter 2 were published as a chapter in the edited volume "Weiqi Legends, Then and Now: Cultural Paradigms in the Game of Go." In *Asian Popular Culture: New, Hybrid, and Alternate Media,* eds. John Lent and Lorna Fitzsimmons, 1–16. New York: Lexington Books (2013).

Library of Congress Cataloging-in-Publication Data

Moskowitz, Marc L.
    Go nation : Chinese masculinities and the game of weiqi in China / Marc L. Moskowitz.
        pages cm.
    Includes bibliographical references and index.
    ISBN 978-0-520-27631-4 (cloth : alk. paper) --
    ISBN 978-0-520-27632-1 (pbk. : alk. paper)
    1. Go (Game)—China.   2. Games—Social aspects—China.   I. Title.
    GV1459.35.C6M67 2013
    794'.4—dc23   2013006681

In keeping with a commitment to support environmentally responsible and sustainable printing practices, UC Press has printed this book on Natures Natural, a fiber that contains 30% post-consumer waste and meets the minimum requirements of ANSI/NISO z39.48-1992 (R 1997) (*Permanence of Paper*).

For Arey Huei-jyun Jhang

CONTENTS

LIST OF ILLUSTRATIONS

PREFACE

Glenn had played more than four hundred [chess] tournament games, which I would come to understand was something like saying he had written four hundred sonnets, in public, while opponents who didn't particularly like him tried to write better sonnets using the same words.

J. C. HALLMAN, The Chess Artist, 2003[1]

There was something unreal about the pictures, which may have come from the face, the ultimate in tragedy, of a man so disciplined in an art that he had lost the better part of reality. Perhaps I had photographed the face of a man meant from the outset for martyrdom to art. It was as if the life of Shūsai, Master of Go, had ended as his art had ended, with that last match.

KAWABATA YASUNARI, The Master of Go, 1951[2]

I'm not sure it's rational—believing as many do that a board game possesses a sort of cosmic power, something commensurate with our capacity for wonder—but I feel it nonetheless.

STEFAN FATSIS, Word Freak: Heartbreak, Triumph, Genius, and Obsession in the World of Competitive Scrabble Players, 2001[3]

The first time I lived in China was in 1988, when I taught English in the city of Xi'an. I had originally planned to stay for two years, but like most of my fellow countrymen I left shortly after the Tiananmen massacre that took place a year later. In those days the streets of China were covered with the swarming flow of uniformly sturdy black bicycles. Steel dividers grounded with concrete slabs provided them with a generous amount of road away from the occasional cars, which tended to be taxis or, infrequently, the black limousines which were the standard model for government officials. At the time there was one Kentucky Fried Chicken in the entire country, which, as the only Western fast food chain to have gained access to the People's Republic of China (PRC), was a symbol of China's opening doors, or corruption by the West, depending on whom one spoke with. At that time, the best places to obtain luxury goods, ranging from cheese to stereos, were called "Friendship Stores." One needed a foreign passport to gain entrance, as well as "Foreign Exchange Notes"—currency designed specifically to charge foreigners several times what the local population paid. For Westerners living in China, it was common practice to make one's money go further by finding a black market that would change currencies for a much higher rate.

Today, China seems less like a transforming nation than a different universe. Cars, though still very much luxury items, now outnumber bicycles by a considerable margin and range from Hyundai to the now-ubiquitous Mercedes-Benz. Shopping malls cover the streets of downtown Beijing and Shanghai, some of which include stores with US$1,000 shoes and designer suits for far more than that. The old Friendship Stores still exist, almost like prehistoric flies in amber that have not changed even though the world has transformed around them. The Friendship Stores' stasis has shifted its role from the highest-end opportunity to buy luxury goods to the feel of a thrift shop in comparison with the newer shopping malls. The grey and uninviting buildings that once seemed such impressive escapes now seem as dated as a 1950s-style diner in the United States, though they lack any of the charm of the intentional construction of nostalgia that such an eatery would offer.

These changes were the result of the economic policies that Deng Xiaoping implemented when he became China's leader in 1978. Making a call for "socialism with Chinese characteristics," he paved the way toward a free market economy. That China is still referred to as a communist state has far more to do with appeasing the government officials who came to power during the establishment of the People's Republic of China than any real commitment to a socialist agenda. Deng implemented policies that would later develop into a seemingly unrestrained capitalist society, the likes of which had not been seen in the United States since before the Great Depression.

Though Deng's economic policies were welcomed by most, many have found the speed of transition to be daunting. As late as the mid-1990s nearly half of China's urban labor pool worked for government-run work units.[4] In this system, there was little incentive to work hard because of what was called the "iron rice bowl." This referred to the idea that, regardless of one's performance, one could not be fired from a government-owned business. In the old system, work units provided everything from housing to health care. After Deng Xiaoping's reforms, the majority of government-owned work units were closed, and their employees were forced to compete in the open market. From 1997 to 2000 alone, twenty-one million of these workers lost their jobs.[5] While most of China's citizens benefited from Deng Xiaoping's economic reforms, many people today feel they have to struggle just to keep up with their previous standard of living.[6]

Even more striking than China's new consumer frenzy is the transformation of people's worldviews about individualism and their place in the world order. In 1988 my Chinese friends occasionally whispered of their discontent about living conditions or the government with a furtive glance over their shoulders. Today, although the government still maintains strict censorship of sensitive topics in its mass media, people openly speak of the 1989 Tiananmen massacre and seem perfectly comfortable criticizing the government in public venues such as restaurants and coffee shops. The only time they might fidget nervously is if one begins to take notes while other people are watching.

This is not to say that the China is free of problems. The PRC is experiencing a level of class inequality that it has not seen since its communist victory in 1949. China is rife with tales of imprisoning dissidents, government corruption, the inhumane exploitation of labor and rural women, and severe air and water pollution. Speculation deals, in which residents are forced out of their homes so that people with government connections can build lucrative new apartment buildings, have generated hundreds of popular protests across the nation. Many people feel that the PRC government is precariously close to losing its legitimacy because of its violation of human rights and because government officials, and their offspring, seem to live beyond the reach of the law. Yet more often than not the abuses that take place are symptoms of an overwhelmed bureaucratic structure and unregulated individual avarice rather than the sinister state malevolence that is so often evoked in Western media's portrayal of China.[7]

Many of the laws that encroach on individual freedoms in China are created because, in a very Confucian sense, both the state and the populace believe that the government should act as a father figure to its citizens. Not unlike a stern patriarch, the government tells its citizenry that it knows best while often pretending not to notice infractions. This includes illegal behavior ranging from accessing prohibited sites on the Internet to intellectual piracy that allows exposure to banned films, music, and books. In a sense, piracy takes on a very different dynamic than in the West, for if China's citizens were truly limited by the government's attempts to control information, life would be far too Orwellian for comfort. As it stands, the rules are bent just enough that in many ways middle-class urbanites' lives are not overly different from our own.

When I was conducting fieldwork for this book I was also filming a documentary on the same topic. To my great surprise I was allowed free rein to film where and when I wanted, with no supervision from government representatives. Though the board game Weiqi is admittedly a particularly safe area of inquiry, the freedom to film on the street with no supervision would have been unthinkable on my first trip to China. In fact, the only interaction I had with government personnel was when a police officer walked up to me as I was filming Weiqi players in a park. Just as I was beginning to panic because he had spent two to three minutes peering over my shoulder, he began giving me detailed advice on what he thought would be a better camera angle.

Because people in China and the United States learn most of what they know about each other from mass media, it is no surprise that we view each other with a mixture of admiration and mistrust. Americans inherit views of Hollywood's portrayal of "China's ancient wisdom" juxtaposed with news coverage centering on inscrutable Chinese who live in a corrupt and easily angered nation. The atrocities of the Tiananmen massacre, and the angry riots in the street after the United States accidentally bombed the Chinese Embassy in Belgrade during a UN operation, fan the flames of America's view that China poses a dire threat in which insincere politeness barely masks a ruthless and hostile other.[8]

China's view of America is no less distorted, for Hollywood's portrayal of the "average" American's life based on affluent Southern Californian lifestyles, in homes that I, for one, could never afford on a professor's salary. People in China envy and mistrust the United States even as many long for its lifestyles. In part this is because of Hollywood's depiction of Americans as rich, exciting, free, unpredictable, and decadent. Chinese news portrays America as a nation that allows its citizens to be ravaged by violent crime, racial tension, and a staggering level of economic hardship for such a prosperous nation. My fieldwork periods were in 2010 and 2011, during which the United States experienced the worst economic crisis since the Great Depression. People in China expressed bewilderment at the American government's inability to pay off its unimaginably high national debt and its failure to heed dire warnings that it was in peril. Because this was also a time in which there was a particularly vicious battle taking place between the Democratic president and the Republican-dominated Congress, most Chinese I spoke with seemed to feel that America had spun out of control.

It is tempting to be critical of China's stance on freedom of speech and information, on dissent, on the exponentially growing disparity between rich and poor, and the sometimes horrific ways that the disenfranchised continue to be abused by those with power. One should not forgive the human rights abuses that do take place. Yet in comparison to the China of my first visit, it is hard not to be impressed at the breathtaking changes that have occurred in urbanites' standards of living, as well as in their general freedom from state intrusion compared with thirty years before. In contrast, Americans' views, ranging from taxes to gun control, do not seem to have changed overly much since the Reagan era. Few, I think, would argue that the average American citizen has a demonstrably better standard of living or more freedom than thirty years ago. While one should not apologize for the abuses that do occur in China, it is important to keep their starting point in mind when assessing the problems that Chinese people face today.

Cinematic fantasies of American and Chinese others, combined with news coverage depicting horrific dystopias, pit the world's two economic superpowers against each other. Yet, as in the United States, people in China are living their daily lives and, for the most part, they are just trying to get by. Like us, they want to be the best fathers and mothers, sons and daughters, that they can be. They are working hard to better their lives and their children's, and they are trying to make their way in an increasingly competitive world.

Perhaps surprisingly, the board game Weiqi is one way to make sense of China's mind-bogglingly fast economic and political transition. People speak of the game as training children in the ways of commerce, social interaction, and proper manhood. University students use it to voice anxieties about the unimaginably competitive nature of the current economy and to find models of behavior that draw on age-old ideals of elite gentlemen who were known to play. Senior citizens use Weiqi to speak of the relatively carefree days of old age and as a tangible example of the relative prosperity and political freedom compared to the tumultuous years of the Cultural Revolution when they came of age. Because Weiqi is such an overwhelmingly male sphere, it is also a means of constructing masculinity. Weiqi's associations with elite culture in the days of old is one of many ways that people are exploring a part of

China's great past because so many of its traditions had been wiped out in the early communist era.

Weiqi is thought to train boys and men to seize the initiative, thereby learning to control their environments and to control other men rather than allowing themselves to be dominated. It is seen as a tool to train them to succeed in business and politics. It is thought to teach them etiquette of Confucian gentlemen so that they would not lose the best parts of what it means to be Chinese in today's global culture. In this setting, Weiqi is believed to help men to retain their dignity, their mastery, their very manhood.

FIELDWORK

I had long toyed with the idea of writing a book on Weiqi. In an addition to a range of informal conversations, I conducted a handful of interviews in Taipei and Shanghai in 2006.[9] The vast majority of this book is drawn from fieldwork in Beijing, however. My first full-time fieldwork on this topic took place in Beijing in July 2010. For three weeks of this period I spent my mornings playing Weiqi at the Wenbo Weiqi School for children and its intensive summer school program. In the afternoons and weekends I frequented a park where a group of twenty to thirty retired senior citizens gathered to play Weiqi on a daily basis.

I returned to Beijing to continue my research from July through December 2011. During this time I continued to visit the park and to interview at children's Weiqi schools. I also expanded my project to include participant observation at Peking University's Weiqi club as well as conducting interviews with several members of Peking University's Weiqi team. I also interviewed a handful of professional Weiqi players.

I began this project with the natural curiosity of someone who grew up playing chess. I had a range of questions about the significance of the game: Who plays Weiqi and what are its cultural connotations? Would the players be stigmatized as neurotic geeks or lauded as noble gentlemen? Would it be a male-dominated game like chess? What was the significance of international competition given the particularly violent conflicts between China and Japan in the twentieth century, as well as the continuing struggle for dominance in East Asia's political economy?

As I learned more about the game, other questions began to emerge: How did Weiqi attain such high status in Confucian-influenced spheres in spite of the fact that Confucius had expressed barely concealed derision for the game and Mencius had outright listed it as an unfilial act? Why did so many people I interviewed say that they learned to play during the Great Proletarian Cultural Revolution (1966–76) given that historically the game was embedded in elite culture? How can the game simultaneously represent the martial prowess of age-old generals, the intellect and self-control of Confucian gentlemen, and a scientific rationality of the new age? What does it mean to be a child in contemporary China or, for that matter, a university student or a senior citizen? How do nationalistic discourses about Weiqi reveal larger tensions with China's East Asian competitors, and in what ways was does this force us to rethink the East–West binary that dominates English-language scholarship? In what ways does this game provide a venue for constructing masculinity that differs from more traditionally studied areas of sexuality or Chinese-style machismo?

What follows is a complicated web of created masculinities that are necessarily born of the particulars of China's historical and present-day cultural contexts. This book focuses on the game of Weiqi, but it is also about what it means to be a man in contemporary China—a nation that has undergone unfathomably radical changes that have presented Chinese boys and men with a and often contradictory set of expectations for manhood.

NOTES ON TERMINOLOGY

The English language use of the term *Go* to refer to this game is a derivation of the Japanese word *igo* and a direct reflection of Japan's centuries-long supremacy in Weiqi, as well as Japan's continued central role in promoting it worldwide. Yet for English speakers the term *Go* is far too easily confused with the verb "to go," and it creates a syntax that borders on the Abbot and Costello skit "Who's on First?" (for example, "go play *Go*"). Trying to find information on *Go* on the Web obtains frustratingly random results. Internet search engines interpret the key words "go game" or "go competitions" as "go to game," presenting links to Web pages on topics ranging from war games to badminton to Las Vegas. At one point in my fieldwork this problem became so pervasive that it had even saturated a Chinese-language server. When I tried to do a Chinese-language search on the words "Korea Weiqi" (*Hanguo Weiqi*) and "Weiqi Korea" (*Weiqi Hanguo*) using the Hong Kong

Google server, I was presented with a page full of links about travel to Korea.[10] Titles for these links included "I can go to Korea" (*Wo hui chu Hanguo*) and "Going to Korea online" (*Qianwang Hanguo zai xian*). They even included an English link for further searches that read "Go Korea," which led to a range of English-language Web pages devoted to the topic of traveling in Korea. Thus, returning to Weiqi's original Chinese name makes sense for the integrity of acknowledging the game's origins, but also to create cleaner English prose and a terminology that works more effectively with today's technology.

Several Japanese terms have become standard English in American Weiqi communities. Readers of earlier drafts of this book found it jarring that I used Chinese terms in some instances and Japanese terms in others, however. For this reason I use Chinese words even when using terms that English-speaking Weiqi players are used to seeing in Japanese (such as *atari, dan, kyu, sente*). All of the relevant Japanese terms and their Chinese equivalents can be found in the glossary at the end of this book.

When people use the Chinese term *Weiqi* in English, it is spelled with an array of romanization styles and forms of capitalization. With the exception of book and article titles, I have standardized this to the pinyin spelling of *Weiqi* in all Chinese instances. When it is a Japanese text I retain the word *Go*.

Because the people I spoke with were excited to be included in the project, I have used their real names whenever possible. In one case I used someone's chosen English name because she requested that I do so. If an account was particularly personal, or if someone voiced an opinion that I felt might cause them trouble, I did not include a name or other identifying markers with that particular statement.

Both Chinese and Japanese surnames precede given names. For example, Wu Qingyuan's surname is Wu. Unless otherwise noted, all of my interviews were conducted in Beijing. Sylvia and Guan Yang's interviews were conducted primarily in English. All other interviews were conducted in Chinese, and, unless otherwise noted, all translations of written texts and interviews are my own.

ACKNOWLEDGMENTS

Acknowledgments are always a daunting task. How does one sum up hours of unpaid labor, breathtaking insights, and life-changing friendships in a few sentences or less? Yet I would be remiss if I did not attempt to express my gratitude in some way. To David K. Jordan, once my dissertation advisor and now my good friend, inspiration, and all-around grounding influence. Joseph Allen, Shawn Bender, Karl Gerth, David K. Jordan, Andrew Morris, Amy O'Brien, John Shepherd, and Peter Shotwell provided thoughtful, admirably thorough, and delightfully insightful comments on an earlier draft of this manuscript. The students in my class Chinese Popular Culture (Fall 2012) were kind enough to give me very helpful comments on the introduction of this book. Jeffrey Wasserstrom offered much needed encouragement. Stacy Eisenstark, at the University of California Press, helped me with all of the important details and paperwork that any new book presents. Pam Suwinsky rescued me whenever I fell into grammatical quagmires. Thanks especially to Reed Malcolm, the UC Press senior editor for anthropology and Asian studies. He gave me exceptionally useful advice, and he immediately recognized the worth of this project at a time when many people I spoke with were scratching their heads in bewilderment at the idea of an anthropological examination of board game culture.

None of this would have been possible without generous funding from a range of sources. The ACLS-NEH (American Council of Learned Societies and the National Endowment for the Humanities) provided me with an American Research in the Humanities in China Fellowship to conduct fieldwork on this topic from July 1, 2011, to December 31, 2011. At the University of South Carolina, Dean Mary Ann Fitzpatrick gave me an additional semester's leave with pay to work on the book in the spring semester of 2012. As consecutive chairs of my department, Anne Kingsolver and Charles Cobb provided additional travel funds as well as much needed encouragement.

I am also grateful to Peking University's Department of Sociology and Anthropology for providing me with affiliation while I was in China. Guo Jie and Guo Jinhua were kind enough to introduce me to the department. Zhu Xiaoyang sponsored me while I was there and gave me many important insights into contemporary Chinese society, as well as feeding me on occasion. Wang Huiqin, Ji Yea Hong, Xiang Xin, Zhang Rui each helped me to arrange an interview. Huang Shan and Hu Shuai helped me to verify several important details at the tail end of my project. Arey Huei-Jyun Jhang served as my research assistant both while I was in China and in the United States, and eased the process of fieldwork considerably.

Many thanks also to Wang Wenbo for allowing me to take classes, interview, and film documentary footage at the Wenbo Weiqi Training Center (*Wenbo weiqi peixun zhongxin*), which I refer to as the Wenbo School. Thanks also to Mike Hong Po, for allowing me to film and interview at the Nie Weiping Classroom (*Nie Weiping Weiqi jiaoshi*). My deepest gratitude belongs to the people I interviewed, who were amazingly gracious in allowing me into their lives. Their candor in our interviews, and their enthusiasm for both my book and film projects, kept me energized and made the process surprisingly fun. Most important, I thank my wife, Arey Huei-jyun Jhang, kindred spirit and fellow guardian of the tomato plants against our sinister four-legged foes (a.k.a. squirrels). You fill my life with love and laughter, and I could not ask for more.

ONE

Introduction

The deepest of all the [Chinese] games is one with more than two hundred pieces, white and black for each side, on a board with more than three hundred squares. ... The mandarins have become so absorbed in this game that some of them occupy most of the day playing it, each match lasting more than one hour. And those who are good at this game, even if they have no other ability, are appreciated by everybody and invited everywhere, and some are chosen as masters to teach this game.

MATEO RICCI, On the Entrance of the Company
of Jesus and Christianity into China, 1610[1]

The art of Go began in China and was transmitted to our country by Grand Minister Kibi. Since that time it has spread, and now everybody plays. Monks who have a talent for it play Go with women and become their lovers. People pass through the world worrying about the moves just as if they were members of the Go Bureau. They put their own lives in jeopardy out of concern for the lives of their stones. Though these addicts are not Buddhist monks, they make do with but one meal a day, and though they are not yamabushi priests, they sit up all night as if waiting for the sunrise.

YAMAOKA GENRIN, *an Edo period
(1603–1868) essayist*[2]

These games were little dramas, in structure almost pure monologues, reflecting the imperiled but brilliant life of the author's mind like a perfect self-portrait.

HERMANN HESSE, The Glass Bead Game, 1943[3]

JULY 8, 2010. That was the day I discovered that I could play Weiqi better than a ten-year-old in China. In 2010 I spent three weeks taking classes at the Wenbo School for children (the Wenbo Weiqi Training Center, *Wenbo weiqi peixun zhongxin*) and its summer school in a different location. In the first week, most of the children were on vacation and the school offered only one beginning and one lower-intermediate class. Much to my surprise, and even more of a shock to my teachers, I turned out to be the strongest player in both classes. Mrs. Wang, the accountant, head administrator, and joint owner of the school with her husband, quickly learned of this. She then began to bring in stronger players, who normally came to the school for private lessons, to test my mettle. When I defeated the first three of these opponents, Mrs. Wang displayed her boundless enthusiasm and began searching in earnest to find me a worthy adversary.

Playing Weiqi in China I suffered the disadvantages of having had no formal training and growing up in a culture that does not commonly play Weiqi—I didn't purchase my first book to study the game until I was thirty-eight years old. To be fair, I had several advantages in these games as well. The most obvious of these was that my classmates were, on average, ten years old. Second, as often happens when I play Weiqi in China, my opponents often started our games in an overly aggressive fashion because they assumed that an American would not recognize the traps of a beginner. Perhaps most important, as word spread of my victories, a growing number of students, teachers, and staff came to watch. This was a tremendous load to bear for a ten-year-old who was attempting to uphold his country's honor. It was very little pressure for a forty-five-year-old American who was so far past his Weiqi prime that the only thing he could do was surpass startlingly low expectations.

After my second day of classes, Mrs. Wang marched in a new opponent to challenge me. He was a stern and focused nine-year-old with a 3-*duan* amateur rating and therefore already a better player than most people would become in their lifetimes. At this point the room was packed full of spectators, including the teachers, several students, and even the female staff who usually showed no interest in the game. My opponent, who had earned a reputation for being something of a Weiqi prodigy, was small in stature but radiated natural intelligence and had honed killer instincts for the game. His intense stare seemed to penetrate the board—an entirely different feel from the other somewhat fidgety students I had played against up to that point. He quickly took the lead. After I conceded my loss halfway through the game he stood up, turned around without a word, and, heedless of his mother's admonition to say good-bye, walked out of the room without a backward glance. I felt as if I had met Bobby Fischer's reincarnated spirit in the Weiqi world, and I tried to suppress a smile.

Weiqi is a board game that originated in China and was already well known in the time of Confucius (551–479 B.C.). Referred to as *Go* in the United States, *Igo* in Japan, and *Baduk* in Korea, the word *Weiqi* is made up of two Chinese characters; *wei* (to surround) and *qi* (logic game).[4] The appellation "surrounding logic game" vividly evokes Weiqi's primary goal, which is to try to take one's opponent's pieces by surrounding them while simultaneously accumulating additional points by encircling empty space on the board. Today, the People's Republic of China (PRC), Japan, South Korea, and Taiwan are the epicenters of the Weiqi universe, although, with the advent of the Internet, it has a steadily growing fan base in the West as well.

I refer to Weiqi as a Chinese game but, in much the same way that the Chinese origins of gunpowder and paper have become largely irrelevant in today's globalized political economy, Weiqi now belongs to several nations. Japan's nearly four centuries of Weiqi supremacy, South Korea's dominance in this sphere from the mid-1980s to approximately 2008 when China became a serious contender, and Taiwan's strong presence in international competitions, have so advanced the theory and practice of the game that it has been transformed into something very new.

Weiqi's popularity in China is often part of a choice to embrace a lifestyle that evokes nostalgia for gentry scholars in imperial times. Its long history has resulted in contemporary dreamscapes that draw on images of noblemen and intellectuals, generals and emperors who played the game. This imagery makes a particularly strong statement in the PRC, where elite culture was dismantled in favor of a new communist utopian movement.

Weiqi embodies mainstream traditionalist ideals in an age in which many people have abandoned the past in favor of more globalized opportunities. Middle-class and elite markers of distinction, including learning English, playing the piano, and studying abroad, are more often than not immersed in Western symbolism.[5] Weiqi's association with historical elite culture aligns it with Chinese tradition. In doing so it offers a very different marker of elite status than most symbolic capital in the PRC.[6]

Weiqi is an iconic reminder of perceived regional differences. In Taiwan, one never sees Weiqi played in parks—the game is too embedded in elite culture. In the PRC, the city of Chengdu is quite famous for the prevalence of Weiqi players in parks and teahouses. In Beijing, where I conducted my research, it is less common to see people playing Weiqi at parks, although those who do so display a remarkable devotion to the game.

China is a game-playing nation. Walking down the streets of Beijing one can see people playing Chinese chess or cards on street corners and in parks. It is not unusual to see people playing cards at restaurants as they enjoy their meals. In public areas such as parks and roadsides Weiqi does not have the ubiquitous presence of Chinese chess and cards, but some parks are known to have groups of retired working-class people playing the game. They are there in stifling hot summer days and on the snow-covered sidewalk in the winters.[7]

Chinese people's love of board games is in part born of a culture that places no stigma on intelligence. There are few of the cultural stereotypes of nerdiness that one might associate with these activities in the United States. Board games admittedly lack the cool factor of rock music or club culture, but in China one rarely sees depictions, so pervasive in the West, of mad genius game players rushing to their doom.[8] Chinese people's appreciation of board games extends to games in general. Outings that include alcohol will inevitably feature drinking games in one form or another. It is a social activity that relieves the strain of witty banter and becomes a way for the entire group to participate. This might include competitive drinking (a game in and of itself) or those on the sidelines cheering them on. Though more sedate, Weiqi in parks evinces a similar sociality. A handful of people play and groups of twenty to thirty bystanders spend the day watching, kibitzing, and perhaps rotating in to play if the mood strikes them.

NEW TECHNOLOGIES

Weiqi is central to China's dreams of self and other, past and present. Given that China has the largest population in the world, it is surprising that there has yet to be an anthropological study of this topic. Television programs, several journals, and an array of instructional books are devoted to instructing players in Weiqi. These texts include issues such as general strategies as well as "life-and-death" problems. The increasingly transnational character of the game includes Internet servers that allow online competition between players from countries as diverse as Brazil, China, and Estonia.

Online reviews of games, as well as sites devoted to teaching Weiqi, have created a contemporary environment that can arguably be considered to be Weiqi's golden age. Though embedded in traditionalist discourses that draw on images of Imperial China's cultured gentlemen, Weiqi has also become part of a far more modern world. With the advent of international competitions, as well as Japanese manga and anime revolving around the game, Weiqi has transformed into an intensely modern transnational experience. This ability to simultaneously represent both the ancient and the futuristic is a vibrant example of how, far from being antagonistic forces, traditionalism and modernity revolve around each other in symbiosis.

In Beijing, most people who play Weiqi online use the Internet server "Tom." Because one must negotiate a densely packed Chinese-language website to find the Tom server, and because one needs a Chinese ID number to register, it is an overwhelmingly Chinese domain. Many people I interviewed in Beijing also use Korean servers or IGS (Internet Go Server, a.k.a. Pandanet).[9] KGS (the Kiseido Go Server) is by far the most popular Weiqi server in the West.[10] The vast majority of Weiqi players on KGS use English as a lingua franca, though one also sees an array of other languages being used as well. As an anthropologist I find KGS to be the most interesting server because of the online community that it has fostered. As with other Weiqi servers, KGS has unicode capability that allows users to communicate in any language by typing comments in a dialogue box to the right of the game. These servers also include the ability to save and edit games. This means that people can review games together or they can entreat, or employ, a stronger player to review their games and point out areas for improvement.

When beginning a game on KGS, it is typical for opponents to exchange casual greetings. This usually takes place in English, with a set of stock phrases such as "Hello," "Enjoy," or "Have fun." The games frequently end with "Thanks," "Bye," or "Good game." Some people enjoy having conversations while they play, whereas others prefer to focus on the game without distractions. When they have finished, many players review their games with their opponents.

One can also watch other people's games, and strong players frequently attract fifty to one hundred spectators. On occasion, two to three hundred people will gather to watch if a game takes place when people are not working and the players are ranked highly enough to draw attention. Spectators often comment in the dialogue box while a game is taking place, though the people playing the game cannot see the comments until they have finished. At its best, the stronger players watching the game point out particularly good and bad moves. Often, the spectators will use the dialogue box to engage in casual banter.

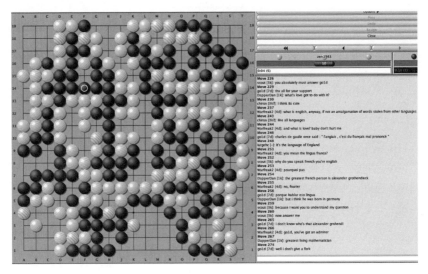

FIGURE 1. KGS game.

Figure 1 depicts a KGS game with 118 spectators. As sometimes happens, those commenting seem to have forgotten about the game altogether, preferring instead to focus on a conversation that they are having about unrelated matters. In this case the spectators primarily use English, but they interject French and Spanish as well. In other instances, there might be several distinct conversations going on at once. In a dialogue box that primarily consists of English, for example, one might also see several people writing Russian while a third group of spectators communicates in Chinese.

As in any online setting, one is occasionally confronted with antisocial behavior, including rude comments. For many, the most frustrating behavior is something called "escaping." This refers to when someone leaves a game before it is finished, which usually occurs when the escaper is losing a game. On IGS, someone who does this automatically forfeits his game. Many people complain, however, that this unduly punishes people with bad Internet connections who try to return after being disconnected only to find an abandoned game.

On KGS nothing will happen if someone leaves one game. If he escapes ten games in a certain period of time, however, his unfinished games will all automatically be forfeited. Unfortunately, there are players who use this system to inflate their ratings in order to play stronger opponents. Their ratings will plummet when they are penalized for previous escapes, at which point they can simply start a new account. The only real deterrent is that many people will not play someone without a rating, and it takes some time and effort to regain one's rank. Escapers are a continual frustration for most players. Yet, given that there are no real repercussions for bad behavior, combined with the ability to hide one's true identity, the relative lack of impolite behavior is in many ways more remarkable than its presence.

Several of the people whom I interviewed were concerned that the Internet was transforming the game in negative ways. Points of criticism included the idea that people seem to take the game less seriously on the Internet. These comments usually took the form of pointing out that games tend to be quicker when playing online. One person I interviewed also confessed that when he played on his lunch break he frequently resigned in the middle of a game simply because he had to go back to work. Others complained that in playing online one does not get the tactile experience of holding the Weiqi stones in one's hand, and that one misses the opportunity to develop strong friendships by having a live partner in the room.

Yet if the Internet does not have the same visceral feel as a live game, or the level of intimacy and friendship that face-to-face interaction might offer, it also has many benefits. Friendships develop on KGS that can arguably be seen as a community, albeit one that is largely made up of people who have never met face to face. Many people I interviewed in China voiced appreciation for the fact that the Internet allowed them to play for free. They also lauded the idea that they could play at four in the morning if they chose to do so.

Many advanced Weiqi players review their games from memory. For those of us without such remarkable skills, online servers allow us to review an accurate record of our games. It is also possible to try out alternative moves, and then find one's place at a different point in the game, without ever becoming confused at the order that was played. If someone has completed a particularly interesting match, or received especially good advice while reviewing it, he can save the game and its commentary on the server. He can also download it to his computer if he so chooses.

More than half a billion people in China have access to the Internet.[11] Weiqi players belonging to the other half of China's population must seek other venues to play. One should remember, however, that for Weiqi players who do have online access, this is not an either/or choice. Many people who use Internet servers also play their opponents in person. Someone might play an online Weiqi game with a stranger and then play the next game with his oldest friend.

Beijing is a large and sprawling city with extreme weather and a dense population. Rather than taking an hour's ride on an uncomfortably hot and thickly packed subway to play Weiqi with a friend, one might arrange to meet on an online server. In China, where traveling abroad still represents a significant expense for even the middle class, the Internet also offers Weiqi players the rare opportunity to play and chat with people from beyond their national borders.

THE RANKING SYSTEM

There are three categories in the Weiqi ranking system. In China the lowest rank is 25 *ji*. From there, the smaller the numeral, the higher the rank. In other words, 2 *ji* is stronger than 3 *ji,* which in turn is a stronger rank than 4 *ji.* The best *ji* rating is 1 *ji.* The next level, the amateur *duan* category, reverses this order in that the weakest amateur *duan* is a 1-*duan* amateur and in China the strongest is a 7-*duan* amateur.[12] The highest category is a 1-*duan* pro to a 9-*duan* pro. A 9-*duan* pro is the pinnacle of the Weiqi sphere—something akin to a Grand Master in the world of chess.[13]

To review, the ranking system is listed from the lowest to the highest ranks:

Ranks in China and Their Stages

25 to 1 *ji*: Beginner.

1- to 4-*duan* amateur: Intermediate.

5- to 7-*duan* amateur: Near professional level.

8-*duan* amateur: Near professional level. This rank is not given in China. It can only be achieved in international competitions.

1- to 9-*duan* pro: Professionally ranked player.

American View of Weiqi Ranks and Their Stages[14]

30 to 20 *ji*: Beginner.

19 to 10 *ji*: Casual player.

9 to 1 *ji*: Intermediate amateur.

1- to 9-*duan* amateur: Advanced amateur.

1- to 9-*duan* pro: Professional player.

To gain an unofficial rank one simply needs to play. Internet servers will rank players compared to how they perform with other opponents at that site. In China, Weiqi schools for children also assign their own ranks based on competitions with students within the schools, or with students from other children's schools. These ranking systems are somewhat unreliable, however, in that children's ranks are highly inflated. For those who gained ranks on the Internet, one must identify the server on which one obtained one's rank, as the levels vary there as well. For example, when asked my rank I would state that I was 2 or 3 *ji* on the KGS server. This would not be the same rank on the IGS server, and would be yet a different rank had I competed at the American Go Association. At the children's school I attended I was ranked as a 1- or 2-amateur *duan* player. Many people I spoke with told me that it was quite normal for children's ranks to be inflated because most teachers at children's schools felt that rising in the ranks helped to encourage amateur students.

From 2010 to 2011 I wavered on the edge between a 2- and a 3-*ji* rank on the Internet Weiqi server KGS. This placed me in a strong intermediate status in the United States, though in China the same rating merely signified a strong beginner. For those in China who took the game seriously, having a *ji* rank was a childhood memory. My level was approximately equal to that of a ten-year-old who had received formal training in the game. I was better than most adults in China who had not taken classes as children but far weaker than adults who took the game seriously. Although my rank was hardly something to boast about in China, it was good enough to favorably surprise most people I interacted with and marked me as an insider of sorts. I was the weakest player at the park, but it was rare that I wouldn't win at least one game on the days that I played. Because I was so decidedly the underdog, and something of an anomaly, people tended to root for me and offer a bit of good-natured teasing to my opponents on the occasions when I won.

I have often heard Western Weiqi players liken earning a *duan* rank to obtaining a black belt in martial arts. Indeed, there are similarities. Years ago, when I began taking tae kwon do classes I had conceptualized black belts as being experts. In contrast, those who had earned black belts often emphasized that this represents a mastery of the basics so that they could then begin to hone their skills into an art. In the same fashion, most Weiqi players in America tend to speak of an amateur *duan* rank as representing an expert level, whereas people in China see it as an intermediate step in which they had developed a firm grasp of the basics. These fundamentals include memorizing set openings, life-and-death situations for particular groups, and set patterns (*dingshi*). Many people I interviewed told me that only after they achieved this could they then start to be creative with the overall flow of the game. Because professional players are much more of a presence in China than in the West, amateur *duan* players in China are more acutely aware of the limitations of their playing strength.

As in Japan and South Korea, to get a professional rank in China one must attend an annual ranking competition that is held by the government. When I was conducting my research, in China one had to be among the top twenty competitors to obtain a professional rank. An age limit was also imposed so that males had to earn a professional rank before they turned seventeen and females had to do so before they turned twenty. Two of the professional ranks were reserved for people who had won a major national or international competition before their twenty-fifth birthdays. At the time of this writing there are approximately 528 professionally ranked players in China. Of those, 285 are actively competing, whereas the others have gone on to other pursuits, which often include teaching Weiqi.[15]

The dividing line between amateur and professional Weiqi players is at times fraught with contradictions. Some people who obtain professional ranks quit in favor of other pursuits, but they will continue to retain their professional ranks for the rest of their lives. There are also famous people with amateur ranks who spend their lives as career Weiqi players, living on prize money from competitions that are open to amateur players. Some career players who have amateur ranks clearly resent being locked out of the professional competitions because they were late bloomers at the game. Others who earn the right to become professional players by winning national or international tournaments opt to retain their amateur status with the rationale that it is better to win a smaller amount of prize money in an amateur competition than to lose at a professional competition.

Because of the prize money offered at professional competitions, the very top players earn an impressive income. The most lucrative competitions include the Ing Cup (US$400,000), Toyota Denso Cup (US$260,000), LG Cup (US$210,000), Samsung Cup (US$170,000), Chu-Lan Cup (US$150,000), and the Fujitsu Cup (US$130,000).[16] One must have a professional rank to enter any of these competitions. Quite often, however, the same dozen players win all of the largest prizes so that there is little prize money left over for anyone else. As a result, the vast majority of professional Weiqi players make their livings by teaching lower-ranking professionals or particularly talented high-ranking amateurs.

At the ages of five through seven, boys only slightly outnumber girls in Weiqi classes. By the time they are nine or ten, it is an almost exclusively male domain, with approximately one female student in a class of fifteen or twenty. The university club I attended generally had between one and three women out of ten to forty club members present at any meeting. In the park, where the regular players were primarily in their sixties and seventies, not once did I see a woman play a game or stop to watch for more than a minute or two.

Of the 528 professionally ranked professional Weiqi players in China, 89 are women. Female professionally ranked players who are still participating in competitions number 42 out of 285. Of the 32 players who have earned the highest rank of 9-*duan* professional in China, only 2 are women.[17] To its credit, China's government has tried to make a place for female players. When I was conducting my fieldwork, three of the twenty professional ranks that were awarded every year were reserved for women. The women played against each other because they could not win in the male competitions. The government has also given women a higher age limit by which they must take the professional exams. Whereas male players must earn the professional *duan* rank before they turn seventeen, women can continue to compete in the professional *duan* rank competitions until they turn twenty. While this has greatly improved women's chances to become professional Weiqi players, for many people I interviewed it also seemed to confirm the belief that men are better at the game than women. Nearly everyone I spoke with in China, including many women, stated that men are superior Weiqi players because they are by nature better than women at logic and spatial comprehension. People also told me that boys are naturally more aggressive—a trait that they felt could be harnessed to be competitive in Weiqi, and in society as a whole. Almost no one raised the issue of gender being shaped by parental or societal expectations.

To fully understand conceptions of men and women in the Weiqi sphere, we must step back to take in a wider view of gender coding in China's culture as a whole. Because of the One-Child Policy, more than 90 percent of urban children have no siblings.[18] For Beijing residents, this has resulted in far greater parental support for daughters in the realm of education and career choices than ever before in China. It is clear, however, that boys and girls are still raised with very different sets of expectations. In part, this is because of an almost universal belief in China that boys and girls are innately different. From a very young age boys are thought to be more logical, outgoing, and prone to making trouble, whereas girls are believed to be emotional, gentle, and docile. Parents socialize their children to successfully maneuver in Chinese culture, with the gender expectations that they will face. Girls are taught that their physical appearance is very important, for example, whereas boys are told that they will be judged on their achievements. Many urban parents now embrace the idea that their daughters should seek university education. Yet both parents and teachers continue to encourage girls to take classes, and to consider careers, that are deemed appropriate to their gender. Attending university is frequently framed in terms of adding to their charm and attractiveness for prospective mates rather than connecting to hopes of future career success.[19]

The restrictions that parental training and expectations impose on girls are self-evident, but they also put a range of constraints on boys. One study found that parents voiced concern when boys were too considerate or gentle, for instance, on the grounds that this was not manly behavior.[20] Boys feel pressured by their parents' expectations that they will accomplish great things in their adulthood, whereas girls are still expected to be caregivers in the family.[21]

As children's primary caretakers, Chinese mothers use a variety of techniques to discipline their children. This includes scolding, threatening, making direct comparisons with other children's (good and bad) behavior, bringing up past offenses, and referencing authority figures or characters from children's media.[22] Boys are subjected to more rigorous disciplining than girls—parents are more likely to use shame to discipline boys, for example.[23] Mothers are also more likely to quote the classics with boys than girls when trying to show them the error of their ways.[24] One study suggests that working-class Chinese mothers respond faster when boys are engaged in dangerous activities than girls. This includes conduct such as refusing to take medicine or playing with electrical wires.[25] The same study found while boys are only slightly more likely than girls to commit breaches of social conventions such as being rude to guests.[26] They are approximately twice as likely to engage in other forms of bad behavior, ranging from dangerous acts to stealing toys or lying.[27]

In China there is a widespread belief that boys are just smarter and better at logic than girls. In an effort to confirm these biases, many point to the fact that there are more men than women in university and high-status occupations.[28] Parents who do support the idea that women should succeed in the public sphere often express the hope that their daughters would learn to "become more like men."[29]

During the breaks at children's Weiqi schools, boys yell, run, and scream with reckless abandon. I never saw the female students participate in the frenetic activities around them. Instead, they tended to quietly talk with the teachers or look on while laughing or rolling their eyes at the boys' antics.

At the Wenbo School summer program, my lone female classmate was a quiet but intense nine-year-old. Most of the students finished a game in approximately twenty or thirty minutes. In contrast, regardless of how much the teacher encouraged her to speed up, she made moves at her own extremely methodical pace, often taking more than three hours a game. To some degree this seemed to be psychological warfare against her male classmates (including me) who would begin to daydream or fidget after a five-minute pause without a move. Yet it was also because, unlike the rest of us who lacked the concentration to focus on any but the most pivotal moves of the game, she read out every single move. Over lunch, one of the teachers told me that my female classmate would never improve if she continued to play so slowly. Still, she defeated me, and many of her other male classmates, through an unparalleled determination complemented with patience and remarkable insight, both on the board and to her opponent's psychology. This combination had allowed her to persevere when her female classmates had dropped out of her classes.

Even adults who are sympathetic to female Weiqi players do not contradict the basic premise that boys are naturally better at the game. This is one emblematic statement from a man who used to teach children Weiqi: "Maybe girls are not as good at logical thinking and they need more encouragement when teaching them. When I was teaching girls I couldn't find the answer. It is easier for them to become discouraged and they are more uncomfortable than boys with criticism. Maybe the critical teaching style is not the only way to do it."

Another example of someone who was sympathetic to women's plight while still reifying gender stereotypes can be seen in this quote from a professionally ranked Weiqi player: "Actually Weiqi is really good for girls to study because if they are not naturally as good at logic it will help train them to be better at it."[30]

As with children's training in general, it is hard not to be struck by how openly people told me that girls are not as talented at the game as boys. Many claimed that it was because girls just aren't very good at logic or spatial cognition. An equal number of people told me that girls aren't aggressive enough to do well at the game. Weiqi teachers frequently made these statements in front of female staff or students who seemed to take the comments in stride. Notably, almost all of the women I spoke with, including several who had become expert Weiqi players, also cited boys' natural aggression and superior ability at logic as the primary reasons that more boys played Weiqi than girls.

Given the ratio of male players to female players, the dearth of female professional Weiqi players, and the fact that Weiqi teachers are daily confronted with female students who seem to progress more slowly than their male counterparts, it is hardly surprising that all of the Weiqi players I spoke with, including female players, agreed that girls just aren't as good at the game. Yet this also speaks to larger cultural understandings of gender that remain unquestioned in relation to motivation or larger social pressures on girls to find other pastimes. It may also be that, consciously or subconsciously, the classes were designed with male students in mind. The teachers' often-critical comments to their students seemed more in keeping with disciplinary techniques for boys, for example. The remarkable amount of leeway for the boys to run, scream, and roughhouse during the breaks also established the Weiqi classroom as a male-dominated domain. That Weiqi helps to discipline boys who are said to be naturally unruly was inevitably one of the first points people brought up in my interviews. Unlike conversations about girls, discussions about boys being aggressive are not framed as a negative trait. Nor is the goal to remove aggression. Instead, Weiqi is seen as a means to harness it for productive ends.

Without exception, the adults I interviewed stated that girls are naturally quiet and fragile and that it would therefore be wrong to hit or scold girls because of their more sensitive temperaments. In contrast, boys were thought to be innately aggressive, rambunctious, and resilient. Most thought that this meant that scolding and spanking them was necessary, but that boys would not be emotionally troubled by these forms of punishment.

Boys were also thought to be able to withstand harsher criticism. At Weiqi schools, the startlingly frank assessment of the children's abilities, and the ways that teachers scolded children when they did not play well, also seemed more appropriate for the cultural context afforded to male interactions. In other words, their Weiqi training matched boys' experiences at their elementary schools and at home. In contrast, the girls may have felt out of place in this relatively hostile environment—increasingly so as the majority of their female classmates dropped out.

Though mothers are no doubt a part of the decision-making process to send their children to Weiqi schools, tales of parental influence consistently referred to fathers' encouragement, and often insistence, that their children study the game. Sylvia, a 3-*duan* amateur and Peking University student who had trained to become a professional Weiqi player as a child, was one such case. Sylvia's father pushed her to train to be a professional Weiqi player in spite of the fact that, as a female, the odds were against her success. Although she did not become a professional Weiqi player, she did enter a traditionally male area of study (biology) at China's preeminent university. In many ways Chinese women's roles have become more traditional in the past two decades as China's population moves away from the gender erasure that took place in the early years of the communist state. Yet cases such as Sylvia's attest to a growing set of options for women, both in and out of the Weiqi sphere.

Fang Weijing is a 2-*duan* professional and Peking University team member. She was also a member of China's national Weiqi team from 2000 until August 2011, and one of four female players to be admitted to China's national team in the first year that women were allowed to join. With full knowledge that most parents would be ecstatic if their children were admitted to Peking University, she smiled when she told me of her parents' unusual preference for her Weiqi career. "My parents were happier about my being ranked as a professional Weiqi player than when I was admitted to Peking University. [She smiles.] They felt that being a Weiqi professional is a more stable career. It's not likely I'd get rich as a Weiqi player, but teaching Weiqi provides a very stable income if you get a high enough rank."[31]

Fang's account depicts parents who are exceptional in encouraging their daughter to enter such a male-dominated sphere. Yet their support of her Weiqi career, as a woman in a very male-oriented world, might also stem from traditionalist assumptions that she would eventually get married and that her husband would be the primary income earner.

As a former member of China's national Weiqi team, Fang Weijing has made a name for herself in mixed doubles competitions. In Weiqi, pairing a man and a woman to take turns making moves is a highly specialized format that evolved out of competitions at formal sporting events. In these cases, because the male teammates are stronger players, and because they are not allowed to communicate with each other during a game, the female teammate's job is in part to follow her male counterpart's lead. She must see the long-term progression of his moves and support his strategy. This is not to downplay the women's achievements in this regard—they are members of the national team, after all. Nonetheless, it does further highlight the fact that even as women have entered Weiqi's professional realm, men continue to dominate the game.

Fang Weijing told me that it was precisely the dearth of female players that drew her to Weiqi. As a child she had debated whether to study Weiqi or Chinese chess, and her elementary school teacher told her that because there were so few female Weiqi players it would be easier to make a name for herself in this field. Because she was recruited during the first year that China's national Weiqi team admitted women, she had a particularly vivid memory for the politics of that time. When I asked her why China waited until the year 2000 to admit female players, she replied, "At that time there were many female professionals in Korea so China felt threatened. That first year there were four female players admitted to the national team. When I first joined the team I was still an amateur player—a 5-*duan* amateur—I didn't even have a professional rank."[32]

As with the men's national team that was established two decades earlier, women's entrance into professional Weiqi was born of international competition. Fang Weijing emphasized that she was still ranked as an amateur player when she was admitted to the team, in part to note the poor state of China's Weiqi only a decade earlier. Her statement also implicitly highlighted the progress that has been made, because today there are a greater number of professionally ranked female players.

In contemporary China, women have more options in sports and a range of other careers. This is by no means an uncomplicated process, for globalization is ushering in an array of contradictory messages for both women and men. It has inspired women to enter the workforce and to become housewives, to rebel against patriarchal control and to embrace it. As with men, rather than providing one template for women to live by, globalization and modernization seem to have created a greater range of choices for women. Expressions of contemporary womanhood are drawn from a mix of iconic images from Imperial China, Republican China, the early communist era, and today's globalized mass media. This includes several models of womanhood ranging from the early communist-era Iron Girls (who were famed for doing men's work such as coal mining), to housewives, to businesswomen. This is not to suggest that a woman is absolutely free to do as she chooses, for who is? In making these decisions she must rely on personal preferences, but she does so in the context of social conditions. These include parental and peer pressure, different regional cultures (Beijing, Shanghai, or Hong Kong, for example), and the economic and educational opportunities available to her. Regardless, if we consider China's population as a whole, there are more options for women than ever before in Chinese history. That women have gained entrance into the Weiqi sphere is no less than a miracle given the cultural biases against them. Yet it is a phenomenon that can also be seen in an array of other occupations and educational settings.

AMBIGUOUS IDENTITIES AND TAIWAN'S WOMEN'S TEAM

Taiwan's Weiqi team is rife with cultural and political ambiguity, stemming from the disputed nature of Taiwan's status as a nation or a Chinese province. Most people in Taiwan continue to think of it as an autonomous nation. It has its own government, military, currency, and distinctive culture, though it has influenced the PRC so much with its popular culture that the cultural divide is less than it once was.[33] In turn, the PRC points to the fact that Taiwan is overwhelmingly ethnically Chinese, and that it was part of China's territory before Japan took it as a colony in 1895. China reclaimed Taiwan after the Second World War under the Kuomintang government that fled the communist revolution in mainland China soon after. The communist-inspired PRC government continues to rule mainland China today. Both Taiwan and the PRC continue to devote a tremendous amount of energy and finances in an attempt to control world opinion on this matter. An uneasy truce has settled in which Taiwan can, for the moment, retain its independence. However, this is at the cost of asserting its nationhood outright—a proclamation for which the PRC has threatened immediate invasion.

The differences in conceptualizing Taiwan are never more apparent than with sports teams. Taiwan, as a sovereign state, has its own teams in both the Asian Games and the Olympics. Yet to assuage the PRC government, the team cannot be called the "Taiwan team." Instead it must go by the moniker of the "Chinese Taipei team." Taiwan, as well as the Olympics and Asian Games administrators, abides by the PRC mandate that Taiwan not proclaim its independence by using the country's name. Still, the very fact that Taiwan has its own team implicitly acknowledges that it is a political entity, for if it is not a separate nation how can China have two teams in the same competition? Taiwan's Weiqi team furthers this ambiguity because traditionally Taiwan's Weiqi players who wanted to compete professionally moved to Japan to train. In part this was because Taiwan was a colony of Japan from 1895 to 1945 and because the two cultures continue to share many commonalities today. In part it also attests to Japan's continued centrality in the Weiqi sphere.

In 2010, the Asian Games, the largest sporting event in East Asia aside from the Olympics, included Weiqi for the first time. South Korea dominated the Weiqi competitions, with three gold medals and one bronze. The PRC had three silver medals, and Taiwan tied with Japan for third place with one bronze medal each. Taiwan's women's team earned its bronze medal. This team included Hsieh Yi-min and Joanne Missingham (Hei Jiajia), who are especially worthy of mention here.

Hsieh Yi-min is a 6-*duan* professional from Taiwan who, in keeping with tradition, moved to Japan to train. Hsieh is notable less because she took this well-traveled path than because of her unprecedented success as a female Weiqi player. She is often referred to as the best female player in Japan, where she has won every important women's division championship. She is also known for holding more simultaneous Weiqi titles than any other woman before her.

Joanne Missingham is a 5-*duan* professional. Missingham was born in Australia to a Taiwanese mother and an Australian father. She moved to Taiwan with her family at the age of four and, unlike earlier generations of Weiqi players in Taiwan, she trained in Taiwan rather than moving to Japan. She was also the first Australian to earn a professional Weiqi rank. Joanne Missingham thereby highlights the Taiwan team's national ambiguity in distinctive ways.

Missingham also holds a unique place in the public imagination because many people in Taiwan and the PRC find her to be physically attractive. Any cursory search on the Web for her name will produce as many pages devoted to her appearance as to her considerable Weiqi achievements. Missingham has used her notoriety to make a call for equality in Weiqi competitions. When she played Weiqi at the 2011 Qiandeng Cup, for example, she learned that, in addition to the prize money, the competition would award US$286 for every game that a male competitor played, whereas the women's division players would be given nothing.[34] In protest, she and the three other female players withdrew from the competition. A week later, while playing at another competition, Missingham held a fan inscribed with the Chinese characters "protest against gender discrimination" (*kangyi xingbie qishi*). This event gained far more press coverage than all but the most prestigious Weiqi competitions. Most of the people I spoke with simply shrugged and said something to the effect of "That's just the way it is" or "Men are better players so they should get more prize money." It seems very likely, then, that the publicity surrounding this event had more to do with a series of photos of the attractive Missingham than a general concern with the gender inequality at the competition. This also points to the ways that Missingham is using her special position in the Weiqi world to achieve greater ends.

Missingham, both by virtue of her mixed race, her Australian nationality, and her physical appearance, is a conceptual anomaly for many. One should not forget, however, that as a Weiqi player Missingham is a force to be reckoned with. She was only sixteen years old when she competed in the 2010 Asian Games, and her star is clearly still rising.

Over the years, Taiwan has also had some remarkably talented male Weiqi players. At the moment, however, both Hsieh and Missingham have become household names in China and Taiwan—even among people who have no interest in the game. In their own ways, both Weiqi players highlight the tensions that surround Taiwan's political status while also contesting gender biases.

CONSTRUCTING MASCULINITIES AND THE WEIQI SPHERE

What does it mean to be a man? In any culture the answer to this question is fraught with an overwhelming range of often-contradictory possibilities. If one explores this in conjunction with the breathtaking cultural changes in China over the past few decades, the complexities of the issue grow exponentially. On the surface, the board game Weiqi might seem to have little to do with constructions of masculinity, since the overtly physical is often privileged in these paradigms. Yet Weiqi continues to be a decidedly male realm that incorporates historical images of the Confucian gentleman, martial strategists, innate genius, and an unforgiving work ethic. It serves as an emblem of intensely male-coded Chinese culture that is both localized and transnational in East Asia's political economy.

The extreme male orientation of Weiqi clubs and schools offers a different construction of masculinity than most gender studies on China, which tend to define manhood in the context of sexual orientation, womanizing, or Chinese-style machismo.[35] These are of course important areas of inquiry, but in examining the ways that men construct cultured personas through this game I hope to address a different set of issues than the current scholarship provides. Other ways to proclaim masculine identities include Confucian filial piety, devoted fatherhood, and being a good husband. They might also feature the embodiment of righteousness, benevolence, intellectual prowess, proper citizenship, and loyalty to one's friends and to the state. Weiqi is an unexamined sphere that incorporates many of these attributes in its imagery, thereby evincing an intricate web of cultural values. These virtues are drawn on to establish the ways that Chinese boys become men, and the manner in which men construct their new identities by incorporating ancient paradigms.

There is surprisingly little scholarship on normative masculinity in China. To the degree that Chinese masculinity has been addressed, it has largely been in the fields of literature and film studies.[36] Anthropological inquiry, and indeed the social sciences as a whole, has been curiously slow in rising to this challenge.[37] As China reclaims its past by moving away from earlier communist ideals, modern constructions of gender are strikingly similar to those in days of old. This includes engaging in ritual (*li*) and the continuation of men's traditional use of women as currencies of exchange.[38] It also features the reemergence of traditional dress, behavior, and vocabulary in an array of dining and drinking establishments.[39] This reemergence of classical etiquette conspicuously manifests itself by appropriating traditionalist forms by self-consciously situating itself before PRC attempts to erase China's past. It is no coincidence that these constructions of masculine identity also hearken back to an era of unquestioned male supremacy at a time when China thought of itself as the undisputed dominant power in the world. Weiqi, as an extension of traditional gentlemanly behavior, is part of this process—a reinvention of tradition as a uniquely modern act.

Because my three primary fieldwork sites included different age groups (children, university students, and retired senior citizens), I was witness to distinct stages in men's lives. Weiqi's imagery shifted in each setting. It was lauded as a disciplinary mechanism that taught logic and proper behavior to children. For university students it was used to critique China's highly competitive political economy and to construct an idealized form of manhood that was based on images of cultured gentlemen from days of old. For the elderly it was an emblem of how much life in China had improved, and for the pleasures of leisure in one's old age.

Economic class was also a point of contrast. The children who could afford Weiqi instruction ranged from decidedly middle class to elite, as did the vast majority of Peking University students. In contrast, the parkgoers were working class and frequently evinced a more openly aggressive masculine ethos. This could be seen in their behavior and speech, but also in their playing styles. Peking University students made moves relatively slowly and cautiously.

If they spoke during a game it was in hushed tones. In contrast, working-class Weiqi players at parks played far more aggressively on the board as their friends loudly commented on their games.

The differences in the cultural meanings of the game were in some ways less remarkable than the commonalities of the themes that these very disparate groups spoke of. People in all three of my primary research sites emphasized the importance of the Weiqi strategy of "seizing the initiative" (*xianshou*), for example. Seizing the initiative represents more than just a playing style. It is a statement of one's place in society, individual psychology, and performance of masculinity. It is an attempt to control a situation, to maximize profit, as well as to dominate, and avoid being dominated, by other men. Weiqi players frequently assert that in teaching this lesson the game builds character and trains one to be a better man.

As my fieldwork in Beijing progressed, it did not take long before patterns emerged that linked individual masculinities with the perceived particularities of nation and race. Beijing residents uniformly spoke of people in Japan as being cautious and contemplative players, of Koreans as being impulsive, intuitive, and aggressive, and of the Chinese style of play as having found the proper balance between the two. These approximations of regionally bound playing styles draw on, and confirm, widespread social stereotypes in China about men in all three cultures that extend beyond the purview of the game.

Many people I interviewed saw Weiqi strategy as a part of a Chinese cultural emphasis on relying on one's intellect rather than physical orientation. Guan Yang, a 4-*duan* amateur and Peking University graduate student, said, "In my twenty years of playing Weiqi I think I have found something of the Chinese character.... We love to compete by mind, by intelligence, not by force. I think you can learn this idea from Weiqi."[40]

As in other areas of the world, China's historical and literary accounts of warfare include tales of daring physical prowess. Yet Odysseus-like figures who win battles through cunning are remarkably prevalent in these accounts. Instead of being something to be ashamed of, intellect, combined with a healthy dose of craftiness, is usually framed as being heroic in these tales. This, in turn, shapes the ways that contemporary men in China think about Weiqi, war, politics, economics, and maneuvering in social hierarchies. Rather than being seen as separate spheres, they are frequently represented as being intricately interlaced, and Weiqi is thought to train a man to maximize his advantage in any situation.

Because of its ancient roots in elite Chinese society, Weiqi is a class marker in the present age and a reminder of China's historical greatness. Parents hope that their sons will profit from emulating historical figures who embodied elite gentlemanly behavior and subtle military strategies. This is as much a part of the rationale for teaching boys Weiqi as the more demonstrable benefits of math and economic strategy for which the game is frequently lauded. In short, Weiqi provides a way of embracing the past to meet the future. It is a means to teach one's sons not only rational thought, but also the proper demeanor and mind-set associated with cultured gentlemen in China's ancient history. In doing so they appropriate the past to help mediate the present moment.

Weiqi is also an emblem of masculine behavior that is grounded in East Asian competition. There is a good deal of scholarship that has explored the ways that Chinese concerns with masculinity are in part a reaction to feeling emasculated by Western Orientalism in both the colonial period and today's global media.[41] However, this is only one set of concerns that vies for attention with emotions arising out of the perceived humiliation of being dominated by Japan in the Pacific War, disempowered by the elite in Imperial China, or monitored in the somewhat Orwellian early decades of the PRC government.

Studies focusing on acts of resistance against the hegemonic West have arguably given it corporeal form. As issues of globalization and localization, Orientalism, and its corresponding forms of resistance have become more central to English-language China studies, there is a danger of losing sight of the fact that there are concerns in China that do not directly relate to the West. It is true that most status symbols in China evoke Western imagery—suits, sports cars, and coffee shops, to name a few. Yet Weiqi is both high status and Chinese and thereby takes on great symbolic force for both the individual and the nation.

In China there is very little separation between conceptions of individuals and society. Rather than extolling notions of Adam Smith's "invisible hand," in which self-interested individuals are thought to balance each other out for a harmonious, just, and profitable society, the Chinese sociopolitical model is based on Confucian conceptions of loyalty, benevolence, and obedience. By extension, the microcosm of a son's filial behavior is intricately linked with the macrocosm of loyalty to the state. In this worldview, a healthy and well-educated son will lead to a robust race and nation. This conceptual framework draws on Confucian theory and, more often than not, defaults to an iconic vision of a cultured gentleman who lives his life beyond reproach. The idealized male citizen who evokes this image continues to occupy a central part of the Chinese worldview today. Conceptions of masculinity are not only discussions of individual psychology and behavior, therefore, but also represent a masculinized nation-state that is based on a nostalgic recreation of the past to suit the modern age.

This book is an effort to see a more personal side of Chinese life. This is not to say that China's political economy can be ignored. Nor is it to suggest that we should neglect Chinese nationalism. Yet for many, if not most people in China, nationalist sentiment is an afterthought. It is naturalized to the point that it goes unquestioned but it remains relatively peripheral to the ways that people live their daily lives. Most people I spoke with were proud that China's economy had overtaken Japan's to become the second largest in the world, and they did not seem displeased to see that America had its own set of problems. Yet at the end of the day, like their American counterparts, they were far more focused on their careers and their families, their pastimes and their romantic relationships, than on anything beyond their nation's borders.

When nationalist sentiments do arise in the Weiqi sphere, it is usually in the form of pride in China's accomplishments. Though their East Asian neighbors are some of their main competitors in economics, politics, and Weiqi, discussions of Japan and Korea are for the most part broached with a remarkable amount of respect; even admiration. Weiqi is a shared culture, a mutual love, and a respected art that teaches a man to respect his rivals. In some ways this results in identifying with fellow Weiqi players more than with many of their countrymen. In the Weiqi sphere, the world is not only divided by nations, but also by those who do or do not play the game.

Multiple Metaphors and Mystical Imaginaries

A CULTURAL HISTORY OF WEIQI

Do not boast of victory, nor complain about defeat! It is proper for a [gentleman (*junzi*)] *to appear modest and generous; only vulgar persons manifest expressions of anger and rage. A good player should not exalt his skills; the beginner should not be timorous, but should sit calmly and breathe regularly: in this way, the battle is half won. A player whose face reveals a disturbed state of mind is already losing.*

ZHANG NI, Weiqi in Thirteen Chapters,
1049–54 A.D.[1]

Thus there are two forms of encirclement by the enemy forces and two forms of encirclement by our own—rather like a game of Weiqi. Campaigns and battles fought by the two sides resemble the capturing of each other's pieces, and the establishment of strongholds by the enemy and of guerilla base areas by us resembles moves to dominate spaces on the board. It is the matter of "dominating the spaces" that the great strategic role of guerilla base areas in the rear of the enemy is revealed.

MAO ZEDONG, Problems of Strategy in Guerilla War
against Japan, 1938[2]

ALL GAMES HAVE THEIR METAPHORS. In the West this is most often evinced by a particular fascination with the thin line between genius and madness. This trope is most often expressed with chess but also with the game Scrabble and even Weiqi as it appears, albeit briefly, in Western movies such as *A Beautiful Mind* and *Pi*. Both films feature brilliant mathematician madmen who are first enamored with, and then humbled by, the game.[3]

In contrast, East Asian writings on games, though acknowledging the eccentricities of gamesters, do not go so far as to depict them as insane and are far more admiring in tone.[4] Instead, the accounts tend to focus on the extreme physical toll of such intense devotion and concentration.[5] Fictional depictions of board games in China also focus on cultural peripherally through poverty linked with the issue of unrecognized and unrewarded genius.[6]

Since the establishment of the People's Republic of China (PRC), Weiqi was transformed from being one of "four arts" (*si yi*) to one of the condemned "four olds" (*si lao*). Later, it came to represent China's reclaiming of lost power, and indeed dignity, in East Asia. Japanese anime and manga have successfully promoted the game to youth throughout the world.[7] Contemporary stories such as the Korean novelist Sung-Hwa Hong's *First Kyu* and the Chinese novelist Shan Sa's *The Girl Who Played Go,* as well as the first cinematic Chinese and Japanese coproduction *The Go Masters,* document and dream about the game.[8]

As Chinese politics have changed over the millennia, so has Weiqi's imagery. Weiqi is a metaphor for everything from Confucian virtue to Buddhist precepts against greed to Maoist military strategy. Fans of the game link it to divination, *The Book of Changes,* and, on one occasion, the genetic code.[9] Chinese and Japanese hagiographies speak of the great Weiqi masters with near-religious awe, lauding their lives as testaments to the balance between innate talent and the seemingly inhuman work ethic that is necessary to rise to the top.[10] One sees Weiqi as a visual metaphor on book covers such as the English-language political science book *Reshaping the Taiwan Strait,* in which Weiqi pieces are placed on a map of the world.[11] Another example is the Chinese-language book *Actually, Cao Cao Was a Management Genius,* in which the Weiqi stones have Chinese characters such as employee (*yongren*), eliminating risk (*paixian*), innovation (*shouquan*), supervision (*yuren*), and delegation of authority (*shouquan*) written on them.[12] This is done to emphasize the complicated logic structure of successful business. Weiqi also sets the backdrop for scenes in historical dramas such as the fourteenth-century historical novel *The Three Kingdoms,* in which the characters Cao Cao and Guangong play the game, and a range of Japanese popular culture has inspired players in China and beyond.[13]

THE RULES

Before we explore Weiqi's metaphors in more depth, it may be helpful to get a sense of how one plays the game and what a finished game looks like. Should you decide you would like to learn the game in earnest, there are several Web venues that provide a more comprehensive step-by-step set of instructions. I provide links to some of these sites on my Web page.[14] One does not need not know how the game is played to understand the overall analysis of this book, however, so the reader can also feel free to skip this section. A quick glance at the illustrations may be helpful in conceptualizing the game, however.

Initially, Weiqi's rules are easier to learn than chess because although chess has only thirty-two pieces, six of them move in very different ways. The pawn is in some ways the trickiest for a beginner because it can move either one or two spaces on its first move, after which it can only move one space at a time, and always forward, unless it is taking a piece in which case it must move diagonally. If it can reach the end of the board then it can transform into any of the more powerful pieces the player chooses with the corresponding moves of that piece. The other five kinds of pieces all have their own style of movements as well.

In English, Weiqi pieces are referred to as a "stones."[15] Each stone works in the same way that every other stone does. They are placed on the intersections of lines on the board, or they are captured and taken off the board, but they never move while they are on the board. Although there are many tricks to the trade, there are only five basic rules of the game: (1) where to place the stones, (2) how to take a stone, (3) learning about something called having "two eyes" (*liang yan*), which defines how to kill a group or keep a group from being killed, (4) not making the same move twice in a row, (5) not putting oneself in a position in which a stone is automatically dead.[16] In other words, one is prohibited from having a group commit suicide. One must also learn to count the points at the end of the game to see who has won.

Weiqi is played on a board with a 19 × 19 grid, and one need only be concerned with surrounding pieces on the vertical and horizontal lines— diagonal pieces do not influence each other. Unlike in chess, black moves first. The stones are either placed on the board or taken off if captured. They never move once they are on the board. If you think of each line as a hallway, the goal is to block all of the hallways so that your opponent cannot retreat.[17] If you are successful at this, then you capture your opponent's stones.

In figure 2, group 1 (top left corner), if black places a stone at A, he will take the white stone because he has blocked all of the vertical and horizontal hallways. When only one stone is needed to kill a group, the group is in danger of being taken (*da chi*). The number of hallway exits that are not blocked are called "liberties" (*qi*). Each of the white groups 1–5 has only one liberty

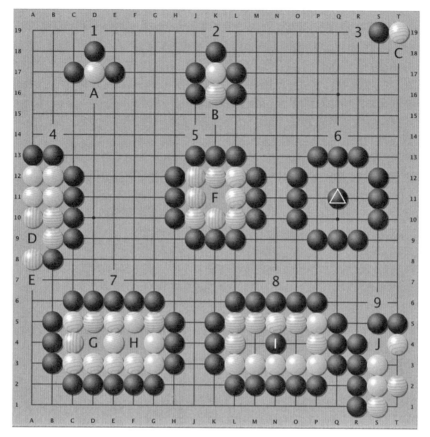

FIGURE 2. How to take one's opponent's stones.

(A through D, and F). To take a group you fill in the last of its liberties. To kill groups 1 through 3 you would place a black stone at A, B, and C, respectively. If it is white's move, white could move to A, B, or C to try to escape.

The outside boundary of the board is like an outer wall that surrounds the hallways. Just as one cannot retreat through a wall, this counts as having blocked hallways along the edge of the board. Group 4 (middle left) also only has one liberty (D). If black plays at D, black will take the seven stones above D, though not the stone below D. If white moves at D first then black can move at E to take all of the white stones.

Group 5 (middle) is tricky because if black places a stone at F he is also completely surrounded. Normally you are not allowed to put a stone in a suicidal position like this. You are only allowed to do this if you are taking the other person's stones, after which your stone is no longer surrounded. In other words, when black places a stone at F he will take the white stones off the board, so that his stone will no longer be in danger and the group will look like group 6 (middle right).

A liberty in the middle of a group is called an "eye" (*yan*). White group 5 has one eye (F), and white group 7 has two eyes (G and H). For the beginning player, the most conceptually difficult part of the game is ascertaining whether or not a group has two eyes. This is important, because if a group has two eyes it can never be taken. For example, white group 7 (bottom left) has two eyes (G and H). If black places a stone in the left eye (G), the black stone is putting itself in danger, but it has not taken the group because the H liberty has not been filled in. This is not allowed, just as putting oneself in check is not allowed in chess. If we try the other eye (H), it has the same result because the liberty G has not been filled in. Because this white group has two eyes, it can never be taken and it will remain as is until the end of the game. When someone cannot take a group of stones it is said to be "alive" (*huo*). If there is no way for the group to obtain two eyes then it is "dead" (*si*). When a group is dead, you do not have to go through the trouble of taking it any more. Thus, one of the primary goals in Weiqi is to make sure that each of your groups has two eyes and to try to limit each of your opponent's groups to one or no eyes.

Group 8 (bottom middle) appears to have two eyes, but if black plays at I then white will either have to fill in its own stones to take it, in which case black could play at I and take the whole group. Alternatively, white can move somewhere else, after which black can fill in white's eye. In other words, if black plays I first, the white group is dead, but if white saves the group by playing at that spot first then this group will be alive. In that case, this white group will remain on the board for the rest of the game (as with group 7 on the bottom left of the board). If black plays I first then there is no need to fill in more of white's liberties because both players should recognize that this group is already dead. The white stones will automatically be taken off the board at the end of the game.

Group 9 (bottom right) has yet to be decided. If white plays at J then it will have two eyes. If black plays at J first, however, then that white group is dead because the top eye would eventually get filled in and would end up looking something like group 4.

In the Japanese counting system (which is the system that is most commonly used in the United States) one counts points according to the spaces that have been surrounded and adds the number of stones one has taken off

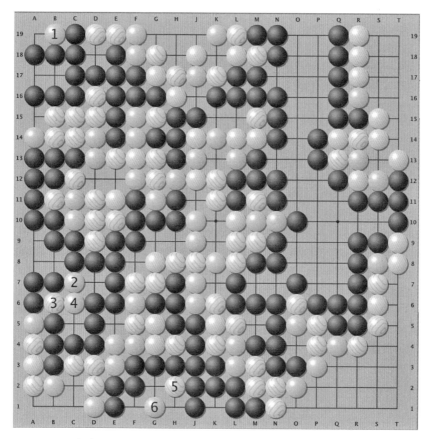

FIGURE 3. Black wins by 2.5 points.

the board. For example, if black takes group 9 by playing at J, the only living group white has on this board is group 7. White would therefore have only two points (from its liberties at G and H), and black would clearly win the game.

Figure 3 is a completed game. In this game I (black) won by 2.5 points on the Internet server KGS (Kiseido Go Server). Because white stones 1–5 are surrounded and do not have two eyes, they are taken off the board at the end of the game before the counting begins. You might ask how I could win by 2.5 stones. The answer is that white is given 6.5 points at the beginning of the game to make up for the fact that black got to make the first move.

Today, the counting system is the only significant variation in Weiqi. Japan uses "territory scoring," in which one counts the surrounded space and adds a point each for any of the stones that were taken during the game. China uses "area scoring," in which one counts both one's stones and the empty spaces one has surrounded, but not the stones one has taken during the game. Because of Japan's prominent place in the Weiqi world, almost everyone outside of China uses the Japanese counting system. The end score is almost identical when using territory scoring or area scoring, but after years of using both systems I still find the Japanese method much easier for counting the points at the end of the game.

There are other smaller details in the game's rules, but for the purposes of this introduction this is enough. If you understand what I have just presented (no easy task, I know) you are essentially now a Weiqi player. Whether or not you were able to understand all of this explanation, you should have a better sense for both the simplicity and the complexity of the game.

WEIQI IN COMPARISON WITH CHESS

Weiqi's significance in Asia is analogous to the role of chess in Cold War politics between the United States and Russia in that it emphasizes both cultural sharing and aggressive competition. There are also several similarities in the nature of the games themselves. Both are games of logic. Neither contains an element of chance other than if one's opponent is careless or when a game develops in ways that neither side anticipated. Both games were historically embedded in elite male culture, and both are immersed in war imagery. Yet if chess represents a war, in which territory and battlegrounds are defined at the outset, Weiqi creates and destroys territories as the game progresses.[18]

Though the computer program Deep Blue defeated world chess champion Gary Kasparov in 1997, computer programmers agree that they are not even close to developing software that can compete with a professional Weiqi player. There are several reasons for this. For one, chess computer programmers have a thirty-year head start. Second, because chess has six different types of pieces, all of varying worth, it is easier to program a computer to prioritize one piece over another. For example, one can assign differing points to the various pieces so that a computer program knows to protect the king at all costs and that a queen is worth more than a pawn. In contrast, all individual Weiqi pieces are alike until they develop in relation to other pieces.

The Weiqi board has a 19 × 19 grid rather than the 8 × 8 squares of a chessboard. Weiqi is therefore more difficult for a computer because there are so many more moves to choose from. On average, a chess player is faced with 25–35 possible moves, as opposed to 200–250 in Weiqi.[19] As a *New York Times* article points out, this poses an exponentially larger problem for computers: "In chess the approximate number of possible board positions after only four moves is typically 35 × 35 × 35 × 35 = 1,500,625. For Go the number is 200 × 200 × 200 × 200 = 1,600,000,000—and far more toward the beginning of a game. Search one ply deeper and the numbers rapidly diverge: about 1.8 billion possible outcomes for chess and 64 trillion for Go."[20]

Several people have emphasized that in fact computer chess does not reason like a human but instead relies on "brute force"—scanning thousands of preexisting games and problem sets to see what move has led to victory in the past.[21] Deep Blue overcomes the challenge of chess because it is able to examine 200 million positions a second.[22]

Even with this amazing capacity, computer programs continue to be overwhelmed by Weiqi because there are so many possible moves. This is not to say that they are not making progress, however. On September 17, 2011, "The Hand" (*benshou*), a computer equivalent to Deep Blue for Weiqi, beat professional Weiqi player Yu Bing in two games on a 9 × 9 board. To achieve this, however, it was given a one-stone handicap (the equivalent of an extra move at the beginning of the game).[23] In addition to the handicap, playing on a 9 × 9 board, which is usually used to train children, puts professionals at a disadvantage because they are used to playing on the 19 × 19 grid.[24] Nevertheless, this marks a significant breakthrough in computer Weiqi and seems to indicate that developing a program to beat humans on a 19 × 19 board is just a matter of time. For now, however, this means that Weiqi is still primarily a human interaction, free of the somewhat stifling pressures of computer analysis that have transformed the nature of chess in recent decades.[25]

Many Weiqi enthusiasts cite the lack of a sophisticated Weiqi computer program to assert that Weiqi is much more complex than chess, but one need not claim one game's superiority over the other. Both games are enjoyable and challenging to any level of player. Both are simple enough that children can learn them yet complex enough that they take a lifetime to master. Few players can truly be said to have mastered either of these games at all.

If many Weiqi players believe it is more challenging than chess, I suspect it is either because they do not fully understand chess or because they understand it too well—that is, like myself, they started at such a young age that they can't remember learning the game. In such cases, the rules of chess are internalized to such an extent that it seems more intuitive for many Westerners, much as I suspect the average East Asian Weiqi player would find Weiqi to be more intuitive than chess because he or she had learned Weiqi as a child. Both games employ similar capacities to problem solve, to think ahead, and to logically and intuitively assess one's opponent's style. In both games one might think out a sequence of several moves that lead to victory, with any deviation from that path leading to failure.

Yet as someone who has played both games for years I confess that I find chess to be more constricted because of the relatively limited range of possible moves and somehow more mechanical. Both games have strokes of genius that are nothing short of art, and both have local strategies that are based on a logical succession of moves. Even so, Weiqi has a more abstract strategy—flows of space that I have yet to fully comprehend despite playing quite regularly for more than a decade.

Like chess, Weiqi is very time consuming. Until the middle of the twentieth century it was not unheard of for games to last several days. Today, one can play a speed game in fifteen minutes, and an average amateur game might last from thirty minutes to an hour. Still, any dedicated player, even as an amateur, has spent countless hours practicing and studying books that include openings, "life-and-death" problems, and general strategies. It is precisely this time investment that helps to mark Weiqi as an elite activity, which is another point of similarity with the role of chess in the West.

As in chess, there are both microcosmic and macrocosmic strategies in Weiqi. In chess one focuses on taking pieces or groups of pieces. In Weiqi one also wants to take one's opponent's pieces (stones), but to win the game one must possess a greater area on the board. Unlike chess, in which the loss of even a single pawn often determines the outcome of the game, in Weiqi there are several battles occurring on the board at one time, and one can lose a fairly large battle and still win the game.

For the most part, board games have been ignored in academic studies, but we should remember that games reflect, teach, and legitimate cultural mores. Mary Flanagan's account of the mid-nineteenth-century French game The Wandering Jew (*Le Juif Errant*), for example, outlines the ways that Jews were portrayed in the game as stereotypes of the day, which ranged from

Moses to ghosts.[26] In this game the Jew also represented the cholera epidemic that followed him around on the board.[27]

More familiar to a contemporary readership is the range of hegemonic instruction of the board game Monopoly, which teaches children the joys of land ownership and to weigh the costs and benefits of high-end investment versus becoming a slumlord. Jail, as both a geographic and allegorical constant, is a relatively benign threat on the board. This teaches children that one must run the risk of imprisonment if one wants to succeed in this capitalist utopia.

Chess is embedded in feudalistic imagery with its knights and bishops, kings and queens. The relative lack of value of the pawns (also read as peasants or foot soldiers) has become synonymous with helpless expendability, as seen in expressions such as "He was only a pawn in their game." In turn, knights and bishops are of less worth than the queen, and the game ends when the king is captured. Significantly, the king's importance results in the game centering on his protection or capture, a fact that highlights his vulnerability and limits his mobility throughout the game. In short, chess can be read as a metaphor for the real political economy of feudal Europe. This is a war of distinctive personalities—the king whose movement is stilted by his very importance, the knight who leaps over other pieces on his trusty steed, the politically oriented bishop who always maneuvers diagonally rather than moving straight ahead, and the queen who pretty much does as she pleases.

In contrast, Weiqi stones are imaginatively flat—they are simply stone-shaped objects without personalities. Yet, for many, the pattern that each game's pieces make on the board evokes the cosmos. Several people I interviewed told me that whereas chess reflects individuals in a highly structured hierarchy, Weiqi emphasizes the worth of social relations. Every piece is equal to every other piece, and they rise in value only as they amass in larger groups—something akin to the importance of one soldier's life to that of a troop to that of a battalion. A well-placed soldier can lead to the downfall of an entire battalion, but on the whole, the larger a group, the more powerful it becomes.

Both games are appealing because they offer tangible victory and defeat. I suggest that this is also a large part of people's love of gambling, sports, and many films in that they provide clear-cut cases of success and loss, which nicely contrast our more ambiguous lives. Of course, the concrete nature of the outcome also adds to the visceral reaction to defeat. This was exactly the problem for John Nash in the movie *A Beautiful Mind,* for example, in that when he lost a game of Weiqi to his nemesis there was no psychological room to maneuver—his loss was incontrovertible.[28]

RELIGIOUS MYSTICISM AND HISTORICAL TELEOLOGIES

According to ancient lore, Weiqi was invented by Emperor Yao somewhere around 2300 B.C. The Emperor Yao mythology was brought up with such remarkable frequency in my interviews that I would be surprised if there was a Weiqi player in China who was not familiar with the tale. In fact, the majority of people I spoke with cited this myth as evidence that the game was several millennia old. This sentiment featured an array of timelines ranging from "at least" three thousand years to five thousand years old. English-language tutorials, books, and Web pages introducing the game rather unquestioningly adopt these claims.[29] Yet this approach loses sight of how malleable oral history can be. It is quite possible that Weiqi was inserted into the legend centuries after the fact.

The first written records of Weiqi date back approximately twenty-five hundred years. Fang Tianfeng is an 8-*duan* pro who teaches Weiqi classes at Peking University, Tsing-Hua University, and Beijing Science University: "It's hard to say exactly when Weiqi appeared. Because the oldest written record is a history book called *The Chronicles of Zuo (Zuo Zhuan)*. This book says, 'This happened in that year, et cetera.' In it there's a line that says, 'The Weiqi player picks up the piece but doesn't know where to play' (*ju qi bu ding*). This is the earliest written record that mentions Weiqi. This was written around 448 B.C., so that was twenty-five hundred years ago. But if Weiqi was around before that or not it is hard to say for sure. This is the earliest reference we've found to date."[30]

The passage from the *Chronicles of Zuo* that Fang Tianfeng is referring to told of a government advisor named Ning Xi who agreed to help Duke Xian take over the State of Wei. Before it mentions Weiqi, it situates the tale in a structure of Confucian understandings. When a man named Dashuwenzi learns of this, he states, "The *Shijing* says 'If I cannot take care of myself, how can I care of my descendants?' Ning Xi is not thinking about his descendants. How can make this promise to the Duke Xian of Wei? A gentleman (*junzi*) should first consider things from all sides. The *Shijing* says, 'One should pay attention to every aspect of everything one does in order not to be trapped in a dangerous situation.'"

Dashuwenzi's reaction is both emotional and rational. It is charged with anger yet seeks to outline historical precedent by referring to older texts. By Chinese standards, his statement is a remarkably straightforward assertion that Ning Xi has failed to live up to historical standards of being a Confucian gentleman (*junzi*). He conceptualizes this as having a responsibility to the past (as seen by his referencing both the *Shijing* and the Confucian conception of rights and obligations). It also looks toward the future in the form of obligation to one's descendants. His statement that "a gentleman should first consider things from all sides" was quoted in several of my interviews about Weiqi, demonstrating the powerful hold that this account has had on the contemporary world. The passage soon goes on to specifically reference Weiqi: "The way Ning Xi is thinking about Duke Xian's attempt to retake the country—his attitude towards this is less cautious than if he were playing a game of Weiqi. In this way, how can he avoid disaster? If someone playing Weiqi picks up a stone and does not know where to play (*ju qi bu ding*) he cannot defeat his opponent. Is it not even worse if he cannot make up his mind who his king is? In this way he cannot avoid disaster. His family has been loyal officers of the state for nine generations. If he destroys this with one decision it is really a shame."[31]

To this day, the classical Chinese saying "to pick up a piece with uncertainty" (*ju qi bu ding*) is used to refer to a situation in which someone hesitates without acting, or acts with no overall plan. Although this is the oldest written record that mentions Weiqi, one should note that in this account the author does not feel it is necessary to explain what Weiqi is, but instead uses the game to illustrate his point. It is clear that the author assumes the reader will understand the reference. It therefore seems reasonable to deduce that the game was already well known when the account was written.

Taking this passage as a whole, one is again confronted with the ways that Weiqi is embedded in conceptions of Confucian gentlemen and becomes representative of proper ways of behavior. The *Zuo Zhuan* account does not imply that Weiqi is of great importance. Yet it suggests that Weiqi is a simplified structure for values that are important to maneuvering in society. This should not be taken lightly, for in this account Weiqi also serves as a basic model for proper gentlemanly behavior and the challenges of maneuvering in perilous political intrigues. Behaving as a Confucian gentleman, then, has remarkable overlap with the strategies of Weiqi. Both necessitate careful consideration of the long-term repercussions of each action. Both advise caution and emphasize the importance of having a well-formed plan before one acts. The fact that the passage is mentioned so often in contemporary China, both in and outside of Weiqi circles, points to its resonance even today.

It is commonly postulated that Weiqi originated as a tool for astrological divination or accounting, but there is no evidence for either. Joseph Needham's statement "The more one investigates the origin of Weiqi in Asia, the more intimate its connection with astrology and astronomy appear to be" is quoted in both Chinese and English writings on the game in an attempt to validate the idea that Weiqi arose out of religious practice.[32] Needham is absolutely correct that some aficionados of the game emphasize its astrological symbolism today, but this is not the same as it arising out of astrological practice. As with using Emperor Yao mythology to establish the game's age, the astrological argument assumes that because contemporary discourse about Weiqi asserts that it had origins in astrology and divination, the game must have originated from astrological and divinatory uses. To date, however, there is no concrete archeological or historical evidence for this theory.

There is no doubt that Weiqi has been deeply immersed in astrological imagery for centuries, however. Zhang Ni's eleventh-century treatise *Weiqi in Thirteen Chapters* (*Qijing Shisan Pian*) is but one example of this: "The three hundred and sixty intersections [on the Weiqi board] correspond to the number of days in a year. Divided into four corners like the four seasons, they have ninety intersections each, like the number of days in a season. There are seventy-two intersections on the sides, like the number of five-day weeks in a year."[33]

Masayoshi Shirakawa outlines some of the Japanese terms that link the game with cosmic significance, using Japanese examples such "the axis of heaven" (*tengen*) and "earth" (*ji*) that link black and white stones with yin and yang.[34] Shirakawa further suggests that ancient 19 × 19 boards only had five handicap points, representing five planets (Jupiter, Mars, Saturn, Venus, and Mercury) or the five elements (wood, fire, earth, metal, and water).[35] He then links the Weiqi board to the calendar because of its 361 intersections, which, he suggests, when added to the four-corner handicap, equal 365 points, which directly corresponds to the calendar.[36] This common trope overlooks the fact that it was only in the Tang Dynasty (618–907 A.D.) that the Weiqi board changed from a 17 × 17 grid with 289 intersections to a

19 × 19 grid with 361 intersections.[37] It seems fairly certain, therefore, that this change marked a growing desire to symbolically link the Weiqi board with the solar calendar after the fact, in an era when it clearly was not being used as a divinatory tool.

Contemporary Weiqi scholars continue to associate the origins of the game with divination, the *I-Ching,* and "the way" (*dao*).[38] Written accounts of Weiqi also link the game to enlightenment. Xie Guofang writes that Weiqi can teach the player to be better person (*rensheng zheli*), for example.[39] He goes on to state that playing Weiqi disciplines the player in language reminiscent of Buddhist meditation practice. Xie lists five stages: first, stillness (*ding*) in that one's body does not move as one plays; second, intellectual focus (*jing*); third, peace (*an*)—the balance of mind and body; fourth, thoughtfulness (*lü*); and fifth, enlightenment (*de*).[40] Xie asserts that if one can achieve the first four stages of playing Weiqi, the fifth stage, that of enlightenment, will be the natural result.[41]

In keeping with this, the highest level of play was traditionally thought to be an aesthetic art form that connected to larger spiritual forces. Often called a "hand conversation" (*shoutan*), winning or losing was thought to be secondary to creating a harmonious balance on the board. The traditional placement of the stone between outstretched pointer and middle fingers further emphasized the game as a ritual.[42]

Fang Tianfeng, the 8-*duan* professional who teaches Weiqi at Peking University, explained the history of the term "hand conversation": "The saying 'hand conversation' is from the East Jin Dynasty. That was just under one thousand years ago. During the Eastern Jin Dynasty there was a group of Buddhist monks. Back then there were a lot of Buddhist monks. One group of monks had taken an oath of silence. No matter what they wouldn't speak. In this group of monks was an expert Weiqi player. He played Weiqi but of course he couldn't speak. So after that, people started to say 'hand conversation.' This is when you can tell what is in someone's heart from the way he plays Weiqi."[43]

Today the term "hand conversation" is commonly heard among Weiqi players around the world. Though I have spoken with one or two people in China who said that one could not really gain insights into someone's personality from their playing style, most insisted on this connection. They further emphasized that one could become emotionally close to people with whom one played Weiqi precisely because of the greater understanding that "hand conversations" provided.

Fang Tianfeng went on to outline the long historical associations with Weiqi and Buddhist enlightenment:

> Buddhism has of course been in China for a very long time. Temple monks also played Weiqi. Because they felt that internal cultivation (xiuxing) was similar to playing Weiqi. So historically most Buddhist monks could play Weiqi. . . . This dates back a long time. For instance, [the famous historical Weiqi player] Zhu Yuanzhang played Weiqi because he was a monk. Many of the temple monks played. This was also true in Japan. In Japan the monks had a saying, "You can only win if you don't care if you win." Their monks also felt that playing Weiqi was a form of internal cultivation. Because if you play it is because you want to win. So playing while eliminating the desire to win is a form of internal cultivation. Only then can you win. So temple monks felt that playing Weiqi helped them in their internal cultivation.[44]

Similarly, in the article "The Art of Black and White" Chen Zu-yan links Weiqi to spirituality, pointing out that poetry about Weiqi often used the game to emphasize "the triviality of victory and defeat."[45] His reasoning is that when one puts the pieces away at the end of the game it "underscores the meaninglessness of fighting, the futility of victory, and the emptiness of life."[46] The roughly equal swirling balance of black and white pieces on the board is also highlighted as representing a harmonic balance of yin and yang.[47]

In addition to the Emperor Yao story, there are several other ancient Chinese myths associated with the game. Perhaps the most famous of these is "The Axe-Handle Story," which tells of a woodsman who, wandering the forest, saw two immortals playing Weiqi. He stopped to watch them play.[48] After some time had passed, one of the immortals looked up and exclaimed, "What? You are still here? Shouldn't you be going home now?" The immortal pointed to the woodsman's axe, the wooden handle of which had rotted away with age. When the woodsman returned home he discovered that so much time had gone by in his absence that everyone he knew had long since perished.

Tang Dynasty poet Meng Jiao (758–814 A.D.) wrote "Rotted Axe Handle Stone" (*Lanke shi*) to describe this legend.[49]

> One day in the heavenly kingdom, a thousand years in the realm of mortals.
> When a game of two opponents is yet unfinished, nothing else has meaning.
> A woodsman returns on his path, an axe handle has been eroded by the wind.
> Only a lone cinnabar bridge remains.

Meng Jiao fuses mythology with the tradition of Weiqi poetry. Bo Juyi (772–846) also wrote poetry that evoked the Daoist imagery of the game.

> *Mountain monks sit playing Weiqi.*
> *Over the board is the bamboo's lucent shade.*
> *No one sees them through the glittering leaves,*
> *But now and then is heard the click of a stone.*[50]

and

> *Willow branch frowning and plum blossom smiling each troubles me.*
> *Poetry creditors and Weiqi enemies all come to haunt me.*[51]

Even critics of the game used Daoism in their condemnation. A sixth-century text, for example, states that Weiqi has a "perverse Dao": "Some believe that criminal law corresponds to Dao because it too is spontaneous. But I say that criminal law, like Weiqi, like fencing and magic practices which confuse the eye, although they are all spontaneous (*ziran*), still have a true Dao only generally speaking, but in their particulars they have a perverse Dao."[52]

Sylvia, a senior at Peking University who trained to become a professional Weiqi player for ten years, had the following to say:

SYLVIA: The Weiqi board is made up of squares—this represents stability and the round pieces represent being dynamic—this is yin and yang.

MOSKOWITZ: Why are the squares stable and the circles dynamic?

SYLVIA: Because you can't have a square wheel, right? Things need to be round to move. Square things are more solid—like a brick.[53]

A question remains as to why there is such a richness of religious and philosophical imagery associated with the game of Weiqi. This may in part reflect a need to legitimate the game in the face of initial Confucian opposition. The nature of the game itself, which brings order out of a seeming chaos of stones, may be a second factor. The fact that political and economic power in Imperial China revolved around scholastic exams that focused on men's poetic and philosophical prowess might also be another facet of this connection. Perhaps most important, there has traditionally been a greater tendency in Chinese culture to use Daoist allegory to highlight the spiritual connectedness of all things. As a result, it is more common for people in China to attribute cosmological significance to board games in general, though this happens more frequently, and with a far wider scope, with Weiqi.[54]

Weiqi's tremendously high place as a symbol of high culture today is perhaps surprising given Confucius' and Mencius' initial ambivalence about the game. Yet although neither Confucius nor Mencius lauded Weiqi as the high art that it would later become, they did not condemn the game as is often asserted today.[55]

The only mention of the game in *The Confucian Analects* is when Confucius states, "It is hard to stand someone who stuffs himself with food and drink all day long without applying himself to anything! Are there not players of [the game] bo and Weiqi? Even doing that would be better than doing nothing at all."[56]

Confucius is indeed a bit dismissive of the game. Yet we should note that he does not evince any real hostility toward it. Similarly, Mencius called Weiqi a "small skill/technique" (*xiao jishu*).[57] This is not necessarily derision, as contemporary Weiqi players sometimes assert. Rather, Mencius uses the game as an exemplar for learning, relating the story of two students who both have the same Weiqi instructor. In this account, only one student masters the game because he concentrates when the other does not. Mencius uses this parable to insist that if a student does not learn, it is in part the teacher's fault but that the student must also take responsibility for his lack of improvement. Given the Confucian emphasis on the value of learning, this can hardly be interpreted as staunch criticism of the game, as is often claimed. As with Confucius' earlier statement, it certainly does not indicate the level of respect that Weiqi would later earn, however.

Mencius' other mention of Weiqi seems more damning. In this case Mencius lists playing Weiqi as part of a second category of five acts of unfilial behavior: "Playing [the game] *bo* and Weiqi, and drinking, and not attending to one's parents' needs, this is the second unfilial act."[58] This quote has become rather infamous in Weiqi circles as an outright condemnation of the game. Linking the games *bo* and Weiqi with alcohol as one category that can produce unfilial behavior seems likely to be a reference to gambling dens, however. This is a clear enough allusion that one modern Chinese version of the classical Chinese text omits the games altogether and simply lists it as a proscription against drinking and gambling.[59]

Betting money on games was common in China's history.[60] This practice can still be found in back rooms of Chinese, Japanese, Korean, and Taiwanese Weiqi clubs.[61] Though often referred to as gambling, in truth it is more akin to pool sharking, for it is based on skill and exploiting opponents' hubris rather than luck. The etiquette of holding a Weiqi piece between an outstretched pointer finger and middle finger as if held by chopsticks is in fact thought to have evolved out of this practice, in that it is harder to cheat because of increased visibility as one places a stone on the board.

Others I spoke with stressed that the issue at hand was excessive devotion to the game, to the point that one neglected one's duties toward one's parents. Indeed, Mencius lists Weiqi as part of one of five categories of unfilial acts. The other four include (1) laziness, (3) greed and favoring one's wife and children over one's parents, (4) pursuing sensual pleasures, and (5) bragging and arguing.

It should be noted, however, that Mencius mentions Weiqi in the act of answering a question about unfilial behavior rather than focusing his attention on the game itself. In other words, he is not asked, "What do you think of Weiqi?" Rather, the game appears in the context of a larger philosophy of treating one's parents well. The second half of his statement about Weiqi is "and not attending to one's parents needs," which clearly lays the emphasis on potential unfilial behavior rather than the game being innately immoral. This stands in marked contrast with Mencius' condemnation of pursuing sensual pleasure (the fourth unfilial act), which he states will result in shaming one's parents, or being a braggart and arguing (the fifth unfilial act), which, he warns, could place them in danger. In other words, the fourth and fifth acts are presented as inherently causing harm to one's parents, whereas the first three categories, of which playing Weiqi while drinking is the second, is listed as unfilial *if* it results in neglecting one's parents. Thus, though Mencius perceived of a danger of Weiqi addicts, gambling gamesters, and alcoholics, this does not necessarily imply a strong condemnation of either drink or Weiqi in moderation. In short, both Confucius and Mencius seemed to view Weiqi as just another game—neither harmful nor overly important in the greater scheme of things.

In large part, contemporary views that Confucius and Mencius derided Weiqi were inherited from later Confucianists who did condemn the game with some vehemence, expressing a clear anxiety that playing Weiqi represented misplaced talent, energy, and time.[62] On occasion, Weiqi was even likened to fox spirits that tempted men away from society to waste their lives on the pleasures of the moment.[63]

By the Tang Dynasty (618–907 A.D.), Weiqi had risen considerably in esteem. In this era, several emperors enjoyed the game, which sparked its widespread popularity.[64] Playing Weiqi was then listed along with calligraphy, playing the lute, and painting as one of the four arts (*si yi*) that any true gentleman should know. China's most famous poets, such as Bo Juyi (772–846 A.D.) and Du Fu (712–70 A.D.) played Weiqi as well as writing poems on the game.[65]

WEIQI'S WAR IMAGERY

Weiqi's war imagery is an iconic reminder of the ways that the game can represent conflict between nations. In fact, one of the early Confucian objections to Weiqi was the degree to which it was steeped in a language of violent warfare.[66] With terms such as "attack and defense" (*gongfang*), "life and death" (*sihuo*), and "invasion" (*qingru*), among a host of others, it is not hard to see why, over the centuries, many Chinese generals have studied the game as a philosophy of war.[67]

Hong Feng is a Weiqi instructor at the Capital Sports Center in Beijing's Science and Engineering University. In our interview he noted the ways that Weiqi had historically been seen as something that could be used to train people in military strategies.

> In ancient China they had a book to teach people to play Weiqi that was forbidden by the government because Weiqi is like a war. People are very smart so if they knew how to play this game they would know strategies that they could be used to fight against the government. Along the same lines, a library reference catalogue placed Weiqi books next to Sunzi's Art of War.
>
> In Sunzi's Art of War there is one war strategy where he said you can win a war without actually fighting. This is the highest form of battle. This is being polite and avoids the road of killing. Weiqi also has a strategy like this.[68]

Zhang Ni's eleventh-century text entitled *The Classic of Weiqi in Thirteen Chapters* is widely recognized as being modeled after Sunzi's *Art of War*.[69] In it, one can find a wide range of statements that are directly inspired by Sunzi's famous treatise:

> The player whose configurations are correct can exercise power over his adversary.[70]

and

> Before attacking to the left, observe the right; before invading the space behind your opponent's lines, observe what is in front of them.[71]

and

When there are many enemy pieces but few of your own in a given territory, first of all carefully consider your own chances of survival. If the opposite situation arises, when your own pieces are numerous and your enemy is in difficulties, exploit that situation to extend your configurations. As the best victory is that gained without fighting, so the best position is one that does not provoke conflict.[72]

As with Hong Feng's statement and Zhang Ni's treatise, Fang Tianfeng, the 8-*duan* pro who teaches Weiqi at Peking University, also emphasized that part of both war and Weiqi strategy is deciding when not to fight. Yet Fang did not imply that this freed Weiqi of its implications for metaphorical violence.

The Weiqi board is like a Chinese map of military battles. As in war sometimes you can take a group but you decide not to. In the old days if you could take a group you just did it and every one would say, "Wow, you are great!" But now you might decide not to take the group because it represents only a small area of territory. And to make that group live your opponent might have to invest a lot more troops to protect it.

So one question is whether or not you should attack—one is how to attack but the other is should you attack at all. Some battles can be won but it is better to ignore them. I can take that group but maybe it isn't in my overall interest so I leave it alone. . . .

Let's take an example from war. In the old days they'd bury a big bomb and it would kill a lot of people—it was very powerful. Now it's different. Now they bury a bomb that is very small. When it blows up it just hurts your leg. Now you're still in a war but you have to save the soldier that was injured. America has a saying "No man left behind" right? So now you need four or five people to save him. He's not dead so you have to send other troops in to save him. Then you have to take care of him so you need a hospital and you have to hire a doctor and a nurse to take care of him, which also takes money. Then when he recovers a bit you have to send him home and the government has to take care of him. But because he's injured he's unhappy. Every day he's out on the street getting drunk—I saw this in an American movie—a veteran was getting drunk on the street and yelling at people. So in the end the government must pay a lot— much more than if you had just killed him. If you had just killed him then they bury him and it's over—he's a hero. The government pays a small amount and its over. But if you just injure him then the government is under a lot more pressure. You are still in the middle of a war but a lot of people have to help that one guy. So from a military perspective it is more powerful to hurt him than to kill him. . . .

Weiqi is the same. Maybe I can win one battle but it harms the rest of the war. This is not good. Because the best way to look at war is to use a Daoist worldview. Laozi's book "The Dao de Qing" outlined this view a long time ago. It may look like you won but whether or not you really are winning is hard to say.[73]

In relating this account, Fang spoke with characteristic vivaciousness that seemed at odds with the grim Machiavellian strategy he was outlining. He expertly tied in an age-old philosophy of the game with contemporary popular culture references from the United States in his explanation. In doing so, he used humor to defuse the trauma of his story. By the end of his account, a seemingly frivolous tale had transformed into a remarkably insightful instruction on both war and Weiqi that also highlighted the overlap between the two.

Chinese scholar Xie Guofeng also uses the game as a metaphor for culturally bound military expansion. Yet Xie's interpretation claims that Chinese expansionism was without violence. He asserts that Europeans and Japanese "take" (*qu*) areas by force, as with chess, in a direct reference to their colonial expansion in the nineteenth and twentieth centuries.[74] In contrast, he states, Chinese surround in the same fashion that China was historically unified by enveloping neighboring kingdoms.[75] Drawing on the fact that the character *Wei* in *Weiqi* means "to surround," Xie goes on to liken Weiqi to the Great Wall that "surrounds" China, concluding, "It is the Chinese government's big Weiqi."[76]

Xie is hardly alone in this interpretation, although it is in fact highly questionable—China's history is rife with violent conflict both in and outside of its borders, after all. Yet if the argument reenvisions China's past in an idyllic gaze, it is nevertheless culturally significant for the frequency with which it arose. Sylvia, a senior at Peking University, made a similar claim.

Western chess is like a battle between two troops. Weiqi is like two entire countries at war. With Weiqi you want to claim territory—you don't always need to fight. You can also negotiate so that one person takes one area while your opponent takes another.

I quit playing Weiqi because you have to be aggressive to win and that is not my personality. It's a little like life—if one country is too peaceful they are likely to be taken advantage of by the other. This is kind of like the way Rome took over Greece in ancient history. But Weiqi also has a more peaceful strategy of just claiming territory without conflict. Basically this is like the way that China took over Japan in ancient history without violence—China just introduced them to cultural ideas. China was already so big that it didn't need to expand—it already had enough land.[77]

Here too Weiqi is used as a reinvention of China's past—one in which China's long history of violence was erased in favor of a constructed image of peaceful benevolence. The tone of accounts such as these is startlingly reminiscent of nineteenth-century European and Japanese rationales for colonial expansion, which they depicted less as violent invasion than a benevolent civilizing process. Today, this logic succinctly summarizes a Chinese worldview that helps to explain the mind-set behind its seemingly aggressive claims to Tibet, Taiwan, and to other contested territories to the south of its borders.

Frequently, those aligning Weiqi with warfare confuse the use of Weiqi as a metaphor to explain political or military theory to laymen, and the idea that Weiqi informed the strategies. Scott Boorman wrote a book comparing Maoist military with Weiqi.[78] Unfortunately he so rigidly asserts that the game is *exactly* like Maoist strategy that many of his finer points are lost. David Lai makes an equally problematic argument that modern Chinese military strategies are informed by Weiqi strategies.[79] Henry Kissinger then appropriates these two scholars' arguments and asserts that China's leaders implemented Weiqi strategy in war. All three of them conflate Mao's use of Weiqi to illustrate a military point with the idea that Weiqi informed Mao's strategies. None of them provides convincing evidence to support their claims.[80]

This is not to discount the idea that Weiqi theory may have been part of a repertoire of conceptualizing contemporary military and political philosophy, just as someone studying warfare and politics in the West might read Machiavelli's work or study Napoleonic war strategies. Yet it is important to question Weiqi's relative importance in relation to contemporary political science, international political thought, or other military strategies that may have played a more central role.

In spite of the limitations of suggesting that Weiqi informs war strategies, Weiqi, as well as Sunzi's *Art of War,* is clearly one way that people in China do think about conflict. There can be little doubt that there is a remarkable overlap between the overall vocabulary and strategies of Weiqi and Chinese discussions of war, diplomacy, and commerce, all of which serve to negotiate conceptual frameworks of relations with their East Asian neighbors.

Drawing on both military and religious imagery of the game, fictional presentations of Weiqi echo tales of ancient martial artists (*wuxia xiaoshuo*) who gained supernatural powers by channeling the natural powers of the universe (*qi*). Chinese martial arts dramas such as these are not merely action tales, therefore, but philosophical guidelines that rest on the notion that the greatest martial artists have acquired a more sophisticated understanding of the universe and, in turn, have transcended the physical boundaries that limit normal men. To cite an example more familiar to Western audiences, Jade Fox, the villain of the movie *Crouching Tiger, Hidden Dragon,* is a skilled martial artist, but her disciple surpasses her because Fox lacks the education to properly understand written instructional texts.[81] These tales of martial arts evoke more than physical mastery, therefore, but a spiritual enlightenment in which intellectual prowess leads to a command of the physical world. Shan Sa's novel *The Girl Who Played Go* is an excellent example of this. Like *Wuxia,* or American westerns for that matter, this contemporary novel about Weiqi features strangers who ride into town to challenge a famous opponent hoping to make names for themselves but inevitably prove only the hero's abilities:[82] "My opponent is a foreigner who came here straight from the station. As the battle intensifies, gentle warmth washes through me. . . . He is bearded and it's hard to tell his age; a long scar runs from the top of his eyebrow and down through his right eye, which he keeps closed. He empties the flask with a grimace. . . . He has been beaten by eighteen points; he heaves a sigh and hands me his candle. Then he stands up, unfolding a giant's frame, gathers his belongings and leaves without a backward glance."[83]

Another example of the *Wuxia* style of narration linked to Weiqi is Guanyu, one of the heroes of the fourteenth-century historical novel *The Three Kingdoms,* who plays Weiqi while a surgeon is removing a poison arrow from his arm.[84] This scene has been depicted in an array of paintings and woodcuts and is well known even outside of Weiqi circles.

In other Chinese and Japanese fictional accounts, Weiqi is less obviously connected with such daring bravado, but these accounts also echo *Wuxia* in that players face horrible physical trauma from the strain of the game and often leave as wounded as if a physical battle had taken place.[85] Yasunari Kawabata's semi-fictional account *The Master of Go,* for example, portrays the incredibly taxing nature of the game and its ill effects on the players' health.[86] It does so in overtly heroic terms that are reminiscent of such tales. The Japanese manga and anime *Hikaru no Go* also draws on this tradition by using visual effects that transform Weiqi competitions into action-packed adventure stories.[87]

The versatility of images surrounding the game of Weiqi is truly astounding. We are witness to a dramatic conceptual shift in Confucian circles: from representing the game as "a small skill" to a wanton waste of one's energies, to one of the four high arts. In turn, Mao Zedong used it as an illustrative point on the nature of war, though it would be castigated as one of the "four olds" in the beginning of the Cultural Revolution in the 1960s, only to be embraced as a symbol of nationalist pride a few years later. Weiqi is an emblem of Buddhist detachment, a Daoist celebration of cosmic significance, and an illustration of both imperial and communist Chinese war strategies. It represents benevolent rule and ruthless attack. It is hyper-historical *and* magnificently modern; mystical *and* superbly scientific in its absolute rationality. Indeed, in examining these juxtapositions it soon becomes clear that the varied metaphors and mystical imaginaries of the game are in themselves as strong an image for yin and yang as the black and white pieces that swirl around each other on the board.

THREE

Nation, Race, and Man

In general, whoever occupies the battleground first and awaits the enemy will be at ease; whoever occupies the battleground afterward and must race to the conflict will be fatigued. Thus one who excels at warfare compels men and is not compelled by other men.

SUNZI, *THE ART OF WAR*, LATE SIXTH CENTURY B.C.[1]

Man makes the moves of Weiqi, which has heaven, earth, and yin and yang—this means that Weiqi is nothing else but the politics of a virtuous king. It is up to the players to decide the outcome of the game, just as the words in "The Analects of Confucius" show: "practice of human-heartedness is up to the free will of the doer." This indicates that Weiqi follows the path of virtue even in its strategies.

BAN GU, *THE MYSTERIOUS GO SUTRA*, 32–92 A.D.[2]

The outsider, who thinks that chess is pure and cerebral, tends to be shocked by such suggestions. But the insider is not shocked, because he knows that chess, like the human brain, is partly reptilian.

MARTIN AMIS, *VISITING MRS. NABOKOV AND OTHER EXCURSIONS*, 1993

MANY PEOPLE I INTERVIEWED MADE direct comparisons with Weiqi strategies and Sunzi's *Art of War*. Sunzi's statement above perfectly captures the nuances of the Weiqi concept of seizing the initiative (*xianshou*), in which the player who can force his opponent to follow his lead is thought to have a tremendous advantage. Similarly, Weiqi rhetoric asserts that one's playing style reflects one's personality and one's place in the world in direct comparison with other men. This form of manhood relies on controlled aggression, the will to maximize one's gain, and the ability to assert one's dominance.

The second opening quote of this chapter, from the two-thousand-year-old *Mysterious Go Sutra*, reminds us of the remarkable ways that Weiqi's imagery is also tied in with the spiritual forces of the universe as well as the ideals of Confucian virtue. Both excerpts speak of manhood, though their conceptualization of this identity is quite different. What, then, does it mean to be a man in China and in what ways does the traditionalist Weiqi realm provide a vocabulary for manhood in the contemporary age? Masculine discourses also extend to national identity and international rivalries. In this worldview, there is remarkable overlap between individual playing styles and national identity.

Anyone familiar with the Cold War politics surrounding Western chess in the 1950s will readily recognize Weiqi's contemporary significance in East Asia. Competitions between China, Japan, South Korea, and Taiwan empha-size a cultural sharing that transcends national borders while simultaneously providing a literal and figurative playing ground for symbolic aggression and nationalistic rivalries. In order to explore these issues in more depth, a closer examination of China's relationship with Japan seems in order. Japan is cen-tral to this discussion in part because it had unrivaled supremacy in the game from the 1600s until the mid-1980s. As such, most Chinese people take a great deal of pride in China's current dominance over Japan in international competitions, whether they are interested in Weiqi or not. The celebration of China's Weiqi ascendance is in part a revisioning of historical power relations between China and Japan—one that is acutely sensitive to Japanese military encroachment during the Pacific War and to its economic dominance until recent years. Much to China's chagrin, however, South Korea was the first to seize the Weiqi throne from Japan, dominating international competitions from the late 1980s until approximately 2008, when China became a rela-tively equal competitor.

China's victories over Japan in this sphere are very much celebrated, but there is also a surprising undercurrent of nostalgic sorrow among older Weiqi players who have watched Japan's greatness fade. Thus, Weiqi competitions are both a point of international rivalry and ping-pong politics, a vestige of age-old hostilities between two nations as well as a reminder of commonali-ties that transcend national borders. Weiqi speaks to the particular histories of China's greatness, Japan's colonial aggression, and South Korea's contem-porary attempt to create a place for itself as it shoulders its way in among these economic giants.

THE SCHOLAR AND THE WARRIOR

One cannot understand contemporary Chinese masculinities or the state without first exploring traditional conceptions of *wen* (the refined and cultured) and *wu* (the martial). In Imperial China, *wen*-style manhood was the ideal, and the more physical orientation of *wu* was stigmatized. Martin Huang emphasizes that martial prowess, for example, was a fairly insignificant factor in the forms of masculinity outlined by Confucius and Mencius.[3] He further suggests that men of learning (*wenshi*) began to replace warrior-style masculinity as a central ideal in Chinese culture as early as the Spring and Autumn Period (722 B.C. to 481 B.C.).[4] In this Confucian worldview, courage had to be tempered with morality lest it degenerate to mere brigandry.[5] True manhood was thereby defined as ethical behavior rather than as physical strength.[6]

Kam Louie suggests that there are other cultural schemas for manhood that can profitably be contrasted with this Chinese model. Greek and Roman culture stressed the importance of mind and body, for example, whereas Jewish culture has traditionally placed far less stress on physical orientation.[7] Louie reminds us that the paradigm of the Western macho male is not overly applicable to China, in that the hyper-masculine tradition was never predominant in the Chinese imaginary.[8] In this framework, the gentle scholar was seen to be no less masculine than the rough soldier.[9] In truth, aggressive masculine behavior or physical orientation that might epitomize the ideal male in the West was thought to be uncouth, even savage, in most of Chinese history.[10] Tang Dynasty (618–907 A.D.) government officials in *wen* positions viewed those who held *wu* posts, such as those in the military, to be inferior, and people entrenched in *wu* culture were careful to legitimate themselves by emphasizing *wen*.[11]

An important figure in historical constructions of Chinese masculinity was the talented scholar (*caizi*). Talented scholars were usually depicted as frail, delicate, handsome, and possessing what in the West might be called a feminine beauty.[12] As Chou Wah-shan notes, in this context, "For a male to be soft, gentle, filial, and subtle is not a deprivation of his manhood but its fulfillment and completion."[13]

In Chinese cinema, the stigma that one sees placed on the effeminate male in the West is perhaps best personified by eunuchs rather than by talented scholars who exemplified viable masculinities. Literal emasculinization has a long history in China. In the Han Dynasty (206 B.C.–220 A.D.), the death sentence was at times commuted to castration. In 98 B.C., for instance, noted historian Sima Qian was sentenced to death; this was later commuted to castration. He spent much of his life justifying why he did not choose death over this humiliating fate.[14] In later history, eunuchs served the emperor, and today their famed corruption and cruelty is often linked with the downfall of the Qing Dynasty and China's perceived humiliation at the hands of the West. Contemporary Chinese-language cinema evinces a remarkable correlation of villainy and third-gender characters—featuring a male character with a dubbed female voice, for example.[15] At times this seems to be a subconscious cultural reference to the historical fear and mistrust of imperial court eunuchs. In contrast, "effeminate" men who were clearly marked as normatively heterosexual in their personas were free of the stigma that such a category might have in the West.

In the Han Dynasty (206 B.C.–220 A.D.), ideal men were portrayed as wearing white face powder.[16] Historical fictions such as the *Three Kingdoms* (1321) depicted idealized men as having "oiled hair, a powdered face, and small gleaming buttocks."[17] Ming (1368–1644) and Qing (1644–1911) Dynasty erotic paintings portrayed young men as so like their female counterparts that the women's bound feet were the only clear marker of their difference.[18] Indeed, literary works usually depicted talented scholars as being handsome and resembling beautiful women.[19] These literary portrayals at times extended to men without learning, such as a merchant or government clerk who might be described as "having dark brows, fine eyes, white teeth, and ruby lips."[20] Ming/Qing fiction often featured explicitly negative depictions of characters who displayed stereotypically rugged physiques or demeanor.[21] In contrast to the talented scholars whose feminine charm was depicted as being virtually irresistible to the fairer sex, macho men such as this were thought to be incapable of attracting women of virtue.[22]

The talented scholar, a staple of romantic roles in Chinese fiction, was frequently juxtaposed with the role of the Confucian gentleman (*junzi*) who was relatively desexualized through an emphasis on duty, loyalty, and proper behavior.[23] The Confucian gentleman is a particularly salient form of masculinity in the Weiqi sphere. This may seem surprising given Confucius' ambivalence about the game, but there is no doubt of its centrality in neo-Confucian constructions that embraced Weiqi as a requisite to becoming a learned gentleman.

The hero *(yingxiong,* a literal translation of which is *ying:* outstanding, *xiong:* male) was another cultural icon for a rugged version of masculinity.[24] Literature valorizing these men of steel was careful to place them at the margins of society, however. *Haohan,* often described as knights-errant but perhaps more akin to Robin Hood figures, were the most notable example of literary depictions of iron men. Most commonly featured in martial arts tales (*wuxia shaoshuo*), such men demonstrated physical prowess through martial arts but also through excess with food and liquor.[25]

Discourses on Chinese men who lived beyond the law revolved around language that stressed these social outcasts' physical orientation in juxtaposition with the civilized *wen*. In late imperial times, Chinese bandits were depicted as uncivilized, "perverse brutes who had not learned the lessons that made men human."[26]

CHINESE MASCULINITIES: INDIVIDUAL FORMATION AND NATIONALIST DISCOURSES

In China, masculinity is at times difficult to separate from nationalist discourses. *Wen/wu* juxtaposition was often aligned along ethnic and national boundaries in that the Chinese Han legitimated their feelings of superiority by contrasting Manchu machismo with the civilized Han Chinese *wen* male.[27] In the words of Frank Dikötter, Republican China depicted Westerners as "drunken, debauched, brutish, and loathsome."[28] Europeans were portrayed as being closer to beasts because of their hairiness.[29] James Watson also suggests that in traditional China and Hong Kong, Europeans were depicted as having a "bizarre appearance and animal like nature."[30] The fact that the Chinese word for "body hair" also means "animal's fur" (*mao*) linguistically solidifies biases that align hairy Westerners with animals. In these contexts, the very *wen* of the Han Chinese equated what in the West would be labeled as effeminate men with positive attributes associated with the best of the Chinese culture, race, and civilization. *Wu,* so prized today, was seen as nothing short of barbaric.

Even amid newfound calls for a more rugged Chinese masculinity, contemporary Chinese portrayals of Western men continue to emphasize the perceived link between physical strength and barbarism. This ranges from analogies of Nazi masculinity to stereotypes of Americans' brute strength.[31] In these depictions, the iconic Western male physique continues to be depicted as being beastly in juxtaposition with the physically fragile but civilized Chinese.[32]

Sartorial choices also came into play. A 1926 Chinese tract wrote of the dichotomy between China and the West. In it, China was depicted as a "civilization formed with gentle culture" that was "feminine by nature" in which "people respect the *yin*, the soft, the maternal."[33] In contrast, the West was found wanting in its perceived attributes that included both dress and behavior, with descriptors such as "barbarian clothes with short trains," "fond of fighting," "a stick always in the hand," "a civilization formed with vehemence and strength," "masculine by nature, people respect the *yang,* the hard, heroic."[34]

Beijing's current concern with masculinity can be seen to be in direct rebellion against nineteenth-century Orientalist discourses in which the Asian other is depicted as feminine and passive, in need of the rational guidance of the male-coded West. As an example of this, Robert Harrist Jr. relates a 1911 account of the sociologist Edward Alsworth Ross, who, on visiting China, mocked Chinese tennis players, saying that their strokes "had the snap of a kitten playing with a ball of yarn."[35] In this Orientalist discourse, Western observers labeled Chinese elite male clothing as women's dress.[36] These sartorial choices emphasize an important conceptual divide, for in China masculinity was marked by strength of character rather than muscle mass.[37]

The People's Republic of China's (PRC's) agenda of celebrating the masculine ethos of the peasant class has merged with attempts to compete with images of masculinity ushered in by Western media that has born the emergence of a more *wu*-oriented ideal.[38] In the 1980s, the Chinese intelligentsia exploited this literature, as well as modern mass-mediated manifestations of the martial arts (*wuxia*) genre. They did so as a call for "a return" to hypermasculinity after feeling castrated by the patriarchal state. Chinese discourses asserting that the Chinese male was impotent and weak were accompanied by a call for new rugged masculinity in cinema.[39]

Post–Cultural Revolution literature in the 1980s marked a new concern with masculinity in relation to modernizing China in the form of "manly men" (*nanzihan*).[40] Such depictions portrayed weak men who yearned to be strong.[41] Rejecting any aspects of self that might be deemed feminine, 1980s literature and film celebrated the *nanzihan* image.[42] New models of manhood came from both the United States and Japan in the forms of actors such as Sylvester Stallone and Takakura Ken.[43] These icons of masculinity were in some ways reminiscent of Cultural Revolution art that imprinted the Chinese imagination with a new vision that celebrated muscular orientation.[44] This too was inevitably framed as wanting to make up for a perceived loss of masculinity that was thought to have been possessed in former times.[45]

Beijing's rock-and-roll movement also emerged in the 1980s, beginning as an underground phenomena but quickly evolving into a medium that sounded remarkably like the state in its rhetorical attempts to reclaim a perceived loss of masculinity in relation to the West.[46] This framework keeps a (self)conscious eye on Western cinematic depictions of iron man masculinity, and through this lens the image of the talented scholar is transformed to a state of lacking what "real men" possess.[47]

In the 1990s idealized masculinity shifted to an image of men who were sexually adventurous and capable in the business world, shedding themselves from Maoist-era manhood that centered on revolutionary fervor and selflessness.[48] In Chinese sports, in which Weiqi is categorized as a subsection, men represent nationhood—a movement that also attempts to do battle with Western Orientalist stereotypes that rendered China weak and feminine.[49] These images were then employed by Japan during its occupation of China in the Pacific War. China's sports reconceptualized manhood, embracing masculinity and propagandizing physical and competitive identities in an attempt to reach full participation in global modernity.[50] This revised masculinity was a conscious construction that was born of the Western introduction of a Far Eastern Olympiad to China.[51] There was a marked presence of foreign sponsorship of the games, tied in with standardized international formats. The Chinese government and press framed the competitions in terms of the athletes' power and fearlessness in helping to construct a masculinist nation-state.[52] Here too, the call for a greater hyper-masculinity was explicitly voiced as a need to counter the imperialist dominance of a feminized China.[53] Martial arts were also heavily embedded in imagery of physical prowess that represents an attempt to recreate male bodies as impenetrable and potent.[54]

Contemporary mass media continue these traditions by attempting to invert Orientalist hierarchies. A staple of Chinese-language cinema is the understated, and underestimated, martial artist who defeats an arrogant and physically larger Western enemy.[55] In turn, there are several television shows and movies that feature the Chinese possession of Western female bodies, which some have argued is a means of overcoming feelings of emasculation evoked from colonial pasts and global modernities.[56]

To some degree Western scholars have been unintentionally complicit in reifying Western-inspired hierarchies. In doing battle with Orientalist discourses in contemporary drama, for example, they have maintained the notion that iron bodies and violent behavior represent true manhood and that other masculinities are something to be ashamed of.[57] In doing so, they stigmatize the more androgynous alternatives that are so celebrated in Chinese mass media.

Fears of emasculation point to colonial and imperialist humiliation at the hands of the West, but they also sprout from the loss of absolute male hegemony in an era that made the abrupt and traumatic discovery that China was not in fact the supreme power in the world. The contemporary embrace of *wen* in China's contemporary soap operas and pop music also linked to women's entrance into the workforce, their corresponding buying power, and the ways in which mass media and other cultural productions adjust to cater to women's desires.

It is important to remember that China has never been temporally or geographically unified in its visions of masculinity. The Ming (1368–1644) and Qing (1644–1911) Dynasties were decidedly more feminine than the Han (206 B.C.–220 A.D.) and Tang (618–908) Dynasties.[58] The Song Dynasty (960–1279) was more feminine still.[59] Southern culture has long been thought to be more feminine than northern culture. Historical precedents include the southern elite males who frequently wore makeup. This dramatically contrasted northern culture, which inherited more rugged roles from Manchu and Mongolian reigns. This north/south divide very much continues today in Chinese-language mass-mediated culture.[60] Beijing, the nation's capital in the north, is especially associated with rugged masculinity that links to its history of imperial rule, Maoist politics, and its place as the current center of government. In contrast, the south, which in the PRC is thought to include Hong Kong and Taiwan, is associated with greater commercial focus as well as with producing some of the most popular movies and popular music. More often than not these media productions include male stars who would be labeled as androgynous men in the United States.

Class difference is also a factor here. For most of Chinese history all but a very small percentage of Chinese voices were silenced. Judging by what one sees in contemporary China, it is quite likely that the working class had a far more rugged form of masculinity than the *wen* elite. Also, as in any society, individual personalities and preferences create a remarkable range of male behaviors.

We should also remember that *yin* and *yang* are relative categories. A man is *yang* to a woman's *yin*. Yet that same man is thought to be *yin* to government officials or men above his station.[61] In traditional China, disgruntled male literati wrote poetry in which they portrayed themselves as abandoned but faithful wives to the government. In doing so they presented loyalty as a feminine virtue.[62] This was done in terms that identified men as part of a spectrum that included women while evincing clear worries of emasculation. The tradition of using women to allegorically protest men's structural weakness at the hands of the state could also be seen in the 1980s Campus Songs movement as well as in contemporary Mandopop. These genres of music frequently feature songs written by men, for women to sing, complaining about men. The songs also give voice to emotions that men cannot viably express in public.[63]

Both *wen* and *wu* have transferred fairly readily to China's contemporary context, and men can choose among several historical models of masculinity, ranging from the talented scholar to the Confucian gentleman and the chivalric *haohan*.[64] *Wen* scholars can be seen in modern academia, and a *wu* ethos is readily found in post-Mao fiction and Hong Kong cinema.[65] Businessmen have shed a stigmatized reputation in both Confucian and Maoist worldviews and have perpetuated *wu* culture while womanizing—a contemporary adaptation of the *haohan* discussed above. [66] These explorations of masculinity are more often than not infused with issues of rugged machismo and a tension between both male bonding and competition.[67] Gang activity, and many contemporary religious practices in China, also evince a remarkable degree of machismo.[68] Hyper-masculine imagery is given legitimacy by religious figures such as the martial deity Guangong and countless literary tales of martial artists and warriors.

Mao Zedong can also be said to have masculinized China's self-image inxd his contributions to evicting the Japanese from China and in maintaining autonomy from the Soviet Union. In addition, Mao's emphasis on modernization, focusing on wealth and power through the accumulation of steel and iron, was a resonant metaphor that countered the Orientalizing feminizing process of Western colonial and imperialist powers.[69]

In spite of an upsurge of masculinist sentiments in the 1980s, other discourses emerged during the same period. Toward the end of that decade there was a marked political shift away from hyper-masculine ethos as the government slowed its glorification of peasant and worker cultures in favor of reembracing education and more traditional markers of elite status.[70] In that same decade, being educated rebounded from a highly stigmatized category during the early communist era to one of the highest attainments for symbolic capital.[71]

Mainstream concerns with masculinity continue to be fraught with a cacophony of contesting expectations. We are witness to contemporary negotiations of manhood, such as the stigmatization of contemporary men in Shanghai, because they are thought to prefer housework and to leave commerce to their women.[72] Yet it is precisely this effeminate ideal that has become a marker of the perfect male in mass-mediated constructions of modernity.[73] Given that the most popular mass media have developed in the south, the caring (*wenrou*) male has become more central to Chinese idealization of manhood at the very same moment that northern cultural spokesmen have intensified their rhetoric lamenting Chinese men's emasculation at the hands of Japan and the West.

Discussions of Chinese masculinity are difficult to separate from nationalist discourses. Several scholars have written on what they see to be a remarkable rise of Chinese nationalism in the nineteenth and twentieth centuries. Yet there is little agreement as to when this began.[74] Henrietta Harrison states that modern nationalism began in the 1860s; Xu Guoqi asserts that a modern concept of Chinese nationalism was born of the first Sino–Japanese War (1894–95); and James Townsend suggests that it began with the establishment of a republic in 1912 and the May Fourth era of 1919.[75] Yet, as William Kirby notes, although China's official statehood did not begin until 1912, Chinese nationalism had existed long before that.[76] To illustrate this point, Kirby reminds us of the anti-Japanese movements and the anti-foreign boycotts in the end of the Qing Dynasty (1644–1912). Shen Zhijia problematizes the issue further by pointing out that while nationalism was an obvious presence in the twentieth century, it was not always clear as to which nation this belonged to.[77] This tension arose because the civil war between the communists and the nationalists created interconnecting but often-contradictory narratives of nationalism.[78] In turn, Xu Guoqi notes that in the early years of the PRC, nationalism could be said to be at war with itself in that it promoted pride in Chinese identity at the same moment that it was attempting to erase its past.[79]

Contemporary Chinese nationalism also takes on several forms. The most noticeable for those in the West is linked to ongoing Chinese resentments concerning the Western economic, military, and political encroachment of colonial and imperialist times. The continued global dominance of the United States also causes Sino–American politics to be fraught with tension. Chinese discourses on this matter range from historical remembrances of the early nineteenth-century unequal treaties in Hong Kong and Shanghai, to more recent events such as in 1999 when the United States accidentally bombed a Chinese embassy in Belgrade during UN operations.[80] Taiwan's continued independence is another rallying point that symbolizes a perceived American interference with Chinese internal affairs.[81] America's attempts to reform Chinese policies in areas ranging from freedom of speech, to copyright protection, to abortion continue to make many people in the PRC feel that the United States is trying to badger China into docility. America's lack of restraint concerning its own deficit, its dearth of environmental responsibility, and its unwillingness to implement gun control do little to convince China that the United States has earned the right to preach to others about a healthy society or global citizenship. Chinese nationalism does indeed emerge in resistance to these issues, but there are other forms of nationalism that are more tightly bound to Asian politics.

ANTI-JAPANESE SENTIMENT AS NATION BUILDING

Scholars writing in English are understandably more sensitive to the issues outlined here, but there are other forms of nationalism in which the West is largely irrelevant. A few examples include reactions to the 1998 Indonesian riot against ethnic Chinese living in Indonesia and several unpleasant events connected to Sino-Japanese relations that I outline below.

Although the United States is the strongest representation of the West as a conceptual category in China, Japan is close enough geographically and culturally that it is a better point of comparison when China is trying to mark its progress.[82] The fact that China overtook Japan as the second-largest world economy in 2010 also fuels the rivalry between the two nations. It does so in ways that arguably surpass China's frustrations with the United States.

It is not hard to spot China's continuing resentment of Japan. Memories of the Japanese invasion of China during the second Sino–Japanese War (1937–45) continue to wreak havoc on contemporary Sino–Japanese relations, and this fans the flames of a particular form Chinese nationalism. Arif Dirlik suggests that because the youth of both China and Japan were not alive during the Second World War they have no real interest in reviving memories of these old tensions.[83] Yet, since the Tiananmen protests of 1989, China's government has systematically highlighted Japan's historical aggression toward China in its patriotic education campaign.[84] Nationalist rhetoric is included in children's curriculum in an array of subjects.[85] Chinese popular culture reifies this sentiment, for China's mass media are saturated with themes of self-sacrificing individuals, love of the motherland, and depictions of a nation that is often at peril from evil Japanese or Western characters.

Another example occurred in 2003 when a Japanese company signed a contract to build a high-speed magnetic bullet train between Beijing and Shanghai for US$12 billion. When it came to the Chinese public's attention that the company that made the successful bid had helped in Japanese military efforts during Japan's invasion of China, this sparked a tremendous amount of online protest. Ten days later, ninety thousand Chinese protesters had signed an online petition complaining that the money was going to a Japanese corporation rather than a Chinese one.[86] This issue gained enough momentum that Beijing authorities sent anti-riot squads to disperse thousands of angry protesters at the final match of the 2004 Asian Soccer Cup.[87]

In 2005, Japan published a middle school history textbook that portrayed Japan's military aggression in the Second World War as efforts to liberate Asia from Western control. The textbook also sparked continued resentment about Japan's lack of a sincere apology for kidnapping women from China and Korea to serve as "comfort women" (women forced into prostitution to serve the Japanese soldiers during the Pacific War). The same textbook also claimed that the Nanjing Massacre, in which Japanese soldiers brutally murdered thousands of civilians, was a "disputed incident." In response, approximately ten thousand Chinese people marched in the streets of Beijing, calling for a boycott of Japanese goods. An estimated twenty thousand demonstrators protested in Shanghai on April 16, 2005, when the Japanese foreign minister Nobutaka Machimura arrived in Beijing for diplomatic talks. On May 23, 2005, the Japanese prime minister Junichiro Koizumi aggravated China's already peaking resentment by speaking out in defense of rituals at the Yasukuni shrine, stating that Japan had the right to honor its war dead and that other countries should not interfere with this process.[88]

Another series of events that aggravated these tensions was in 1996 and 2012 when Japan's right-wing factions attempted to claim the Diaoyu Islands. The Diaoyu Islands are made up of uninhabitable volcanic rock that protrudes from the ocean. They have no worth of their own, but they mark both fishing and oil rights for the area. Long contested ground among the PRC, Japan, and Taiwan, the act of building a structure on the islands set off a wave of nationalistic outcry in both the PRC and Taiwan.

China's government officials and its popular press frequently deride Japanese as "monsters" who owe a blood debt to China.[89] These outcries carry a shared theme of wanting to punish rather than forgive the Japanese.[90] In turn, Japan's government officials have been terse in expressing their remorse to China, grumbling that China would not really accept an apology so that there is no reason to try any further.[91] Chinese nationalist reactions to Japan are both personal and political.[92] They are personal in that they represent very real emotions concerning memories of the atrocities committed by the Japanese, and they are political because they are often used in expertly calculating ways to attain diplomatic advantage or to maximize business deals.[93] In a sense, China and Japan are still in what amounts to a cold war that must be mediated as they attempt to do business together.[94] Even as China stresses its long relationship with Japan in an effort to highlight their friendly relations, it frequently does so while framing the discourse in terms of Japan's two-thousand-year "cultural indebtedness" to China.[95] Weiqi, as a game that spread from China to Japan over a millennium ago, is part of this discourse—one in which Japan's long-time supremacy had been a particular point of shame for China.

JAPAN'S WEIQI LEGACY

Although China invented Weiqi well over two millennia ago, Japan had almost four centuries of uncontested supremacy in the game. This began in 1612 with the establishment of four state-sponsored Weiqi "Houses," which were competitive schools that developed the game to a standard it had never before achieved. Today, Japan's central place in the Weiqi sphere is largely attributed to the Four Houses' contributions to the theory of the game, and people in China often begrudgingly refer to Japan as Weiqi's foster mother (*yangmu*).[96] In part because of this history, and in part because of a continued promotion of the game internationally, most Weiqi players outside of China and Korea have learned the Japanese terms for describing moves and strategies in the game.

Teacher Wang, my first Weiqi instructor at a children's Weiqi school where I engaged in participant observation, said the following about Japan's contributions to the game: "Weiqi began three or four thousand years ago. You can say it was created in China but in fact it was created before China existed when you think about it. You could say that contemporary Weiqi was really created in Japan during the four houses period. They changed the theory of the game to make it like the Weiqi we play today."[97]

Japan had so established itself as the world's Weiqi epicenter that the vast majority of notable players from other countries such as China, South Korea, or Taiwan moved to Japan at a young age to perfect their skills. Perhaps the best example of this is Wu Qingyuan (known as Go Seigen in the United States and Japan), who was one of the best players that has ever lived.

Born in 1914 in China, Wu Qingyuan was discovered as a Weiqi prodigy, and in 1926 he moved to Japan under the sponsorship of Baron Ōkura. Wu spent most of his life in Japan, including during its war with China. He transformed the theory of the game by emphasizing the importance of the center of the board. His story has also captured the minds of most Weiqi players, because, in a sense, he belonged to both nations.

Other notable examples of Japan's intense draw on the world's players included South Korean Chō Chikun, who began studying in Japan at the age of six; Rin Kaihō (Lin Haifeng) from Taiwan; Michael Redman from the United States; and a host of others. Today, players in the PRC and South Korea train in their home nations, but Taiwan's best players have continued the tradition of moving to Japan to study the game—to the point that Taiwan's team has been referred to as "virtually a second Japanese team."[98]

In short, for close to four hundred years Japan had the same draw on the best Weiqi players that the United States has on baseball players from across the globe. In part, the Weiqi professionals went to Japan because there was more money to be had and because it was more prestigious. More important, they went because this was the environment that would best allow them to develop their skills to their fullest potential.

MASTERING EAST ASIA: NATIONAL RIVALRIES AND INTERNATIONAL COMPETITIONS

In Imperial China, Weiqi had never been an income generator as it has come to be in modern competitions, but the best players could find wealthy patrons in much the same way that someone in literary or artistic circles might.[99] It was only in 1956 that the PRC established Weiqi as an official national sport (*tiyu, yundong*). Chen Yi, China's foreign minister from 1958 to 1972, was largely responsible for the promotion of the game during this period. In explanation of his endorsement of the game, Chen Yi stated that China's Weiqi was far behind that of Japan: "Weiqi originated in China, but the level in Japan now is higher than in China. Without fail, we must catch up with, then surpass Japan."[100]

It would be hard to argue with Chen's assessment of the relative strengths of China and Japan at that time. As telling evidence of just how far China had fallen behind, one need only look at the PRC's first tournament with Japan in 1961, when China's national team lost thirty-two games to two, with one tie. In 1966 Japan won thirty-four to five, with one tie.

At its peak, the Cultural Revolution (1966–76) resulted in the closing of most Weiqi schools, as well as the disbanding of the professional team.[101] Yet there were several high-level party cadres that continued to promote the game, which assured its resilience through this tumultuous time. Chen Yi is best known for this, but Mao Zedong also demonstrated a remarkable comfort level in referring to the game. Even people who had been put in reeducation camps in remote areas of the country were allowed to play Weiqi, and, because there was little else to do, those who learned the game often became quite skilled.[102] As part of the Cultural Revolution, Mao called for urban youth to be sent down to the countryside to learn proper proletarian thought. Although these "sent-down youth" were usually from urban well-to-do families, many of them became permanent members of the working class. As one of many paradoxes of the Cultural Revolution, therefore, it created a setting that promoted this elite game among a wider range of class strata.

In 1972, when the Cultural Revolution was waning, the PRC reinstated its national team, and Weiqi schools began springing up throughout China.[103] Weiqi players and government officials alike renewed the call to catch up with Japan for the sake of national honor.[104] It was in this same year that Weiqi competitions with Japan resumed.

It was only in 1984 that Nie Weiping became the first Chinese-trained player to win in formal competitions between China and Japan. As such he was hurtled into stardom that reached far beyond the Weiqi sphere. Not unlike American reactions to Bobby Fisher's world title victory against his Russian opponent Boris Spassky in 1972, when Nie defeated the Japanese team it inspired intense interest in Weiqi across China. His victory also fanned the flames of nationalist pride that sought to bring China to ascendency in the region. Many people I spoke with in China told me that Nie Weiping's first victories inspired them to learn how to play.

When I asked people in Beijing to name three of the most important Weiqi players throughout the world, Nie Weiping was on virtually every person's list. Most noted, however, that this was less because he had transformed people's conceptions of the game, as Wu Qingyuan had done, than because of his role in leading China toward its first victories against Japan.[105] Sun Yiguo, a career Weiqi player, explained Nie Weiping's importance to Weiqi, and to China more generally:[106] "China's excitement about Weiqi over recent years is all because of Nie Weiping. And his contribution is not only in the world of Weiqi. Many people know about Nie Weiping, he is famous across the nation. His greatest contribution was that he was an inspiration to

China's people. And this wasn't only about Weiqi. Because during the Cultural Revolution everything was erased. So we all needed something to inspire us to have faith in the future. That's really the most important thing that he did."[107]

Nie Weiping's victories marked the turning point in China's Weiqi sphere, but this would continue to be an arduous struggle. In the late 1980s, South Korean Weiqi players had become so strong at the game that it was only in 1995 that Nie Weiping and Ma Xiaochun became the first Chinese players to win international competitions that included both Japanese and South Korean players. Although many would argue that South Korea still dominates the Weiqi sphere, most people I spoke with in China insisted that beginning in 2008 China had reached an even footing in international competitions.

CONCEPTUALIZING NATIONS, RETHINKING PLAY

Xu Wu makes the important distinction that China sees itself less as a rising power than as a returning power, noting that this has profound implications on the nation's psyche.[108] In this context it is no coincidence that Weiqi is increasingly popular, for it evokes nostalgia for an era of China's greatness, when it was the undisputed center of its universe. Weiqi is symbolically associated with this golden age. In this context, international competitions link to feelings of emasculation by, or dominance of, other nations.

In 2010, China displaced Japan as the world's second-largest economy. China's Weiqi ascendency is another point of quantifiable comparison and rivalry between the two nations. Weiqi competitions are perhaps a less dramatic form of nationalism than angry mobs in the street, but they are no less significant in reaching the psyche of Chinese pride. Yet Weiqi can also be a venue for ping-pong politics by offering a setting for international dialogue and cooperation in the organization of the competitions. It also serves as an important reminder of shared culture amid other tensions in the political economy.

National styles of play seemingly confirm broader stereotypes about cultural differences among men from China, Japan, and Korea. People I interviewed in China consistently told me that Japanese Weiqi players are too reserved, Koreans are too aggressive, and China is striving for the balance between excess and restraint. Guan Yang is a graduate student at Peking University who studied Weiqi at a professional school as a child. He put this sentiment most succinctly when he told me the following: "People say that in Japan Weiqi is regarded as an art, in China it is regarded as a sport, and in Korea it is regarded as a fight."[109]

In my interviews, the three nation's differing styles of play were universally agreed upon. Several of the people I spoke with were able to point to practical reasons why Japan had fallen behind China and South Korea, as well as explaining the different national styles of play. They provided examples that included connecting Japan's poor performance in international competitions with economic considerations. They pointed out that Japan's domestic competitions had more prize money, for example. In their view, it was rational that Japan's players would prioritize domestic competitions when there was a conflict in schedule. Guan Yang was able to point to several other practical reasons as to why Japanese players had fallen behind China and South Korea:

> In China, Weiqi is like a sports team. You have a game every week and the government gives prizes to the winners. So if you don't win you don't get money. People also make money by teaching students or writing for magazines.
>
> In Japan there are more players than in China so professionals can make a good income by teaching amateurs. So their lives are a little too easy—they needn't worry about their incomes so they are not as hungry to win as in China. That's why they have fallen behind China and Korea. ... Another reason is China is better because our population is so big. Even if only one percent of the populations in Japan and China take the game seriously, that means there are a lot more players in China, right?[110]

Sylvia, a Peking University student who had also studied to be a professional Weiqi player as a child, emphasized the importance of national training: "We all have schools of thought where we learn. So if you are learning Weiqi in Korea your teachers will teach you to play aggressively. If you are learning in Japan people will teach you to be more careful."[111]

Teacher Zhuang, who had been working at a Weiqi school for two years, suggested that the main reason that Japan has fallen behind in competitions is that its players often don't receive proper training or funding until they have already made names for themselves. This usually doesn't happen until they are in their mid-thirties, which, he suggested, is already nearing the end of one's greatest abilities. In contrast, he pointed out, China and South Korea begin training promising students when they are still children, which gives them a tremendous competitive edge later in life.[112] Teacher Wang, a Weiqi instructor at a different children's Weiqi school, had another explanation: "Part of this has to do with the time allowed in a game. In Japan, players take two days to play so they really think things out. In Korea professional games are limited to three hours so Koreans would often just throw in a stone even though they can't read the outcomes—they are more willing to gamble on a good play than Japanese."[113]

These accounts list a range of practical reasons for different national playing styles. Yet more often than not the people I interviewed, including those I just quoted, highlighted the difference as a matter of national character that helps to shape individuals' personalities. Liu Xiaoguan, a 9-*duan* professional Weiqi player, and one of the most famous Weiqi players in China, linked Weiqi with Chinese cultural characteristics:

> *There is a lot of overlap with way Chinese people play, with the way Asian people play, and Chinese ways of thinking in general. . . . For instance, Asians aren't as direct as Westerners, right? Westerners just say what they are thinking, right? Asians are less direct. They may start by hinting at something they want to say later on. First they will look to the situation on their left and their right, and only then will they ask the question they really want to ask. They are much more cautious and will think about the repercussions of whatever they are saying. You have to understand this to really understand Weiqi. If you understand this then you can better understand how we think about things. So if you can learn to understand the way people think when they play Weiqi, this can help you to understand Chinese culture and ways of thinking.*[114]

Liu Xiaoguan used Western culture as a contrast to Chinese and/or Asian culture because he was speaking with me and was hoping to explain things by using points of reference that he felt that I, as an American, would understand. The idea that Westerners are more direct than Chinese people comes up quite frequently in China, both in and out of Weiqi settings. Suggesting that Weiqi reflects this difference seemed to be a polite way to tell me that Chinese people are more contemplative and sophisticated.[115] The statement highlights prevalent beliefs that Weiqi reflects Chinese thinking in ways that are both profound and difficult to fully express.

Far more common than using Western culture as a point of contrast was a highly prevalent emphasis of the idea that different playing styles exemplify cultural differences across China, Japan, and South Korea. Liu Xiaoguan expanded on what he saw as Japanese and Korean characteristics in relation to their different playing styles.

You could say that Japan is a little conservative. They have a hard time changing their old set opening patterns (dingshi). This is the Japanese character (minzu xiguan). If they have a way of doing something and you tell them that there is a better way to do it, it is very hard for them to change. Weiqi is the same. In comparison, Chinese and Korean thinking is more open—more willing to dare to change, to break with established traditions. Japanese conservativism influences their organizational structure [he points to the Weiqi board]. They tend to hold on to the ways of their predecessors. They try hard to protect tradition. But in China and Korea the younger professionals' level is better. They are more assertive and they have taken the old ways and changed everything.

Koreans don't really like using set opening patterns. They've completely broken away from these set opening patterns. They just put their personalities into their style of play. . . . In Japan, there are a lot set opening patterns of play (dingshi). To see someone's personality expressed in one's style of play like this is more rare because they still emulate the old masters, they still think the old ways are the best.[116]

Hong Feng, a Weiqi instructor at the Capital Sports Center in Beijing's Science and Engineering University, contextualized Japan's playing style with historical precedent.

Japanese have a strong sense of playing established moves. In traditional Japan they had a government title called "Benyinfang." The Benyinfang were like aristocrats in that the title was inherited—the son will inherit the father's title and the grandchild will then inherit it generation after generation. The whole family would do this—their government would give them 200 duan [1,000 kilograms] of grain to eat. When someone else played them Weiqi, if that person's level was lower, they might play for a while and then be sent away to think about their moves. They'd tell him, "You come back later to finish the game."

In those days one game might take a whole year. Then they wrote down set opening patterns (dingshi). This was like a bible for Weiqi and it said this is right and that is wrong and you have to respect these rules because some ancestor said that was how you play. So the Japanese style of play has more set rules. Their tradition of abiding by those rules is very strong. Koreans are more rebellious. They say, "I don't care what anyone else says I just want to win." So they don't have as many rules.[117]

As demonstrated in these two quotes, most of the people I interviewed spoke of differing styles of play as reflecting nationally bound cultural characteristics that manifested themselves in individual personalities. Outside of Weiqi contexts, people in China also depicted Japanese men as passive and in far more negative ways—as being sexually perverted because of their repressed personalities, for example. Similarly, conversations I had with people who did not frequently play Weiqi often spoke of Korean men in openly derisive tones. The most commonly voiced stereotypes are that Korean men are violent, misogynist, loud, and bad drivers. People in China seem half outraged, half amused, when they go on to say that Korean's claim that Chinese cultural icons, ranging from Confucius to Weiqi, originated in Korea. Conversations about the conservative Weiqi playing style of Japanese men and the aggressive playing style of Korean men who disregard traditions thereby overlap with larger cultural identities in the eyes of people in China. I should emphasize, however, that the underlying sentiment was far more forgiving, even affectionate, in Weiqi circles.

AN UNEXPECTED NOSTALGIA FOR
THE JAPANESE ERA

When I first began this project I confess that I was expecting to encounter a rather uniform nationalistic hatred of Japanese players. This assumption was born of years of hearing Chinese people express remarkably angry and at times racist rhetoric about Japanese people. Chinese views such as this were the result of widespread resentment about the atrocities that Japanese soldiers committed during its occupation of China, Japan's continued refusal to offer a sincere apology, and, to some degree, because of Japan's remarkable economic success. In both my formal interviews and informal conversations I found that while Weiqi players were not without their biases about Japan, for the most part they were far more respectful of Japanese people than the other Chinese people I spoke with. They frequently spoke of Japan's more reserved playing style and character, but I never heard them make comments that matched the vitriolic diatribes I had heard outside of Weiqi circles.

It was hardly surprising that people in the PRC celebrated overtaking Japan in Weiqi. Yet, for many who had been raised studying the games of Japan's great masters, this was also nuanced with a certain sorrow for what was also recognized as the end of an important era in the Weiqi realm. Weiqi players in their twenties and younger had grown up studying Korean players' games, whereas those in their thirties and older had studied the Japanese masters. The differing emotional connections to Japan and Korea are a reminder of the tensions of a generation gap that is arguably more pronounced in China than in most other nations. To some extent, for the older generation, the fall of Japan represents nostalgia for their lost youth. What is at stake, then, is not just proving China to be the most powerful nation, both in the Weiqi sphere and beyond. Equally important are the ways that Weiqi allows for the transcendence of national rivalries at the same moment that it seems to support them. The following commentary in *The Weiqi Report* (*Weiqi bao*) evinces some of these ambiguities.

> *"The Sad Song of Japan's Weiqi" (Riben Weiqi de beige)*
>
> *Japan lost again! The sad song of the utterly defeated reverberated around the rafters of the Toyota cup. All of Japan's players were also defeated in all sixteen of the playoff games in the recently finished Samsung Cup competition. Not one survived, and yet again they had no choice but to play the sad song lamenting their lost battle. . . . Japan's Weiqi has been embarrassed in this way too many times to count. . . . Japan's Weiqi is clearly on its deathbed. People have never thought this way about Japan's Weiqi before. . . .*
>
> *Japan's Weiqi already has a long history. But regardless of whether or not one is talking about small battles on part of the board or overall strategies for the board as a whole, they seem to suffer from a kind of diseases that has weakened the bones or "calcium deficiency." They show such feebleness they seem anemic. Their immune system is so frail that they can't fight back, to the point that they just can't keep up with the tempo of China and South Korea. . . . (Z. Huang 2004)*

The author of this article speaks of Japan's fall in a tone of mixed anger and despair. The military terminology he uses might be interpreted as a celebration of China's victories were it not for the overall tone of disappointment. The article's illness metaphors accentuate that the author's anger is more akin to the frustration of watching an elderly family member's physical and mental decline. It then goes on to expand on its battle metaphors in conjunction with this seeming frailty.

> *Even the top Japanese players—the very best, those who have great abilities and achievements—one by one they still fall in battle to Chinese and Korean players who use the Japanese players for target practice (jidaozhigui). . . . [118]*
>
> *The fast decline of Japanese Weiqi isn't really good for the development of Weiqi in the rest of the world. The Japanese are so proud of their race that there is no way they will accept that they are losing. They will certainly make the appropriate changes to adjust to work at improving and make every effort to return to their old position [of greatness] in future international competitions. Could the Japanese Weiqi team one day be as good as its Olympic sports? Will they explode on a scene where no one expects much of them anymore and return to the strength of their younger days to create another great era? Or will Japan continue to play the role of servant (xiao sanzi) to China and Korea? Someday history will tell.[119]*

In this set of comments, the editorial's continued themes of war and illness are tied into claims of China's national superiority. The author suggests that people speak of Japan's weakness in the game as a marker of Japan's patriotic decline. By its logical inverse, this implies that China's strength in the game attests to its nationalistic fervor. The article's concluding remark that Japan is too proud to not want to catch up with Weiqi also strongly associates superiority in the game with the health of the race and the strength of the nation.

If the themes in Huang's editorial confirm this chapter's discussion of warlike nationalism in the Weiqi imaginary, one should also note the ways in which it subverts these very sentiments. The article does not bask in the glory of China overtaking Japan. Rather, it laments the loss of a worthy adversary, perhaps in some sense even a father figure, in the world of Weiqi. It has the feel of a spectator watching his favorite boxer get knocked to the ground and shouting "Get up!" with both rage and concern at the athlete's ruin. Japan's failures in international Weiqi competitions are portrayed in unmistakable tones of frustration, anger, and grief. When he uses the term "song of sorrow" he speaks of the dirge that the Japanese should sing for their own state of affairs. Yet it also seems to refer to the sentiments of the author, who also seems to long for Japan to return to its former greatness.

In the end of the article the author asserts that it is not healthy for the Weiqi world to have such lopsided competitions. The inference here is that one grows strongest from having worthy adversaries. In this sense, the article tacitly acknowledges that Japan's history of defeating China in Weiqi was beneficial to the higher cause of Weiqi, beyond the disputes of individual nations. I can think of no other venue in which Japan's decline would be cause for anything other than celebration in China. As such, we are witness to the fact that although Weiqi is certainly a venue for nationalistic rivalries, it can also be a free space to transcend those borders in the shared appreciation of, and membership in, an increasingly international community of Weiqi players in East Asia.

Japanese mass-mediated productions that China's younger generation has been raised on are also surprisingly critical of nationalist ideologies. The first Chinese and Japanese coproduced film, *The Go Masters,* for example, uses Weiqi as the backdrop of a drama that juxtaposes the warm friendship evoked with the battle on the board with the divisive and inevitably calumnious war between China and Japan.[120] *The Go Masters* emphasizes the harm that the war had on both individuals and families in both nations. The film uses Weiqi to emphasize a shared culture that transforms the conceptualization of the

Sino–Japanese War into a dialogue reminiscent of the American Civil War in which brother was pitted against brother. This has a very different feel than the rhetoric of racial and cultural difference that was employed during the war, or that sometimes informs discussions in contemporary China.

Similarly, the Japanese Weiqi manga *Hikaru no Go* repeatedly mocks Japanese nationalism at Weiqi tournaments, choosing instead to embrace Weiqi players from all over the world.[121] The game thereby becomes an emblem for setting aside one's differences even as one is engaged in fierce competition, of transcending regionally bound conflicts, yet doing so with decidedly nationalistic vocabulary.

In focusing on a sphere that is so firmly grounded in East Asia, international Weiqi competitions and their cultural significance force us to rethink the East/West binary of the majority of English-language scholarship on Chinese nationalism. We have also seen the ways in which international Weiqi competitions simultaneously support and undermine nationalistic rivalries. Chinese discussions of national styles of play come to represent culturally defined personalities and, in a very Confucian sense, link individual manhood directly with a masculinized state. In this depiction Japan is reserved, artistic, impractical; South Korea is aggressive and focused on winning at any cost; and China, according to the people I interviewed in Beijing, is striving for the happy balance between the two. These discourses on national styles of play come to represent different cultural models for individual personalities belonging to particular groups that merge conceptions of nation, race, and man.

FOUR

Becoming Men

CHILDREN'S TRAINING IN CONTEMPORARY CHINA

Confucius said, "I consider my behavior three times a day" (Kongzi yue: wuri sanxing wu shen). In the same way, with Weiqi one must consider what you are doing—how to find shortcuts, how to improve.

Interview, Sylvia, Peking University
Student, July 16, 2010

He just doesn't seem like a chess player until you see him settle in front of the board, his body stiffening a little, his face becoming serene and ageless, the little boy taking leave for a time while Josh muses over ancient, difficult ideas.

FRED WAITZKIN, *Searching for Bobby Fischer,* 1984[1]

TEACHING CHILDREN WEIQI IS PART of a larger discourse on training boys to become men who will thrive in China's highly competitive economy. This has been linked with the concept of *suzhi* (often defined as "quality"), which is more often than not associated with middle-class aesthetics, consumerism, and a grueling work ethic. *Suzhi* is used by the Chinese government, popular press, and educational leaders to encourage its citizenry to be industrious, to seek education, and to behave in a genteel fashion. *Suzhi* is also used in disciplining children to become model citizens. In elementary school classes, for example, children are exposed to expectations of continual self-evaluation of their abilities, diligence, and striving to overcome their own shortcomings.[2] In turn, teachers and parents are also disciplined. They must adjust their behavior to become proper role models, and they are bound to the children's grueling schedules. This often includes school during the day and intensive tutoring and study during the evenings, weekends, and vacations. Weiqi training is a subset of this disciplinary process—one that is thought to train young minds and bodies to face the challenges of today's competitive society.

71

In contemporary China, middle-class only children from the cities have become symbols of modernity as well as the hopes of the nation.[3] Yet Weiqi's revival can also be said to be born of contemporary fears of these very same youths. Today's children are often referred to as "Little Emperors" spoiled only children who came of age during China's One-Child Policy. As a result, an entire social fabric has been turned on its head. Suddenly, instead of two parents having eight or nine children to support them in their old age, China's typical family structure is referred to as 4–2–1 (four grandparents, two parents, one child). The most fundamental tenets of Chinese society have revolved around a two-millennia-long Confucian notion of the centrality of family relations for individual happiness and societal harmony. In the context of the One-Child Policy, this familial focus was confronted with a nation of only children who must live up to the hopes and dreams of their parents. Adding to this, China's recent prosperity has resulted in a dramatic shift in values. In urban centers throughout China, parents who grew up in the austere early communist era, where self-sacrifice was the mantra of the day, are raising a nation of Little Emperors who are given what they want before they even ask. Not surprisingly, the Little Emperor Syndrome has caused a tremendous amount of angst about China's future.[4]

It is in this anxiety-filled context that parents decide to send their children to Weiqi schools. Most people told me that because of increasing demands in the workplace, fewer adults play Weiqi than they did ten years earlier. Yet they were quick to point out that the number of children who study the game is growing exponentially. An increasing number of parents are sending their children to Weiqi schools because they think that it will give their offspring a competitive edge later in life. It is also widely believed that Weiqi teaches children mathematics and logic in a fun and interesting way. Perhaps more important, Weiqi represents a discipline and behavior associated with an idyllic, if somewhat invented, past—a time before the complexities of today's global political economy. It harkens back to a day when hard work and endurance were some of the most defining components of proper manhood, and an era when China was unquestionably the leader in its known world.

WEIQI TEACHERS AND THE CONFUCIAN IDEAL

One of Weiqi's disciplining structures is the way that it trains its players in Confucian behavior. That Confucian imagery is embedded in the game is not hard to see. Confucianism emphasizes ritual and is firmly grounded in the belief that behavior, ranging from filial piety to ceremonies, both shapes and reflects morality.

These disciplinary mechanisms also have a strong influence on the teachers. Any instructor knows that an important part of teaching is leading by example. In this sense, the children were not the only ones to be disciplined. The teachers conformed to a remarkably similar mode of self-presentation, both in the classroom and outside of it. This behavior can best be described as a modern manifestation of iconic Confucian gentleman from days of old.

In 2010 I attended the Wenbo Weiqi Training Center (*Wenbo weiqi peixun zhongxin*), which I refer to as the Wenbo School for short. This children's Weiqi school was named after the owner and manager, Wang Wenbo. Wang Wenbo was a quiet and warm person whose persona evoked the paradigm of the cultured gentleman—a worldview that asserts that morality, intellect, and bodily actions (ritual and behavior) can never be truly separate. Calm, reserved, and exuding care for others, Wang Wenbo daily escorted the students up the street to eat lunch at the school cafeteria. He was always the first to take plates of food to the students who waited at the tables, and the last one to get his own meal.

At the Wenbo School, all of the teachers were male, and all of them spoke with a gentle dignity. Most of the instructors were in their forties or fifties. Although some of the teachers snuck off during breaks to have a quick smoke, I never saw them partake of this activity in front of the children or even keep their cigarettes in a place that the children could see them (such as the customary placement in a shirt pocket). In part, they behaved in a manner that they felt was fitting for their roles as teachers but, with the exception of smoking, their personalities did not markedly change when the students were not in the vicinity. Instead, a certain personality type seemed to gravitate to the Weiqi realm, and, as in any subculture, this was accompanied by a slow acclimation to the behavior of others in this sphere.

The reserved demeanor of the teachers stood out in marked contrast to other forms of manhood in China—businessmen are extroverted to a fault, for example. The Confucian model for an ideal teacher was not limited to instilling knowledge alone, then, the way education is often thought of in the West. Rather, the Confucian model is to teach the whole person, in whom intellect, behavior, and morality are one. Academia in the West is historically born of the priesthood, so in some sense this is familiar territory. Yet in China this is carried out to a much greater degree, for teachers are expected to embody a personhood that is inseparable from their behavior in the class-room. Perhaps the closest equivalent in the West would be elite boarding schools' objective of molding their students' characters and providing them with an education, as well as the subsequent monitoring of their teachers' behavior.

Children's Weiqi teachers embodied models of Confucian masculinity for their students to emulate, even though their backgrounds did not always fit this model. Their previous occupations ranged from construction work to white-collar employment at a computer company. None of the teachers I spoke with at this school had taken lessons themselves as children.

My first Weiqi instructor, Teacher Wang, is a *6-duan* amateur, which places him among a very privileged few at the top rungs of amateur Weiqi players and signifies that he had won a national tournament at some point in his career.[5] He met the owner of the school because they play at the same Weiqi club, which in turn led to his employment at the school. He was a construction worker before he retired. I had the impression that this occupa-tion was less because of inclination than because of the misfortune of Cultural Revolution politics. Teacher Wang learned to play Weiqi when he was sixteen years old as a Sent-Down Youth during the Cultural Revolution. He improved by playing with friends and reading books. Notably introverted with adults, Teacher Wang exuded a grandfatherly gentle charm and was clearly most at home when interacting with the children.

Teacher Li, who in his mid-thirties was the youngest of the teachers at the school, has a quiet and reserved dignity that evokes images of this earlier time. Like many men in Beijing, he has a surprisingly deep voice for such a thin man. In addition to his quiet dignified countenance, he would slowly saunter down the street as we escorted the children to the cafeteria. His hands were inevitably held behind his back, much in the fashion of a tradi-tional Chinese gentleman. As with Wang Wenbo and Teacher Wang, Teacher Li's quiet reserve, as much as his skills as a Weiqi player, legitimated his role as a teacher at the school.

The Weiqi instructors' embodiment of Confucian behavior helped to reinforce the iconic link of Weiqi with historical gentlemen of learning. In this context, the teachers' behavior became an unspoken means of leading by example. The aim, then, was to train the children to excel in Weiqi but also to embody the ethos of great men of history. In setting an example, the teach-ers were disciplined no less than the children. To the degree that the adults who played Weiqi were also drawn to these images, it was a fairly painless disciplinary process. Yet in noting the acceptable range of behavior one gains a better sense of the forms of manhood that are offered in this sphere.

MODERNIZING INFLUENCES: WEIQI SCHOOLS AS CORPORATE STRUCTURES

In addition to my 2010 and 2011 interviews at the Wenbo School, in 2011 I conducted interviews at two branches of the Nie Weiping Classroom (*Nie Weiping Weiqi Jiaoshi*). The school was named after China's most famous Weiqi player, Nie Weiping, who, in exchange for the use of his name and occasional guest appearances, had been given stock in the franchise.

Hong Po is the CEO of the Nie Weiping Classroom franchise. According to Hong Po, the Nie Weiping Classroom has schools in two hundred cities across China, with a total of fifteen hundred to sixteen hundred students and sixty teachers.[6] It has seven branches in Beijing alone. The Nie Weiping Classroom franchise focuses on young beginning players, but it is also affiliated with the Nie Weiping Center of Learning (*Nie Weiping Weiqi Daochang*), which trains students who hope to become professional players. The Nie Weiping Center of Learning already has twelve branches in Beijing.

Hong Po listed the Nie Weiping franchise's achievements with clear pride. "Our lowest ranking students are four years old. When they come they can't play Weiqi at all. The highest, if we count the entire Nie Weiping franchise, well it is very high. Our school has a brother institution called Nie Weiping Weiqi Center of Learning. This school has trained one hundred professional players in China. Teacher Nie Weiping has trained some of the most famous players in China. For instance, Chang Hao, and Gu Li—Teacher Nie trained both of them. They all trained in our school. At this point we have trained half of China's professional players."

Compared to the decidedly family-run flavor of the Wenbo School, the Nie Weiping Classroom made no effort to hide the fact that it was built on a business model. In a two-hour weekly meeting I attended that included teachers from all of the Nie Weiping Classroom Beijing branches, Hong Po spent approximately one hour and forty minutes talking about business strategies. This primarily consisted of instructing the teachers on how to sell the various packages available to the parents. This included reviewing the relative costs and benefits of each package, in which signing up for more classes meant a cheaper per-class fee. He instructed them on the exact phrasing of

FIGURE 4. The Nie Weiping Classroom Weiqi competition to attain a rank.

the sales pitch so that the parents would feel they were getting a special deal. He then provided several examples of common things that parents might say and the proper response to each of the parents' worries or objections. Although he did not go into the specifics of the incentive plan for the teachers during that meeting, he made it clear that a substantial part of their salaries relied on commissions. After the marketing portion of the meeting, Hong Po spent approximately ten minutes talking about children's education. He used the final ten minutes to discuss the logistics of an upcoming tournament which ended up including approximately 280 students from all of the Nie Weiping Classroom Beijing branches.

Hong Po freely admitted that he was drawn to his current profession because he saw it as a wide-open market. Nevertheless, of the children's educators I spoke with, he was by far the most adept at articulating the more erudite aspects of children's education. In explaining his school's learning objectives, for example, he began with a brief overview of Montessori's theories of discovering children's latent talent. He then went on to contrast this with traditional Chinese views on children's education: "In traditional China we had our own methods regarding children's development. They thought that to help children grow up it was a step to increase their abilities (*nengli*) and enhance their vitality (*shengming li*). Now what was the concept of vitality and ability about? In fact it was taking a concept to become ability. For instance, when we read books we attain knowledge. But this is not true ability. You cannot gain ability from reading books. You just have a concept. Afterwards you have to have action with repeated practice. Only then can you make your ideas become abilities. This process is embodied in Weiqi. Any child who studies to any level of skill on the board is taking a concept and putting it into action."[7]

By drawing on well-known Western educational theory and what he depicted as traditional Chinese thought, Hong Po placed himself firmly at the center of a new hybrid culture in contemporary China. This aligned Weiqi perfectly at the crossroads of past, present, and future, suggesting that Weiqi could help children to mediate all three.

Hong Po stressed that fulfillment comes from a combination of thought and action. To some degree his view of traditional conceptions of childhood training is remarkably revisionist in that the West was in fact far more oriented toward a practical implementation of knowledge. In contrast, the traditional Chinese scholastic system was rather infamous for not training its bureaucrats in any practical matters at all. In spite of its remarkable durability over the millennia, this system had the obvious drawback that China's governing body was made up of people who had been trained in thoroughly impractical knowledge such as being able to write eloquent poetry. Hong Po's conception of China's traditional education sounded more like an MBA class at the Wharton School than traditional Chinese thought. Yet on another level, Hong Po's analysis also built on Confucian doctrine in which there was very little division between one's demeanor, intellect, and morality.

Talking to Wang Wenbo from the Wenbo School and Hong Po from the Nie Weiping Classroom were very different experiences. Unlike the Confucian ethos that was cultivated at the Wenbo School, which was very much a family-run operation, the Nie Weiping Classroom thrived on its modern corporate image. Though evoking traditionalist imagery in his speeches, Hong Po was less a representative of the Confucian model than a natural salesman. If Wang Wenbo radiated an endearingly introverted sincerity, Hong Po oozed confidence and charm.

The physical environments of the two schools I have mentioned, as well as a third I will present in a moment, were in some sense similar. All of the classrooms were filled with tables that were covered with Weiqi boards. Each of them contained a blackboard-sized magnetic chart that was set up vertically for class demonstrations. Yet on another level the physical environments also spoke to the schools' different orientations. The Wenbo School was a modest building in a traditional area of town. Renting space in an elementary

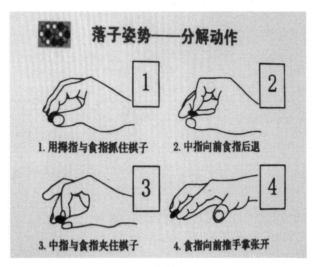

FIGURE 5. Poster A: How to hold a Weiqi stone. Nie Weiping
Classroom.

school to hold its intensive summer program, the underlying message seemed
to be that the school was part of the community. In contrast, the Nie Weiping
Classroom's branches were in the most upscale parts of Beijing. Their classrooms sparkled with cleanliness, fresh paint, and evoked a sense of a new and
well-organized franchise.

At the Nie Weiping Classroom, posters hung on the walls that featured
children's cartoons labeled with instructional messages. Figure 5 is a poster
that shows the children how to properly hold the Weiqi stones. It reads as
follows:

> *1. Grasp the Weiqi stone between your thumb and index finger.*
> *2. Use your middle finger to move the stone to the back of your index finger.*
> *3. Grip the stone between your middle finger and your index finger.*
> *4. Spread your middle finger and index finger out to place a stone on the board.*

This sign instructs the children that the proper way to hold a Weiqi stone is
between one's outstretched pointer and middle fingers. When I asked Hong
Po why people did this, he emphasized the importance of teaching the children proper etiquette when they played: "Playing Weiqi has its own rituals.
This is one of Weiqi's rituals. For instance, before you play a game you should
bow to your opponent and greet them, saying 'Thank you for your instruction' (*qing duo zhi zhao*)."[8]

FIGURE 6. Poster B (*top half*): Weiqi etiquette. Nie Weiping Classroom.

I had asked many people in China about the origins of this hand position for holding a Weiqi stone. A few people told me that if one's fingers were outstretched in this manner it was harder to cheat because it was far more difficult to obstruct one's opponent's view of the board. The vast majority of them simply shrugged and told me that it was the polite thing to do. True to form, however, Hong Po had a more eloquent explanation:

This is called, "The crane bows its head" (he diantou). China has a bird called a crane. [He raises his hand as if he were holding a Weiqi stone.] It is like a crane raising its head. Every time you place a stone on the board it is like the crane is lowering its head. [He lowers his hand like a crane bowing its head.] . . . This is the crane's beak. Then it lowers its head and gently places the stone on the board. [He lowers his hand again.] In Chinese culture this is a very beautiful thing. So when you play Weiqi, every time you place a stone on the board you are demonstrating your respect for your opponent.[9]

A second poster had two cartoons. In the top half (figure 6) a grandfatherly figure could be seen playing Weiqi with a virile middle-aged man performing karate in the background. Rather than expounding on the martial imagery of the game, or the intellectual power that might be implied by the picture, the caption extols the students to be polite while playing. It states:

“礼貌” 开始　“礼貌” 结束

白棋罐方座位为“上位”。
黑棋罐方座位为“下位”。
对局开始前，棋力较弱或
年龄较小者，应提前坐在
“下位”以示尊敬之意。

对局开始前，双方应相互
行礼表示友好；对局进行
之中，因故必须离开或返
回座位时永应向对手敬礼
示意。

FIGURE 7. Poster B (*bottom half*): Teaching children to bow. Nie Weiping Classroom.

[ABOVE, IN BLACK]: *Weiqi is something a gentleman strives to master; etiquette is the basis of its way.*

[BELOW, IN RED]: *It begins with manners and it ends with manners.*

The bottom half of the poster (figure 7) features cartoon depictions of a cute dog and turtle bowing as they begin their Weiqi game.

[ON THE LEFT]: *The person playing white will be in the "superior seat." The person playing black will be in the "subordinate seat." Before you begin, the person who is the weaker player or who is younger should sit in the subordinate seat to show your respect.*

[ON THE RIGHT]: *Before opponents begin to play both sides should bow as a friendly greeting. Once you have started to play, if you must leave your seat or when you come back to your seat you should bow again to show your respect.*

The text instructs the children on the relative hierarchy of black and white. Although the poster does not explain why, this is based on the idea that the weaker player should take black because it gets the first move. The seemingly whimsical posters spoke volumes as to the cultural values that were being instilled into the children. Both posters emphasize the importance of ritual behavior, in which physical control becomes an emblem for good manners and for the embodiment of civility.

The etiquette for holding the stone is indeed the norm in China as well as outside of its borders. The bowing and ritualized speech that Hong Po outlined, however, is in fact from Japan. Except in the Nie Weiping Classroom I did not see anyone bow before or after a game. Similarly, I had never heard or read any Chinese statements about the crane bowing its head as a symbol of respect. I suspect that this account is from Japan. Just as Hong Po had merged Western and Chinese traditions in speaking of educational models, here he merges Chinese and Japanese traditions to become something new. That he does not credit Japan with the origins of much of the etiquette he is teaching his students can no doubt be linked to his awareness of the widespread anti-Japanese sentiment in China. The ensuing hybridity creates new cultural forms with an aim of teaching children proper behavior and, in a sense, adopting the most poetic imagery from each tradition and claiming them as its own.

At the Wenbo School, the teachers had all met while playing at the same Weiqi club. Old friends with the owner of the school, the teachers had been hand-picked for their expert skills as well as for being kindred spirits. In contrast with the middle-aged teachers at the Wenbo School, most of the Nie Weiping Classroom teachers had just graduated from university. In marked contrast with the other schools I visited, several of the teachers at the Nie Weiping Classroom were female. When I remarked on the unusual presence of female teachers, I was told that it was because the school primarily taught young children and that women were more appropriate for this age group. Several of the teachers I spoke with were also from remote and poorer areas of the country, such as Inner Mongolia or the countryside outside of Harbin. I suspect that all of these factors were related to their relatively low salaries. Yet it should be noted that all of the teachers I spoke with at the Nie Weiping Classroom were college graduates, which attested both to the school's symbolic capital and its efforts to present an image of quality and middle-class values (*suzhi*) in its learning environment. Unlike the Wenbo School, where the teachers had been "Weiqi friends" (*qiyou*) before working together, the Nie Weiping classroom was, for the most part, an association of twenty-somethings who had no connections with each other before obtaining their jobs.

The Nie Weiping Classroom also engaged in far more aggressive advertising, and a substantial part of the teachers' salaries was based on commissions. At one of the branches I witnessed a handsome and confident twenty-three-year-old calling people at home in an effort to sell them one of the package

FIGURE 8. Teacher Dang shows my classmates some life-and-death problems on the magnetic board. Wenbo School.

plans that offered discounts that varied according to how many classes were paid for in advance. The Nie Weiping Classroom's Web page was a masterpiece that included photos of happy children receiving prizes and a Western news crew filming their classes. The Nie Weiping Classroom was built on the fame of the person it was named after, which gave the school a prestige that was hard to compete with.

A third point of comparison is a children's Weiqi training center that I will call School X. School X was located in the back streets of a business district. The school was housed in one of the traditional four-story buildings that lined these back alleys, in block-long enclosures surrounded by a wall and a guard. Outside, a man and a woman were selling vegetables from a horse-drawn cart. School X was more expensive than the Wenbo School, but it was remarkably unkempt.[10] To get to the classrooms one had to walk up five flights of dimly lit and poorly cleaned stairways. The classroom I visited was small and cramped, and only one of its four fluorescent lights worked. The ensuing dim lighting seemed to affect the energy level of the students, who were decidedly lethargic. Part of the students' subdued manner might also have been a result of the fact that, unlike the other schools I had visited, some of the children's mothers sat in the back of the class.

In spite of the marked difference in the ethos of the three children's schools, their teaching methods were almost identical. Classes consisted of (1) playing the game with a classmate, (2) reviewing standardized opening moves, (3) engaging in a second period of playing against a classmate, (4) a teacher-led review of a student's game in front of the class, in which he pointed out where they played well, where they made mistakes, and how they could have played better. The only significant differences I saw were the schools' policies toward the students' parents. At the Wenbo School, parents dropped their children off in the morning and appeared again only at the end of the day. In contrast, the Nie Weiping Classroom had a free class designed for parents who wanted to learn the game for the sake of their children. At School X some of the mothers sat in on their children's classes.

The remarkable standardization of the teaching methodology is all the more impressive when one considers the range of self-presentation of the schools themselves. The uniformity of these well-established techniques created a symbolically viable sense of employing a proven educational model that the training was based on. This methodology was focused on the goal of teaching the game, but it also spoke to a shared understanding of the best way to educate the children and, in turn, to mold them into the adults that they would become.

THE STUDENTS

During the school year, children can take Weiqi classes in the afternoons and on the weekends. In summer vacation the Weiqi schools offer half-day classes from Monday through Friday, and many of the children were enrolled in both the morning and afternoon classes. The Wenbo School held an intensive summer session in an elementary school's otherwise unused classrooms. For all intents and purposes it served as a second branch of the school because its different location drew on a disparate, though sometimes overlapping, student body. This program, where I spent two-thirds of my time during my 2010 fieldwork, ran five classes simultaneously. It had enough students who did not go home after the morning sessions that the teachers would line them up in pairs and walk around the corner to the school cafeteria. By virtue of my age I assisted the teachers in passing out the food to the students and sat with the teachers while eating. This gave me the opportunity to hear the teachers' views on the game and their students.

FIGURE 9. One of my favorite opponents. Wenbo School.

The beginning class was made up of five-year-olds who ranged from 25 *ji* to 2 *ji*. The strongest class ranged in age from ten- to thirteen-year-olds with 3- to 5-*duan* amateur ratings. My class ranged from eight- to eleven-year-olds with ratings from 1 *ji* to 2-*duan* amateurs. This represented a substantial inflation for children's rates. At that time I was only ranked at 3 *ji* on the online Weiqi server KGS (Kiseido Go Server). Having witnessed children's games at several Weiqi schools in Beijing, I can say that this inflation of children's rates is the norm. Most of my classmates were between nine and eleven years old, though there was one high school–aged student in each of my classes.

At the first branch of the Wenbo School, my oldest classmate was a recent high school graduate who was readying himself to attend Qing-hwa University in the fall. My second oldest classmate was an eleven-year-old who radiated likeability with his quiet charm. While other students used the breaks to roughhouse or simply run up and down the hallways, he would stay behind and play Five in a Row (*wuziqi*) with me—a game that has approximately the same level of complexity as checkers. With each victory he would quietly glow with pride, and with each loss he would offer a sorrowful smile to show that there were no hard feelings. Because our Five in a Row games would not influence the level of Weiqi classes I would be enrolled in, I often let him win. The only exception to this was when a group of our classmates gathered to give him advice, in which case he and the other children were having so much fun that they didn't seem to care who won or lost.

The boys at these schools clearly loved to play Weiqi, but almost all of the ones that I spoke with emphasized that they were taking summer classes because their fathers wanted them to. Most of their fathers played the game but not their mothers. Part of the training, therefore, was to follow a path to manhood in which their fathers, and the male teachers, served as examples.

Many of the students were in Weiqi classes from 8:30 in the morning to 4:30 in the afternoon. As such, during the breaks the boys understandably showed no interest in playing more Weiqi in their free time. Instead, they amused themselves by playing cards or using the Weiqi set for other games akin to Othello, checkers, or even marbles in which they flicked one piece across the board with their fingers with the goal of knocking their opponents' pieces off the board. They also played a rock-paper-scissors game in which every time someone won he was allowed to move a certain number of spaces to try to take his opponent's pieces by landing on them like checkers.

On the breaks, the boys in my class were as rowdy as other children of their age. They took turns practicing their karate kicks on each other, screamed loudly as they chased each other around the room, and occasionally threw things at each other. At first glance, this behavior belied the oft-repeated mantra that Weiqi taught children discipline and proper manners. Yet amid this seeming chaos was a remarkable amount of control. Not once in all this tumultuous anarchy did I see anyone run into a Weiqi board while people were still playing. Clearly there were unspoken limits to their rambunctious behavior. On one occasion, a boy was running around the room screaming that he was going to beat up a classmate whom he was chasing. Yet when two of his classmates grabbed the fleeing culprit (who was guilty of what, I do not know) the pursuer stopped and, seemingly losing interest, just walked away. In another instance two boys were taking turns kicking each other with surprising force. I was sure that their game would escalate into a real fight, but as soon as one of them stopped the other immediately desisted as well.

I only saw serious disciplinary problems once during my fieldwork. The boy, whom I will call Rocky, was fiercely intelligent and not a bad player for his age, but he was spoiling for trouble from the start of the day. Although he was already a disciplinary problem, I turned out to be the catalyst for many of the conflicts that were to come. This began when I caught him trying to cheat by attempting to take some of my pieces off the board that he had not earned, clearly hoping that I wouldn't notice because his hands moved so quickly.

This was the only time I witnessed such an action in China. After being chastened by our teacher, who had overheard our conversation, Rocky spent the rest of the morning singing songs that mocked Americans and Japanese. He also whiled away the time throwing pens, Weiqi pieces, and whatever else he could grab at our eighteen-year-old classmate who had tried to intervene on my behalf. Rocky generally acted like a little gangster, and if he does follow that path I suspect that between his bellicose behavior and being very smart in spite of it all he will probably go far. I could barely repress a smile when his father came to pick him up after class in a police uniform.

It is not easy to keep young boys still. Most of the teachers hit the boys on occasion, but never very hard and only after they had repeatedly warned the student to behave. The boys seemed so remarkably unfazed by this that I can only guess that they were used to such behavior in their regular schools as well, and likely were getting much worst at home.

During the three weeks that I took classes, a handful of the boys tested the teachers with minor acts of resistance. A teacher's first response was to ask the offending student to sit still or be quiet. After issuing this warning two or three times, the teacher would angrily tell the child to move seats to separate him from his peers. More often than not the boy would ignore this instruction but would stop his disruptive behavior and the teacher would not insist on the student changing seats. It was only after repeatedly making noise or disrupting the class that a teacher really put his foot down. Usually all but one or two particularly unruly boys would give the teacher their full attention, and for the most part even the difficult students would usually limit themselves to staring off into space rather than causing overt disruption.

Weiqi is supposed to teach children to be good sports, but if that was the case it occurred much later in life for the nine- and ten-year-olds in my classes.

My classmates were not above using psychological warfare and frequently taunted their opponents by bringing up previously played bad moves or the games that their opponents had lost in the past. On the completion of a game, students often raised their hands yelling, "Teacher, I won," for all the class to hear.[11] They would frequently kibitz, though this was discouraged. Especially when one of them played against me, they would often gang up, freely giving each other advice in the hopes of symbolically crushing me on the board. This was, of course, a double victory for them because I was both an American and an adult.

Overall, the students were surprisingly attentive during class, however. This was no small feat considering that the all-day classes took place during the children's summer vacations. In part this is because a large portion of the classes was devoted to just playing the game. Another reason was that my classmates were interested in the subject matter. A third was that they and their peers were also taking other classes, ranging from piano to English to tennis. This effort to better themselves and to increase their chances of one day getting into a good university was part of their world. In this setting, they were fully aware of the fact that the alternative to their Weiqi classes would not be free time. Rather, it would be enduring lessons in another subject.

One of the daily exercises consisted of two students going to the front of the room to review their game from memory for the rest of the class to see. This was something that the teachers could effortlessly do, that most of my classmates could do with some degree of certainty, and that the younger students and I were hopeless at. Standing at the front of the class, two students would replay their games from memory by placing large Weiqi pieces on a magnetic board at the front of the classroom. As they did so the teacher stood beside them, commenting on particularly good and bad moves and suggesting alternative sequences.

I was struck by the ease with which people could remember a series of two hundred moves on a 19 × 19 grid with seemingly infinite possibilities. I asked Sylvia, the Peking University student who trained to be a professional Weiqi player as a child, if she could replay a game from memory: "Yes, I can remember a whole game from memory because I can look at what would have been a rational choice in a given move. If my opponent or I made that move it is easy to remember. If we did not make that move that is also easy to remember because it stands out as unusual. So it's not like trying to remember a bunch of random patterns. It's harder to remember other people's games because you don't know what they are thinking."[12]

A year later, when the topic came up again, she said the following:

There was a very famous player in Japan who could count three hundred moves in his head and think about all kinds of different alternatives that his opponent might come up with. So maybe he makes a different move and you have a totally different situation so the professional has to think ahead for every possibility. They can think ahead two hundred steps. Me, I can think out maybe one hundred steps ahead. And sometimes I would memorize famous players' games—I would mimic them and learn from them—try to understand why they made certain moves. Some of these games had more than two hundred moves and I had to memorize the whole game.[13]

There is some evidence that long-term Weiqi players experience white matter neuroplastic changes in their brains.[14] This is not unique to Weiqi players. Piano players experience a slightly different set of changes, for example, as do those who practice meditation, experience long-term painful stimulation, or suffer from chronic schizophrenia.[15] Scientists conducting these studies had expected to find that Weiqi influenced frontal lobe function in what has been called the "general intelligence domain" but instead found that neither Weiqi nor chess did so.[16] Rather than activating areas of the brain that are associated with logic or computation, both games primarily influence spatial mechanisms.[17] Weiqi increases right-brain dominance more than does chess, however.[18] Because research on brain function tends to focus on professional players and those studying to become professional players, there is a bit of a chicken-and-egg problem here. In other words, there is a possibility that preselection is at work because talented players are discovered at a very young age.[19] Left brain–dominant people might therefore be weeded out from the pool of Weiqi players by virtue of not playing Weiqi in the first place. Regardless, there seems to be evidence that Weiqi players rely heavily on spatial recognition and the memory of certain patterns as well as the possibility that there are minor physiological changes when learning the game at a young age.[20]

WEIQI AS A DISCIPLINARY MECHANISM

According to Chinese mythology, the legendary emperor Yao (2357–56 B.C.) created the game of Weiqi to train his son, who was, according to varying accounts, dim witted, unruly, or simply uninterested in the responsibilities that came with the throne. The unifying theme of all of the versions of the tale is that Weiqi is a valuable instructional tool to teach children lessons that expand beyond the board. In this framework, the game is lauded for teaching concentration, logic, war strategies, and ways to control an unruly empire.[21]

A good deal of the neo-Confucian praise of Weiqi can be heard in contemporary Chinese discussions of the game's benefits for children. Many assert that Weiqi teaches people not to be greedy, so that in mastering Weiqi one also learns to be a good leader in the government.[22] It is also thought that children who play Weiqi become more mature than those in their age cohort who do not learn the game.[23] Others seek to prove Weiqi's worth by connecting it with larger life lessons. For example, a book devoted to good parenting and sparking children's interest in the game states that it instructs children on how to persevere in the face of hardship as well as teaching them how to be good sports.[24] The book goes on to assert that Weiqi provides the opportunity for children to make good friends, that it is a healthy and entertaining way for a family to share time together, that it teaches cooperation, and that it has scientifically proven effects on improving intelligence and spatial comprehension.[25] The authors further assert that Weiqi teaches children knowledge (*zhishi*), widens their experience of the world (*jianshi*), and inspires daring combined with superior judgment (*danshi*).[26] Weiqi enthusiasts also feel that the game will help children learn the basic rules of commerce in that it teaches them to invest in several areas (of the board) while also instructing them in the perils of becoming too attached to one investment.[27] Other people I interviewed praised the game for developing children's memory, concentration, logic, and basic math skills.[28]

Sylvia, told me the following: "Weiqi teaches children to be wise and to be rational. . . . The game is good for children because they can learn math. They learn to count points up at the end of the game to see who won, to assess who is ahead or behind during the game and to adjust their behavior accordingly. For instance, it makes them think, 'Should I be peaceful and just hold on to what I have because I'm ahead or should I be more aggressive because I'm behind?' The first thing Weiqi teaches children is to assess their situation rationally—to know what decisions to make in life."[29]

The idea that Weiqi not only helps children to use logic but also assists in their ability to face challenges in their adult lives, was ubiquitous among the Weiqi players I spoke with. Liu Xiaoguan, a 9-*duan* professional, learned to play Weiqi when he was thirteen years old. This is much later in life than most professional players begin, but, in spite of this, he strongly believes in the benefits of the game for children.

For children, playing Weiqi helps their logical thinking. It develops their intelligence. . . . If they develop their intelligence, they can think about what to do when they run into difficult situations. . . . So a child who has studied Weiqi understands what to do. He or she will definitely be able to handle situations better than someone who has not studied Weiqi—and they will be smarter. They can think about problems and will know the best way to solve those problems. Because when they play Weiqi their teachers . . . instruct the children to think about what kind of result their actions will get, or that if they want something to happen later they need to do a, b, or c now.[30]

Teacher Zhuang is a twenty-one-year-old 4-*duan* amateur who works at the central branch of the Nie Weiping Classroom franchise. He also extolled the benefits of Weiqi for children: "Weiqi helps develop children's ability to contemplate (*siwei nengli*). It develops their ability to observe. It trains them to be creative. Weiqi is a competition so it teaches children to work hard in training themselves step by step so that they can grow up well, to develop their ability to strike or take action (*daji de nengli*)."[31]

All of these statements, and many more that I could not include here for want of space, further attest to the fact that Weiqi is not conceptualized as being merely a game. Everyone I spoke with believed that it was self-evident that Weiqi training helps students learn logic and concentration. Many people also emphasized that Weiqi helps boys to grow into men who would be better prepared for the challenges of China's new political economy. An important part of this preparation was disciplining the children's minds and bodies. This included teaching them to sit still and to concentrate for hours at a time as well as to accept losing games and cooperate with other children.

Coming from an American school system, it was hard for me not to be struck by the brutal honesty of the teachers in China. In reviewing games, the instructors provided comments ranging from "Good move" to "This is terrible." In conversations with me, or with the children themselves, the teachers would assess the students' strengths and weaknesses with equal candor. On several occasions a teacher might evaluate my classmates' abilities with a statement such as "He is not really very talented at this" while the student was listening. Learning to withstand this candor is perhaps an unintended part of the range of endurance that Weiqi schools teach.

The teachers' remarkably frank approach is part of Beijing's more direct culture as a whole. At a park I frequented where senior citizens gathered to play, my first attempts to say thank you after a game were met with loud laughter by my opponents and people watching the game. Because I had spent far more time in Taiwan, which has been heavily influenced by both Japanese and American styles of etiquette, I had fallen into Taiwan's habit of being what in the People's Republic of China (PRC) was deemed as overly polite and formal. In the PRC "Thank you" (*xiexie*) is reserved for sincere moments of gratitude. Part of what I was witnessing with the children's training, therefore, was simply a different etiquette than I had grown accustomed to in other Chinese-speaking regions. Within this setting, enduring criticism, while never enjoyable, did not carry the emotional impact that it might have had in a country with a less direct cultural milieu.

In truth, it did not take long for me to gain an appreciation for this style of education. If one could expect the teachers to be blunt when assessing one's shortcomings, one could also have faith in their compliments on good play. If the teachers were at times brutally honest, their comments were always within the realm of expected etiquette and, as such, were not traumatic in the ways that similar comments might have been in other cultural settings.

There was only one occasion when I saw a teacher really lose his temper. In this instance he angrily berated a student who had not come to class for several weeks, saying, "What were you thinking with that move? You really aren't improving any more!" In tones of unmistakable anger he went on to criticize the student for a very uncomfortable three minutes. This was all the more surprising because this instructor was usually one of the most gentle and caring of the teachers I met. What, then, was the reason for this sudden outbreak? What seemed to be happening was that the teacher felt that it was no sin to lack talent, but to not live up to one's ability was seen as a slight to the teacher who invested his time into the students. It was also clear that his anger arose in large part because of a frustrated sense of helplessness in watching the student fail to live up to his potential.

WEIQI AS SPORT: BEYOND THE CARTESIAN DIVIDE

Weiqi is categorized as a sport (*yundong, tiyu*) in China, whereas attempts to give chess this label in the United States have been met with mirth.[32] To buy a Weiqi set in the PRC, one does not go to a game store or, as would be the case in Taiwan, a stationery store. In the PRC one purchases a Weiqi set in a sporting goods store. Categorizing Weiqi as a sport results in China's Weiqi foundation being housed in the same building complex as other sports teams. The Weiqi players also dined in the same cafeteria as the other sports team members at China's national sports center. This represents a different way of seeing both sports and games of intellect than in the West—a worldview that does not create as great a distinction between behavior and thought, or between corporeal and cerebral concerns.

That Weiqi is categorized as a sport extends to conceptual frameworks about children's instruction, because in teaching them the mental discipline of the game one must necessarily also train them in physical endurance. Perhaps the most overt form of this is in teaching them to sit still for hours at a time. Teacher Zhuang used physical sports as an analogy for the need for children's daily training in the basics: "To learn Weiqi they need to review old games and to train. If they do this, their skill will rise quite quickly. For instance, I like to watch the NBA. When you watch the NBA the fun part is watching the amazingly difficult parts. But to be in the NBA they have to practice the basics every day. They have to practice their hoop shots and they have to practice passing the ball. This is very important. So the most important thing with my Weiqi students is to keep them interested so that they practice every day."[33]

The hours of study and concentration that Weiqi training necessitates are also linked to a worldview in which a Cartesian divide between mind and body is all but meaningless. The Japanese novel *The Master of Go,* for example, forcefully depicts the bodily harm that the stress of the game has on Weiqi players, ranging from extreme fatigue to severe stomach pains.[34] In this context the game becomes more like a martial art than a board game competition.

bell hooks critiques Western notions of metaphysical dualism in which mind and body are split.[35] She makes a call to recognize the ways in which intellect and passion are not antagonistic forces.[36] This worldview is far less controversial in China, where Daoist traditions conceptualize mind and body as being in very close symbiosis. One sees this in martial arts dramas (*wuxia*), in which mastery of written texts is a central part of attaining a higher level of expertise in physical combat. Thus, martial arts are seen to be more than merely a physical equation but one in which the master gains supernatural control through channeling *Qi* energy as both a physical and spiritual exercise.

Teacher Dang, who was my main instructor at the Wenbo School, once told me that as one becomes better at the game, there comes serenity in the quiet moments shared with friends. Although I am only an intermediate player even by Western standards, I have been fortunate enough to have experienced moments such as this. I have also had games that quickened my heartbeat in anticipation of an opponent's move that would lead to a dramatic victory or defeat—a surprisingly visceral reaction to the intellectual stimulation provided by the game. In the park I frequented, one of the elderly members of the Weiqi group told me that he liked to watch the game but could no longer play because he had had some serious heart problems the year before. He believed that the excitement of winning or losing could put him in physical jeopardy.

An essential component to training children in this context was a disciplining of the students in the classroom. Applying Susan Brownell's analysis of Chinese sports to Weiqi, the grueling disciplinary structure could be seen as a means of control in which body and personhood become one.[37] Endurance and relentless self-improvement are fundamental parts of Weiqi training and part of middle-class and elite children's educations as a whole— an ethos that is linked to the strength of the nation.[38]

Guan Yang, a Peking University graduate student who had trained in a professional Weiqi school as a child, expressed concern about how hard children were being pushed in contemporary China.

> *Many Chinese children must have a hobby—it's not necessarily that they want to have a hobby. Because China is so competitive, parents want their children to succeed early in life.*
>
> *For instance, on Monday they might have a dance class, on Tuesdays and Wednesdays a Weiqi class, and on other days they might have yet another class. My child is only one year old but I worry a bit—children work much harder than in our parents' generation.*[39]

Guan Yang's statement was confirmed by one of my high school–aged classmates. He told me that he took Weiqi lessons in the morning, badminton lessons in the afternoon, and was about to begin taking driving lessons on the weekends. He clearly enjoyed all of his classes, and when I commented that it was a remarkably structured schedule for a summer vacation he laughed, "This is definitely less work than preparing for college entrance exams." In short, childhood and adolescence are seen less as periods of carefree youth than a time for relentless self-improvement in order to prepare for the highly competitive nature of adulthood.

DISCIPLINING PARENTS

Weiqi shapes both children and their teachers. Yet this picture would not be complete if we did not also acknowledge the disciplinary effects on the parents. In the School X class that I visited, two mothers sat in the back of the room. During class one mother attentively watched as the teacher explained problem sets on the board. After class she told me, "I know how to play too. I want to be able to play it with my son. Weiqi is very good for their concentration and logic. It helps them not only with Weiqi but also with their other studies. My son first took Weiqi in a class at his elementary school and then became interested in it. So we come here every Saturday to study the game."[40]

The other mother just seemed to daydream during class, and she was quite frank in telling me that she had no interest in the game: "I don't understand the game but my son has taken an interest. He took a Weiqi class at his elementary school and really liked it. He was the best in the class and asked me if he could take lessons so I said okay but just one day a week because he is busy. He is in third grade in elementary school, which is from nine to five, and then after that he takes one to two hours of English a day so I want him to focus on that. But he likes Weiqi so I said it was okay to take lessons."[41]

Although all classroom settings are fecund fields for an analysis of cultural disciplinary structures, this school's Weiqi classes seemed particularly ripe for the picking. The children were watched both by the teacher and the parents, which seemed to result in a particularly sedate, almost grim, ethos. The teacher was also under more surveillance than at the other schools I interviewed in that the mothers, who were not paying a small sum, were also monitoring their behavior. Yet one should not overlook the significant time commitment that the mothers made in attending Weiqi classes. Neither of the women I quote here professed to have an interest in the game beyond its connection to their sons' welfare. If they monitored the children, as well as the instructors, the mothers were also under the watchful eye of their offspring and the teachers. The mothers also had to sit through the three-and-a-half-hour lessons while trying, with a greater or lesser degree of success, to look attentive.

As with other issues in these classrooms, this disciplinary structure was part of a larger social ethos rather than being particular to Weiqi. Near the apartment building where I lived, for example, there was an English school that taught students in rooms with large windows facing the street. Passing by, I often saw mothers sitting in the back of closet-sized classrooms, looking on attentively as their children received private lessons. A mother would watch each tutorial, sitting two or three feet behind her child. Beyond the added dimension of studying in a panopticon that was clearly designed to advertise the fact that they had foreign teachers, the physical proximity of the mothers and their attentive gaze must have put a tremendous pressure on both the teachers and pupils. If a mother or other third party could not be present, the school monitored both the foreign teacher and the student with a small camcorder mounted on a tripod. I do not know if this was to record the lessons for the student to review, to monitor the teacher's behavior, or, most likely, both. Regardless of the stated intent, the remarkable lack of privacy and the hierarchical supervision could not help but to add a tremendous amount of pressure on everyone involved. Based on my admittedly superficial understanding from my passing view from outside, it seemed to stifle the interactions of the teachers and students to a remarkable degree.

The pressures that people in China face in relation to societal expectations of good parenting should not be understated. Sun Yiguo is a career Weiqi player who discussed his feelings on childrearing.

> *I think maybe I'm a bad father.* [He smiles mischievously.] *Because I talk with my friends and they say my ideas about parenting are very strange. Because I want to be like my parents. When I was a child they didn't have any demands of us. They would say, "As long as you are all happy." They wouldn't ask about my grades. If I said they were good my parents would praise me. If they were bad my parents wouldn't say anything. I have the same attitude towards my child.*
>
> *But in China this is not a very popular view. Because now the competition is very fierce. So many parents want their children to train hard. Every week they go to classes* [in addition to their normal school classes] *and the parents go with them. Being a parent is really a hardship. I don't want to live this kind of life. A child's life is his own. In China many children don't have any time of their own, they have no time to be children.*[42]

Sun Yiguo grew up during the Cultural Revolution. In this context it makes sense that his parents were unconcerned with his academic progress. Nor is it surprising that they were loath to criticize their son, who, given the political climate of the time, could have wielded a tremendous amount of political power over his parents had he chosen to do so. Yet on another level, Sun Yiguo's statement spoke to very real pressures that are distinctive to China's contemporary political economy. In addition to his concern that children were being overworked, was a tangible resentment about the fact that he too was burdened by the responsibility. He was remarkably frank in stating that he had neither the time nor the desire to escort his son to all of his tutorials.

Anne Allison has written on the pressures that Japanese mothers face in making their children's school lunches.[43] She suggests that this invokes a range of disciplinary mechanisms on the children, who must consume the food in a timely fashion, but also on the mothers who have to spend two hours a day making the lunch boxes and who are judged by a range of aesthetic choices made in designing the food.[44] As Allison also argues, the significant time commitment to make these lunch boxes also limits mothers' employment possibilities beyond the familial sphere and supports the patriarchal agenda of the state.[45] Similarly, in the above quote, Sun Yiguo outlines the challenges that Chinese children face and the ways that parents are also disciplined in the name of their children's welfare. Although he plays down his own willingness to take part in this system, he and his wife had moved into an apartment complex that was adjacent to his son's high school. In spite of Sun Yiguo's claims of disinterest, this was one of the best schools in the country. This lends further support to the idea that it is impossible for parents to fully reject their roles in this system, even when they are ambivalent about the process.

Weiqi schools are a window view into China's family-oriented disciplinary structures. These cultural mores shape the lives of children in powerful and gendered ways. Yet parents and teachers are also disciplined by the mechanisms created to educate their children. With a very real threat that the children will not be able to thrive in China's exceptionally competitive environment, the students, teachers, and parents are all under a tremendous amount of pressure for the children to succeed. This stress was in many ways elevated by the remarkable uniformity of opinion concerning what counts as success in China, where quality of life is measured far more by quantifiable markers of achievement and status than by abstract sentiments of well-being.

At the end of the day, however, this system is centered on developing the boys' potential. Because endurance, intellect, and perseverance are common themes in training boys in China, the Weiqi schools are but one part of a larger gendered whole. Yet in constructing masculinity, few things exemplify the reemergence of age-old ideals in China's new political economy as well as this particular sphere. If these boys are successful, when they come of age they will become university students. It is there that one sees the results of this rigorous identity formation as they look back on their childhood training to better understand the men that they have become.

FIVE

A Certain Man

UNIVERSITY STUDENTS, AMATEURS,
AND PROFESSIONALS

Display profits to entice them. Create disorder and take them. If they are substantial, prepare for them; if they are strong, avoid them. If they are angry, perturb them; be deferential to foster their arrogance.

SUN-TZU, *The Art of War,* 722–481 B.C.[1]

In the same way that danger may lurk behind peace and serenity, remaining inactive means being annihilated. Remember the words contained in the Yijing: "The gentleman (junzi) is at peace but does not forget the danger; he affirms his position but does not forget the possibility of being destroyed!"

ZHANG NI, *The Classic of Weiqi in Thirteen Chapters,*
1049–54 A.D.[2]

WEIQI IS THOUGHT TO ATTRACT a particular kind of man and, in turn, to train him to become certain—to address the world with confidence and to fearlessly rely on his intellect to overcome all obstacles. One of the central tenets of being a Confucian gentleman is to display an unwavering integrity. For Peking University students, the idea that a proper man should consistently display virtue and strength also arose with remarkable frequency. Regardless of whether or not they play Weiqi, Peking University students represent the ideal personhoods associated with Weiqi, for they have overcome incredible odds to gain entrance to one of China's most prestigious universities. This same determination and honed intellect has led them into a world of startlingly high expectations, however, and the majority of students I spoke with were anything but certain that they could live up to people's hopes for them.

One of the greatest challenges facing China today is a dramatic increase in class inequality in conjunction with rampant corruption. Urban salaries are disproportionally outpacing rural ones, and new class tensions have arisen that include a widespread belief that the extremely rich have obtained their wealth through immoral means.[3] In court cases concerning murder or grievous injury, for example, judges take into account financial reparations made to families, which has seemingly confirmed the suspicion that the rich can even buy their way out of serious prison sentences.[4]

The 1997 per capita income in rural areas was US$2,090 and US$5,160 in urban areas, accounting for 2.47 times the rural income. In 2007 the rural per capita income had doubled to US$4,140, while in urban areas it had almost tripled to US$13,786.[5] As part of the same development in China's contemporary political economy, university education is increasingly becoming a domain of the elite.[6] At Peking University, the children of workers and farmers represented 30 percent of the student body in 1957, 64 percent in 1960, and 78 percent in 1974.[7] By 1990, this had fallen to 21 percent, and the offspring of white-collar workers and state officials represented a clear majority of university students.[8] Because of better educational resources available in the cities, there has also been a dramatic shift in favor of urban applicants.[9]

With an eye to children's eventual need to apply to university, many parents are increasingly devoting resources to pay for tutors as well as breathtakingly high tuitions and additional "donations" to prep schools.[10] They are also buying houses near the best schools.[11] Children are competing at an increasingly young age, and many parents complain that sending one's child to a good elementary school is more expensive than a prestigious university.[12] Rampant corruption inevitably favors families who have more powerful connections (*guanxi*) or can afford to rely on all-out bribery.[13] Even with connections this is a difficult process. Wu Xiaoxin tells of a head teacher at a prominent prep school who was only able to admit 100 of the 1,100 applicants who had special connections backing them.[14] In other cases, outright fraud ensued, such as in Chongqing when thirty-one students were discovered to be lying about their minority status to gain extra points on their university examinations.[15] Others were discovered to have forged documents attesting to their achievements in sports or literary endeavors.[16]

Those applying to university can add bonus points to their university entrance exams if they have "special talents" ranging from sports to musical achievements. As of 2009 there were 192 categories, including Weiqi, that earned bonus points for the university entrance exam. This accounts for 35 percent of the total university entrants in China, most of whom come from privileged classes.[17] All of this shifts the conceptualization of university entrance from an individualistic meritocracy to competition between families who draw on their entire social and economic resources.[18] This is tragic for those who were passed over for students with better connections, or who could not afford the expense of paying tutors to acquire skills that would earn them extra points on the entrance exam. For those who are admitted to university, it increases a sense of indebtedness to one's parents that adds to the pressure of living up to their expectations.

In China, middle-class success and higher education are not only viewed as representing the acquirement of technical skills and a certain lifestyle. They are also equated with having developed higher aesthetic tastes and a more moral character. This moral nuance intensifies the already overwhelming pressure on university students who feel that they have to live up to parental and societal expectations that they become successful. This is especially true because success is defined by a remarkably narrow definition that hones on one's career.

More often than not, these goals are associated with being "middle class." It should be noted, however, that in the People's Republic of China (PRC) this term has much more to do with elite lifestyles of consumption and higher educational levels than having average incomes. China's National Bureau of Statistics defined "middle class" as having an income between US$7,250 (60,000 RMB [*renimbi*]) and US$62,000 (500,000 RMB),[19] even though China's per capita GDP is only US$8,400 (5,880 RMB).[20] Tellingly, many people in this economic category respond that they do not know whether they are middle class or not.[21] In this income range, 92 percent have college degrees and 19 percent have master's degrees, although only 4 percent of China's population have university degrees.[22] The term "middle class" has thereby come to represent possessing a university degree and a familiarity with global culture. It is also marked by a range of consumer habits that might include sporting designer clothing, dining on expensive international foods, or spending US$31 (200 RMB) to take someone to a movie. Essentially, then, in China the term "middle class" evokes an image of someone who can live a

Western middle-class lifestyle, though this in fact marks them as decidedly elite in China.

The term *suzhi* is usually defined in English as "quality" and is often used in conjunction with "good taste" (*pingwei, gediao*). It denotes a heightened aesthetic appreciation and, to a certain degree, a greater moral worth. *Suzhi* discourse is ubiquitous in China when discussing children's education, the middle class, or modernist goals to become global citizens. The term is applied to individuals and, in a very Confucian sense, is thereby seen to indicate the overall quality of the nation. It represents a relentless call for self-improvement and combines ethical behavior and hard work with the ability to demonstrate middle-class tastes and values through one's consumerism.

In the PRC, the concept of *suzhi* arose in the 1970s in relation to a eugenicist goal of population control. The government argued that in reducing family size one could focus on developing one's children to their fullest potential. In turn, this was thought to lead to a healthier nation and race. In the 1980s and 1990s, the government attempted to stimulate the economy by using *suzhi* as a modernizing discourse in which China's citizenry was encouraged to become participants in consumer culture.[23] While ostensibly a marker of etiquette, *suzhi* quickly shifted to represent one's worth as part of a process of class stratification.[24]

Suzhi discourse is more often than not related to the middle-class appropriation of Western lifestyles and consumer habits, but it has influenced people from all walks of life. The government has used this concept to encourage poor and rural people to modify their behavior to become more like the middle class. This, in turn, is used to legitimate middle-class feelings of superiority.[25] *Suzhi* also provides a rationale to claim moral superiority over the rich who seemed to have gained their wealth overnight by using their connections rather than through hard work or education.[26] Urbanites criticize their rural counterparts as lacking *suzhi,* and the Women's Federation opines that its primary goal is to raise women's *suzhi*.[27] Rural people who migrate to cities for employment take pains to improve their *suzhi* by changing the ways that they dress, speak, and act in an effort to be more like the people from the cities.[28] Intrinsically embedded in discourses of modernity and civilization, *suzhi* has become a keyword for individual and social progress.[29]

Suzhi is a decidedly PRC term, though its basic modernizing agenda can also be seen in other Chinese-speaking areas. David Schak's work on civil society in Taiwan, for example, painstakingly outlines a modernization process that has quite similar goals with the *suzhi* movement in the PRC, though the vocabulary and the role of the government in implementing modernizing and civil society agendas varies on different sides of the strait.[30]

Yet in my first week in Beijing, the word *suzhi* arose more frequently than I had heard it in ten years of living in Taipei. It speaks to a profound sense among many Chinese that the PRC needs to catch up to global standards of etiquette—an idea that has saturated governmental discourse and popular consciousness to a startling degree. I have seen poorer people apologize for not being *suzhi* when they ask questions that more educated people might find inappropriate, for example. Other modernizing discourses complement this. Subways and busses feature video advertisements that ask people to behave properly in order to advance the state of the nation to become more civilized (*wenming*). As they do so, they flaunt the modern-looking subway as youthful employees gaze proudly, heads tilted toward the horizon, or smiling directly at the viewer.

Several scholars have examined the troubling implications of *suzhi* discourse in shaping a citizenry that conforms to a neoliberal agenda.[31] Yet, as Andrew Kipnis has suggested, one should be wary of conflating *suzhi* and neoliberalism, for there are many areas in which they do not overlap.[32] He also warns that using the term neoliberalism in very different political economies all but loses its meaning. Reagan's neoliberal agenda is very different from the process that has been labeled as "neoliberalism" in northern Europe or contemporary China, for example.[33] Another pitfall is the degree to which the term *neoliberalism* is tainted by an air of moral condemnation, which clouds rational analysis of the issues.[34] The major difference between Kipnis and those he critiques on this point seems to be that whereas Ann Anagnost and others focus on the ways that *suzhi* discourse disciplines individuals as subjects for the workforce, Kipnis locates it instead in the larger governmental framework.[35]

Suzhi discourse lauds individual self-discipline with an aim to improvement.[36] It also legitimizes a highly structured learning environment for children that lasts from when they rise in the morning to when they go to sleep.[37] *Suzhi* is certainly used as a disciplinary mechanism that helps to train its citizens in consumerism and global concepts of the workplace, but it also marks the beginnings of a civil society. In creating a social ethos in which strangers matter, *suzhi* discourse introduces a conception that was largely absent in Confucian doctrine or traditional Chinese society.[38]

The five Confucian relationships (Lord/Vassal, Father/Son, Husband/Wife, Elder Brother/Younger Brother, Friend/Friend) claimed that proper behavior in one relationship would lead to a harmonious balance in all five. In other words, if a father and son treated each other as they should, then they would naturally behave properly in the other relationships as well. In doing so, society, the government, and the very heavens would work smoothly. It is important that all of these relationships are with known personages, with an equally defined set of expected behavior according to one's place in the hierarchy. A significant lacuna in Confucian doctrine is in its lack of attention to how to treat strangers. In spite of its disciplinary nature, the concept of *suzhi* has also helped to create a stronger civil society, enforcing a worldview that certain behavior, ranging from not standing in line to spitting in the street, reflects badly on the individual who disregards the needs of the people around him.

The tension between a traditional disregard for strangers and this new emerging form of civil society continues today, but *suzhi* discourse has indeed made great strides in this area. Subway and bus lines in China can at times still be a bit of a push and a shove. Yet they are nothing compared to the three-hour-long wait to buy train tickets that I experienced in 1988. At that time, rather than lining up, the person who was strong enough to push to the front of the crowd was the one who obtained the tickets, which were in short supply. Young children had "split pants" that were open at the rear end, and the children were trained in Pavlovian fashion to urinate when their parents whistled. This took place in public venues ranging from the street to on busses and trains. Living in Xi'an in 1988, my casual mention of the use of diapers in the United States was met with disgust that Americans allowed their infants to sit in their own urine and feces. The idea of public sanitation came a very distant second to the perceived health risks of such action on their own children.

In contrast, during my 2010 and 2011 research in Beijing, I only saw one child urinating on public transportation. Whereas in 1988 this was seen as a perfectly natural event, in 2011 my fellow subway passengers looked positively disgusted at the act, and the rural-looking grandmother accompanying the child was noticeably embarrassed. Though many Westerners opine that China still has a long way to go in creating an ordered and sanitary society, most Chinese people I spoke with agreed that great strides have been made in this area.

Work on civil society has pointed out that, throughout Chinese history, theories of individual morality have been far more centrally tied to the government than in the West.[39] Some have suggested that this results in a Chinese worldview of "obligation and interdependence rather than [Western notions of] rights and responsibilities."[40] One might suggest that this is largely an issue of differing rhetorics in that many Chinese people display highly individualistic self-interest just as most Westerners are bound in an intricate web of social relationships.[41] Yet the two ideologies may indeed create a differentiated conceptualization of state, society, and the individual. The Chinese worldview draws on Confucian paradigms in which family relationships are a microcosm of the bond between state and citizen.

Suzhi is also a marker of class distinction that carries a moral valance. China's highly competitive job market is a pressure cooker by any standards, but *suzhi* discourse implies that those who have not become middle class are not *suzhi,* and those who lack *suzhi* have not developed themselves to their full intellectual and moral potential. This puts enormous pressure on university students in general, but especially on students at the most prestigious schools, for whom parents, peers, and society have the greatest expectations. Sayings such as, "Oh well, you tried your best" or "I just want my children to be happy regardless of what jobs they get" are about as alien to people in China as any other idea that one could think up.

Xue Lei, the captain of Peking University's Weiqi team, was one of many university students I spoke with who told me that he was anxious about his future job prospects. In the United States, when faced with my students' job related angst, I usually try to calm their nerves by reminding them that they are young. I suggest that if they find they have chosen the wrong career they still have plenty of time to change their minds. Usually my students in the United States tangibly breathe a sigh of relief when I say this. In this instance, however, the same statement was greeted with the polite pause that so often signifies disagreement in China. Sighing, he responded as follows: "That may be true in the U.S. but there just aren't that many jobs in China. I'm not sure there really is that much leeway to change one's mind if one is lucky enough to get a job at all."[42]

If I had to pick one theme that arose in my discussions with Peking University students, it would be their fear that the job market had become so competitive that even if they had perfect scholastic records they would not find good jobs when they graduated. In their conversations, being economically viable seemed to come in as a distant second to the fear that they would not live up to the expectations of parents, peers, and society as a whole.

This is not to imply that university students are resentful of the pressures placed on them. In many cases they are appreciative of the investments that their parents have made and are anxious to live up to their expectations. Yu Rongxin, a 5-*duan* amateur on the Peking University team, hopes to go to the United States to pursue a master's degree or an MBA. He emphasized that parental pressure can be a good thing: "When my father was seven or eight years old he had to start working as a farmer to help his family survive. So their lives were much harder than ours. . . . My father told me that his greatest desire is that our family improves every generation. He said that he has already taken us from being a farmer's family to living in the city—and he sent me to a very good university. He told me that he feels like he already did a pretty good job and that now that he has done his part he can put his hopes on me."

When I asked him if he felt pressured by his father's expectations, he replied:

> It is a little bit of pressure but this is not necessarily a bad thing. Often a little bit of pressure is a kind of motivation. Many students give up if they are left to their own devises. Especially in middle school and high school—at that age it is very easy to make wrong decisions. And at that time if they walk down the wrong road it will have a very bad influence on their futures. So on the one hand my parents put their hopes in me, which is a bit of pressure. But that kind of pressure made me avoid those kinds of wrong choices and encouraged me to walk down a more proper road. Of course I think the most important thing is if a student wants to study hard or he motivates himself, but if parents give their children a little bit of pressure this can make you even better.[43]

Yu Rongxin's account highlighted the love and appreciation that many university students have for their parents. He acknowledged that he was under a great deal of pressure to succeed, but he also emphasized that he had become a better person for it. In other cases, however, the idea of living up to people's expectations led to clear anxiety. As but one example of this, I had been talking quite comfortably with a Peking University student for several minutes. When the conversation veered to his career prospects he suddenly started nervously pulling at tufts of his hair, though he was seemingly unaware that he was doing so: "Yes, expectations are very high, especially for people who are not from big cities. Because then it isn't just the parents that care if you succeed or not. The whole village is really counting on you. And it's a lot harder to succeed when you are from a small village because you don't have the connections that people who grew up in a city do. It is much more pressure with far less chance of success when you think about it."[44]

The Chinese cultural emphasis on group orientation has many benefits. Many Chinese people living in the United States, for example, feel that America's individualistic orientation has made it an emotionally cold and uninviting place. They speak affectionately of being part of the larger whole that their kin and friend networks provide in China, and many long for the hustle and bustle of densely populated communities.

The downside to China's group ethos can be seen in situations in which people not only experience the pressure to succeed for their own well-being but must carry the weight of the success and failure of their families. In some cases, such as the account above, this extends to the needs of an entire village. How, then, do they mediate between individual desires and the expectations of others? How do they prepare themselves to meet the challenges of today's market economy in an overpopulated nation of overachievers? Weiqi provides one solution because it introduces a highly disciplined work ethic and a focus on intellectual pursuits at a young age. At the same moment it soothes by evoking images of an admittedly created idyllic past in which cultured gentlemen had more time to focus on sociality as well as individual and societal well-being.

WEIQI'S *SUZHI* DISCOURSE

The associations of Weiqi with being a cultured gentleman draw heavily on traditional Confucian doctrine and modern *suzhi* discourse. Liu Xiaoguan, a 9-*duan* professional and one of the most famous Weiqi players in China, used *suzhi*, Chinese culture, and Weiqi in remarkably fluid ways: "Weiqi has a lot of connection to Chinese culture. For instance, the way Chinese people think is similar to the way we play Weiqi. . . . This is an Eastern person's way of thinking that is not the same as the way people think in the West. When you look at the way people play Weiqi one gets a sense of *suzhi*, their aesthetics (*pingwei*). Aesthetics are very important in China. So Weiqi is a way of better understanding Chinese thinking."[45]

Linking the aesthetics of the Weiqi board with larger issues tying into Chinese identity, Liu Xiaoguan emphasized that if one hopes to understand China one must see the importance of *suzhi*. People in the PRC often link the playing styles of China, Japan, and South Korea with distinctive regionally bound cultural identities. Here, Liu envisions one's playing style as an accurate reflection of Chinese thought. In his account, conceptions of *suzhi* and aesthetics are the defining factors of Weiqi's cultural ethos, and that of Chinese culture as a whole.

Hong Feng, a Weiqi instructor at the Capital Sports Center in Beijing's Science and Engineering University, also linked Weiqi to *suzhi:* "One form of *suzhi* is developing one's muscles. For instance, to train one's body to run fast or to become stronger. This is the body's *suzhi*. Another form of *suzhi* refers to someone's cultural development. This would include being polite. Weiqi is one kind of polite behavior. We have a phrase called 'hand conversation' (*shoutan*). When two people play Weiqi they don't speak. Their conversation is on the board; it's the way they play. When I play, if I put the stone in a certain place this expresses my respect. 'I played here—look at that. I'm sorry, I played this stone in your area.' This is a kind of 'hand conversation.'"[46]

As with Liu Xiaoguan's account, Hong Feng links *suzhi* with Chinese identity in relation to the way one plays Weiqi. Though *suzhi* only gained momentum in the second half of the twentieth century, Hong Feng's description connects this relatively new movement with the traditional conception of "hand conversation" that dates back hundreds of years. In this context, part of Chinese identity is depicted as being in a continuous flow from past to present. It demonstrates the ways in which the modern moment is defined by events of a bygone age.

Fang Tianfeng is an 8-*duan* professional and Weiqi instructor at Peking University, Qing-hwa University, and Beijing Science University. In our interview he outlined how conceptions of the Confucian elite have inspired contemporary university students to learn the game: "In my beginning class, around 90 percent of the university students don't know how to play at all. They are in the class because of the traditional concept that one should know the four arts; calligraphy, music, Weiqi, and art. The traditional idea in China was that educated people should be able to play a musical instrument, write calligraphy, paint, and play a board game. . . . In the old days the game was just Weiqi, but now it can also be Chinese chess or Western chess, it all counts. So they feel that they should improve their music, calligraphy, painting, and games."[47]

As with Hong Feng's account, Fan Tianfeng highlights the ways in which old paradigms are adopted in modern contexts. He notes that university students hope to embrace age-old identities linked to the iconic Confucian scholar. Although one might suggest that these students are performing a role, this is such an important part of their identity formation that it becomes a very real part of who they are. In the same fashion, the men on the university Weiqi team had not merely mastered Weiqi's techniques. Rather, these students' soft-spoken and dignified demeanor was a modern-day embodiment of this age-old ideal of what it meant to be a gentleman.

Even members of the working class linked *suzhi* with Weiqi. In an interview I conducted at a park where a group of working-class retirees play Weiqi, two of the park regulars enthusiastically emphasized this point.

> MR. MA: People who play Chinese chess are less cultured (*wenmiao*) than people who play Weiqi. . . . People who play Weiqi are more civilized (*wenming*).
>
> LITTLE LIU: There are no bad people who play Weiqi! People who play Weiqi put their hearts into the game. There are no bad people who play Weiqi!
>
> MR. MA: Yes, we just play all day like crazy people!
>
> LITTLE LIU: Regardless of whether you are someone with rights and power (*gaoguanzhidi*) or a hoodlum (*liumang*), people who play Weiqi have a Chinese-style pure mind. For instance, it gives you the morality of being filial.
>
> MR. MA: The way you solve problems in Weiqi is like solving problems in life—you deal with difficult situations in the same way.[48]

In this interview, Mr. Ma and Little Liu spoke with great enthusiasm, often interrupting each other or speaking at the same time. One of the more striking aspects of this conversation was the degree to which these working-class men, who were arguably stigmatized by *suzhi* discourse, readily drew on Weiqi's associations with *suzhi* and the game's iconic links with the ethos of Confucian elites in Imperial China.

THE PEKING UNIVERSITY WEIQI TEAM, RANKS, AND THE AMATEUR/PROFESSIONAL DIVIDE

By adding extra points to talented Weiqi-players' college entrance examinations, and in rare cases waiving the test altogether, Peking University had recruited a Weiqi team with astonishing talent. It is widely recognized as one of the best university teams in the country and an impressive seven of the fourteen members of the team have professional ranks. One of the team members confessed to not having to take the university entrance exam because the university wanted to recruit strong players for its team. It was more usual for team members to have points added to their university entrance exam scores. At the time of my research, only two of the team members, both lower-ranking amateur women, had been accepted to Peking University with no points added to their entrance examination scores. This is common university admissions practice for Weiqi and other sports, but Peking University also had the draw of being the most prestigious university in the country.

Many of the team members, and several other people I interviewed, had trained to become professional Weiqi players as children. In their accounts it soon became clear that studying to become a professional Weiqi player was one of the most competitive careers in the country, and that the chances of becoming good enough to live on one's winnings was very slim indeed. During my fieldwork, in China's close to 1.3 billion population, only twenty people were given professional ranks a year. This was done so as not to overwhelm the system with people attempting to compete in professional competitions. The ranks were awarded in a government-run annual competition, and all twenty positions were age restricted. Because female players tend not to be as strong as their male counterparts, three of the positions were reserved for women under the age of twenty. Fifteen of the openings were held for men under the age of seventeen. Two of the openings were reserved for people who were between eighteen and twenty-four years old who had won a national or international competition. The age limit has varied over the years—so much so that almost no one I interviewed could agree on what the limit was at that time. Yet it seems fairly certain that some form of age restriction will remain in place for the foreseeable future.

The most lucrative and prestigious competitions are limited to players with professional rankings. In recent years, however, some people who had earned the right to have a professional rank by winning a national competition opted to retain their amateur status instead. Their reasoning was that it was better to win a little prize money at an amateur competition than to lose at a professional competition.

Most people I spoke with complained about the current ranking system and the rather draconian enforcement of the age limit. The rationale for keeping the system centers around the unwieldiness of opening competitions

FIGURE 10. The twenty-fifth annual board game competition between Peking University and Qing-hwa University.

to the thousands of players in the general population who might otherwise want to compete. In recent years, in order to accommodate a larger number of players in amateur competitions, initial tournament playoffs have been held on online servers. The obvious drawback to this method is that although each competitor has an ID and password, it is possible, and some have said common, to have a friend or classmate play in one's stead. Many expressed a hope to see a system more akin to international chess or baseball in which one's cumulative score is kept according to one's overall games rather than a one-time success or failure in an annual professional exam. Some journalists and Weiqi commentators have used such a system to evaluate professional players' relative strengths. For the foreseeable future, however, the traditional *duan* ranking system and age limits define who will be allowed to compete in the most prestigious and lucrative competitions.

The current ranking system has created many paradoxes. Sun Yiguo is a 7-*duan* amateur and a semi-retired career Weiqi player who won an international championship held in Japan in 1993. In 1999 he defeated a 9-*duan* professional in a national championship.[49] In large part because of severe health issues when he was younger, he was unsuccessful in obtaining a professional rank, although he had made his career playing in amateur tournaments. In other words, he had effectively been banned from participation in the most prestigious and lucrative tournaments, though he was skilled enough to earn his sole income from Weiqi competitions, and he had proven to be a worthy adversary to professionally ranked players.

On the flip side of the coin was Xue Lei, a *4-duan* professional who was the captain of Peking University's Weiqi team. Xue Lei had given up his career as a Weiqi player when he decided to become a university student, although he would be allowed to hold onto his professional rank for the rest of his life. This was a point that he was clearly ambivalent about.

> *In truth, a professionally ranked player is not always better than an amateur. For instance, in a match between a 6-duan amateur and a 1-duan pro, you don't always know who will win. . . . Many people with a professional rank—for instance me, but also many other people—we have a professional rank but for us Weiqi has already become a hobby. We don't rely on winning prize money for a living. Someone who lives on his winnings is the true definition of a professional. . . .*
>
> *On the other hand, there are people like Ye Yuqing, one of the best amateur players in China right now. He doesn't have a professional ranking—he is an 8-duan amateur—but Weiqi is his profession. He doesn't rely on a job to make a living. Instead he goes to competitions. Every year he goes to sixty or eighty formal competitions, maybe more. People like him are the real professionals because he has turned Weiqi into his profession. There is no separation between Weiqi and the rest of his life.*[50]

Xue Lei's teammate Yu Rongxin is a *5-duan* amateur who scored twenty-ninth place in the annual competition to gain a professional rank and thereby lost his chance to become a professional Weiqi player. After trying unsuccessfully to pass the exam the following year, he discontinued his Weiqi training to return to his studies. Yu Rongxin also noted that the division between the skills of a high-level amateur and a low-level professional is not always clear.

> *Maybe someone in the competition to become a professional is unlucky or doesn't perform well on that one day. Because there is only one chance a year, so if he doesn't perform as well as usual on that one day he will never achieve a professional rank. This doesn't necessarily reflect his overall skill. I think this is the first reason that the skill level between an amateur and professional is not always clear.*
>
> *The other reason is that the duan rankings are not very fair. You can only go up, you cannot go down. Maybe one year you do particularly well. So your rank goes up but your level of skill hasn't really gone up. Maybe someone just played especially well in one competition and achieved the duan rank. After that day if he loses a lot of games his level goes down but his duan rank is the same. So sometimes a duan rank is not overly accurate.*[51]

The finality of not meeting the age limit for an annual competition dashed many people's hopes. Wang Wenbo is the owner of the Wenbo Weiqi School for children, which I attended in my first fieldwork period. He told me of his son who was enrolled in a full-time Weiqi school and was training with the hope of becoming a professional player: "My son started attending that Weiqi school at the age of six and is now seventeen years old. He lives at his Weiqi school with his classmates. In all of China only twenty people a year will earn the right to be professional players. So becoming a professional Weiqi player in China is six times harder than getting into Peking University, and that is almost impossible in and of itself. Of course I hope my son will succeed but if he doesn't make it as a professional he will come work at the school with me so in a way it is win-win. The important thing is that he continues to improve because this will be useful either way."[52]

At the time of that interview Wang Wenbo's son was only a 3-*duan* amateur at the age of sixteen. As such, that year's annual ranking competition would be his last chance unless he could win a national championship before he turned twenty-five. When I mentioned the case of Wang Wenbo's son to Sylvia, she sadly shook her head. "If he isn't a professional before he turns seventeen it will never happen. If you want to be a professional you have to sacrifice your normal education. Becoming a professional is a tremendous time investment. It takes two hours for one good game, then an hour to review the game, and then more time to train. This includes studying life-and-death problems but also trying to learn ways to maximize benefit, to understand the implications of each move on the whole board."[53] Most people I spoke with agreed with Sylvia's assessment that becoming a professional Weiqi player was challenging enough that one should just give up if one had not done so before one turned seventeen.

When I interviewed Wang Wenbo a year later, it turned out that their dire predictions were true, although his son had progressed far more than might have been expected:

My son's case is a story in and of itself. Because I have always loved Weiqi I started teaching him to play at the age of five. At the age of six a new school opened up that I think is now the best children's Weiqi school in China—no, in the world. . . . They take classes with professional Weiqi players. When this school opened up I thought it was really a dream come true so I enrolled my son in the school.

He has been studying there since the first year that they opened. Since then China's Weiqi has gotten better and better. My son has studied this game over ten years now but it has become increasingly competitive to become a professional as China's Weiqi has improved. As for his level, it is not the best. When he competed in the national competition to become a professional he ranked thirty-nine. This is still not bad when you think about it because these days there are a lot of people competing to become professionals.[54]

Wang Wenbo's conversation then turned to the concept of *suzhi*.

Even though he didn't become a professional, at some point he can come to my school to teach. But he needs more education before he can do this. My son has spent the last decade improving his Weiqi skills but he has not really had the time to develop his academic learning. So I think that his Weiqi level is already not bad but when he has raised his overall education, his suzhi, then I would like him to come here and teach. I would like him to go to university first because at my school we don't only teach students Weiqi but how to be better people, and to do that you need a well-balanced education. Also, when he is in university he can continue to take part in Weiqi competitions so this story is not over yet. It is really my dream to work together with my son. My wife also works here handling the administration, so if my son also worked here we would really have a family business.[55]

Yu Rongxin also spoke of his failure to earn a professional rank at the annual competition.

I am from Liaonian in Shengyang. I trained in Weiqi for eight years and then when I was in the first year of middle school I participated in the national competition for professional ranks but I didn't do well. So in my second year of middle school I moved back home and went back to school. Weiqi used to be my profession but now it's just my hobby.

When I was younger I was Shanlian province's champion several times. Then I went to the national competition for establishing a professional rank. The top twenty competitors became professionally ranked but my best score was twenty-ninth place so I didn't make it. It's really a pity.[56]

These accounts speak to the ways that Weiqi is a microcosm of China's intensely competitive society. Even on attaining the much-coveted professional rank it was clear that one could not rest on one's laurels. In their mid-twenties, Xue Lei and Fang Weijing had already earned Weiqi ranks that had been achieved by fewer than four hundred people in China's 1.3 billion population. Yet, even with their remarkably impressive ranks, they would have had to accomplish far more if they were to make a livable wage from competitions. It was also clear, however, that even though the Peking University students I interviewed had gone on to other pursuits, their Weiqi training had provided them with tools that would help them succeed in later life. The relentless work ethic and cerebral focus of Weiqi training instilled in them study habits that had helped them to gain entrance to China's preeminent university, for example. With that training they had also learned the philosophy of Weiqi players throughout history, which they drew on to confront the challenges of the modern age.

That people who trained to become professional Weiqi players would have to sacrifice their education was taken as a given. Even if the people I interviewed had gone on to do great things, the trauma of leaving behind their Weiqi training, in which they had invested so much time, energy, and passion, was very clear. These accounts were deeply emotional in the telling. Wang Wenbo related his account of his son ranking thirty-ninth place in the competition to be a professional Weiqi player when the cut off was the top twenty players. Yu Rongxin, in taking twenty-ninth place, missed his chance even more narrowly. Sylvia related her sorrow at having to quit Weiqi training. These were more than just stories of competitions. They were tales of all-or-nothing dramas that defined the players' lives forever. For these individuals, and their families, Weiqi was more than a game—it was a rare chance to fulfill a dream rather than simply finding a job to earn a living. While no one I spoke with felt that they had made a wrong choice in giving up their Weiqi careers in order to go to university, they did express a tangible sense of loss when they told me of their experiences in doing so.

PROFESSIONAL TRAINING

Several of the people I interviewed told me of the arduous path to becoming a professional. Fang Weijing was one of three female members of Peking University's Weiqi team. She was also the only person I met who was attempting to keep up with the herculean task of being a full-time student at Peking University while continuing to compete in professional Weiqi competitions. This was all the more challenging because, like other professional Weiqi players, she had dropped out of high school to train. This was taking its toll, however. In 2011 she did not compete well enough to remain on the national team and worried that, because she was so spread out, her grades were not up to a level that she could get into graduate school.

I decided to become a professional around 1998. Because studying in school is also very hard you can't really do both. In the end you have to decide if you want to continue to study Weiqi or if you want to go to school. So I decided to study Weiqi. Now there are other training centers (daochang) but at that time the only place to study to become a professional was in Beijing. So I moved to Beijing in 1998 and studied nothing but Weiqi for two years.

After I had become part of the national team I took some culture classes. Culture classes are academic classes like normal students take. But we studied them differently from normal students. They study all day. Our main job was to study Weiqi and the culture courses were something we did on the side. Usually we would take the culture classes two mornings a week and one evening.[57]

Several of the people I interviewed had dropped out of school as children in order to focus on their Weiqi training. Xue Lei was a twenty-four-year-old 4-*duan* professional who gave up his Weiqi career to go to Peking University. In Peking University's Weiqi circles he was something of a hero because he held the highest Weiqi rank at the university. His popularity was accentuated by his quiet but charismatic charm.

> XUE: I started playing Weiqi when I was five years old. At that time it was just for fun, I didn't think about becoming a professional. But after that I got more interested and when I was eleven years old I passed the test to become ranked as a professional player. From when I was nine years old to after I became ranked as a professional I studied Weiqi all day every day. Professional sports, like basketball for instance, was the same.
>
> MOSKOWITZ: How old were you when you got your different ranks?
>
> XUE: I was twelve when I became a 1-*duan* pro, fourteen when I became a 2-*duan* pro, sixteen when became a 3-*duan*, and nineteen years old when I became a 4-*duan*.
>
> MOSKOWITZ: So why did you decide . . .
>
> XUE: To go to university?
>
> MOSKOWITZ: Yes.
>
> XUE: Actually the answer is very easy. In Weiqi it is very difficult to advance to the top *duan* professional levels. . . . So I made a decision. In part this was because it is so hard to advance to the next level in Weiqi, but it was also because going to university is important. When I studied Weiqi I was completely focused on my training and I didn't go to school. Now I want to make up for this. . . .
>
>   For five years, around the time I obtained a professional rank, I did nothing but study Weiqi, I didn't go to school. At that time this was a pretty normal thing to do if you wanted to become a professional player. Because many people dream of becoming a professional Weiqi player and supporting themselves with this career. But when they do this they are giving up a lot. At the least they are giving up their opportunity to study

in school. Personally I think this is not very good. Everyone puts their hopes on this one thing and it is not every healthy—even to the point that their parents might move to Beijing with them so that they can study Weiqi. So their investment is very great and if they don't pass the test, it is a very risky decision. Because every year there are only around twenty people who pass and a great many more are eliminated. In the end this isn't a very good way to invest in their futures.[58]

Sylvia, a 3-*duan* amateur, related her own experiences of studying to be a professional player when she was a child, and her sorrow that she did not continue on this path as an adult.

> I was enrolled in elementary school but I often had to skip classes so that I could focus on Weiqi. I would skip school every Tuesday and Friday afternoon to take Weiqi classes. I took a one-hour bus ride to the Weiqi school and then took three hours of classes. Then I'd take the one-hour bus ride home. . . .
> My father treated me very harshly—he wanted me to be a professional. . . . I cried a lot. And I sacrificed a lot of my free time. Because other kids were playing outside and I had to stay inside and study my life and death problems. . . . When I was in primary school my father never cared what I learned in school but he cared what I learned at the Weiqi school. I really spent a lot of time practicing. When I was nine years old and I didn't have to worry too much about school, my schedule was as follows: When I woke up I would practice life and death Weiqi problems for about one hour. Then I'd have breakfast. Then I'd go to school. On Tuesday and Friday afternoons I'd go to the Weiqi school. On other afternoons after I got home from school I would practice until it was time for dinner and then I'd study Weiqi again from seven to nine.[59]

As in the examples above, in many ways people who attended Weiqi training centers with the intention to become professionals lost much of their childhoods to arduous study. Many of them had dropped out of school to focus on their Weiqi training. As children, all of them had trained from morning to night, on school days, weekends, and vacations. The Weiqi world is an intensified microcosm of a larger whole; normal students must also endure remarkably challenging study schedules. This grueling environment for children and adolescents is something that adults in China are very concerned about. Yet even those who have misgivings about this system have little choice but to comply. Given China's highly competitive economy, parents must urge their children to work ever harder if they hope to succeed in later life.

There is little doubt that this system has broken many spirits and left many children with fewer economic resources or less committed parents

behind. Yet the Weiqi players I interviewed at Peking University had benefited from this system as well. They had obtained impressive markers of success, such as being admitted to the most prestigious university in the nation.
They had also become remarkable people, with exceptional intelligence, an
enviable range of talents, and a phenomenal work ethic. The Chinese view
that the strength of individuals leads to the vitality of the nation is embodied in these remarkable young men and women. If one wonders at China's
impressive economic achievements in the past two decades, the reason why,
I think, is here.

FACING THE FUTURE

I have often heard people in China say that the PRC's transformation from
an agricultural economy to an urban industrial society occurred in one
generation. They told me that China had gone through more or less the
same process in thirty years that the West had gone through in two centuries. Adding to the speed of cultural and economic change, China's wildly
tumultuous twentieth century was rife with war and political upheaval.
Most agree that people in China are better off today than they were thirty
years ago, but there is also a pervasive sense of uncertainty born of an economic structure that began only in 1979. China's free market economy is
continually metamorphosing to meet the demands of an overwhelming
global economy that has added to people's angst about the future. Weiqi is
often used as a metaphor for the uncertainties of life and the long-term
consequences of one's actions. In characteristic fashion, Sylvia littered her
example with old proverbs (*chengyu*): "People use Weiqi as metaphors for
ways of life. For instance: 'One wrong step, everything will be wrong after'
(*Yi bu cuo, bu bu cuo*). Or, 'One wrong step, lose the whole board' (*Quan
pan jiesu*)."[60]

The people I interviewed used Weiqi to celebrate a relentless work ethic
and unflinching intellectual development, while at times also critiquing the
perils of the modern economy. As in Sylvia's statement, many students I
spoke with (both in and out of Weiqi circles) felt that one mistake would lead
to eventual disaster in their lives. Sylvia was exceptionally adept at employing
age-old Weiqi proverbs to gain insights into the modern condition. On
one level her statement was a warning that one must consider each action
carefully. But on another it spoke of the ways that Weiqi taught her to face

difficult situations with dignity and to carefully analyze situations in order to maximize the potential benefits that each new challenge might offer.

When Liu Rongxin graduated from Peking University in 2010 she became a journalist who covered Weiqi professionals for *Sina Sports*. She exhibited little of the angst that the other Peking University students I interviewed exhibited. In large part this was because she had already found employment. Yet Liu also spoke of the uncertainties of the market by contrasting it with the earlier work unit system.

> MOSKOWITZ: What are your plans for the future?
>
> LIU: I will continue to do my current work.
>
> MOSKOWITZ: What about ten years from now?
>
> LIU: Ten years from now is harder to say because the world around us is changing so quickly. The things I do today, maybe I won't want to do them tomorrow. This is also because there are a lot more choices today than there used to be. In my parents' generation, their first work unit would be the place they would be employed for the rest of their lives. But now is not the same. Now, unless someone is still employed at a work unit, this will not happen. I may work for one company today and then after a few years I will go to a different company. I think America is also like this. It is a normal situation, if you are in a company, you don't really know where you will be tomorrow.[61]

Liu took the uncertainties of China's new economy in stride with remarkable poise. Most people seemed far less confident of their futures, however. The Peking University team and club members I spoke with looked forward to graduating with a mixed sense of anticipation and dread. When I asked Xue Lei about his plans when he graduated he responded:

> XUE: Now I am in my second year of my MA program. So I still have a little less than two years to go. When I get my MA I will look for work. What kind of work I will find, only time will tell. I haven't really figured that out yet. But I think the opportunities of working with Weiqi are not many. Because there aren't many ways to make money with Weiqi.
>
> MOSKOWITZ: Do you think it will be hard to find work?
>
> XUE: I think there's a lot of pressure. . . . One of the most tiring things is to decide what one wants to do. Because being a Peking University student and living in Beijing there are a lot of choices. So sometimes I don't know what I want to do. But time waits for no man. I haven't really figured this out yet. I will think about it but right now I just need to study. Right now I need to improve myself.[62]

Being admitted to a prestigious university and finding a good job requires a relentless work ethic, charm, connections, and a bit of good luck. In contemporary China there is a pervasive sense of not knowing what the future will bring. Conversations about this are usually accompanied by assertions that one must continuously struggle just to maintain one's place. To meet these challenges, the people I interviewed drew on the wisdom of Weiqi masters and Confucian theorists spanning across two millennia. Most Weiqi players in China believe that studying the game teaches one to face these pressures and that, in turn, Weiqi has many of the same strategies as life. Though I have made an effort to include women's voices here, the idealized Chinese citizen was usually envisioned as a modern manifestation of a Confucian gentleman. These men of learning emphasized the importance of developing iron wills and unwavering integrity. In this way, contemporary Weiqi players learn to be a certain kind of man in a largely uncertain world.

SIX

Retirement and Constructions of Masculinity among Working-Class Weiqi Players

"No art or learning is to be pursued halfheartedly," His Highness replied, "but each has its professional teachers, and any art worth learning will certainly reward more or less generously the effort made to study it. It is the art of the brush and the game of Go that most startlingly reveal natural talent, because there are otherwise quite tedious people who paint or play very well, almost without training.

MURASAKI SHIKIBU, *The Tale of Genji*, 1008 A.D.[1]

He had a convincing resemblance to an escaped convict: worn-out army pants dyed black, rubber shoes a size too large, and a face in great need of a haircut and washing. But his appearance did not matter once he entered the club. Everybody treated him as the master.

HONG SUNG-HWA, *First Kyu*, 1999[2]

FIRST CONTACT

ON MY FIRST DAY AT the park I accepted an offer to play a game of Weiqi with seventy-two-year-old Mr. Yu. Because I had watched him lose to a much stronger opponent I had underestimated him. Because I am American he underestimated me. The result was a strange beginning, full of unreasonable moves on both sides. A stream of passersby stopped to watch because of the anomaly of my presence in this decidedly non-Western arena. For the same reason, a crowd of Weiqi-playing regulars at the park gathered to provide a steady commentary to the effect of "Hey, the foreigner can actually play." My opponent also endured a bit of good-natured teasing on how shameful it would be to lose to a foreigner. I didn't have time to pay any of the onlookers any heed. I missed dealing a crushing blow to my opponent by one move, and after that the tides turned and I was less concerned with winning and more determined to lose by a respectable margin. It was a relatively cool 90-degree summer day, and when it began to sprinkle we played on like everyone else. In the end I lost, but by a margin that earned me a certain level of respect, though admittedly establishing me as the weakest player in the park.

An hour later the rains became torrential and we all ran to the front of a high-end restaurant that had a living room–sized enclave that protected us from the elements. As customers pounded on the story-high doors to be allowed entrance, the Weiqi players and other pedestrians hid from the rain and talked. Some did so animatedly, others spoke in hushed tones that one could barely make out over the thundering cascade of water pouring down outside. By the end of the day, the park regulars had taken me under their wing with a certain avuncular benevolence.

RETIREMENT

In 2006 the number of people in China over the age of fifty-nine numbered 130 million, accounting for 10 percent of its total 1.3 billion population.[3] This number is predicted to reach 336 million by 2030.[4] In Beijing alone there are an estimated 1.7 million people who are sixty or older, accounting for 12.5 percent of its population.[5] China's life expectancy for men is seventy years of age; for women it is seventy-four.[6]

Since Deng Xiaoping's reign, the state apparatus has been largely been dismantled in favor of (relatively) free market capitalism. This has had a tremendous effect on raising many urban residents' standard of living. Yet it has also led to considerable diminishment of many of the state support systems for the elderly. By Chinese law, children are required to care for their parents, but there is still a wide range of behaviors, depending on the individuals involved. Most retired people do indeed rely on kin for support, but urbanization, modernization, and the new economy have put a strain on the reliability of these networks.[7] To ensure that younger generations can find employment, the state enforces a mandatory retirement age of sixty for men and fifty-five for women. This means that many are expected to find hobbies to keep themselves busy for decades after retirement.

Joel Savishinsky points out that retirement is not a single event but rather an ongoing process.[8] People anticipate retirement long before it occurs—and they continue to be influenced by events that took place while they were working for years after they retire.[9] Similarly, my fieldwork challenged my notions of what it means to be old. At the older end of the spectrum, I was interviewing men in their seventies who had been playing Weiqi on a daily basis in the park for years. However, two of the regular players were not yet of official retirement age—one was forty-six and one was in his early fifties. Two men in their thirties also frequently came to watch games, although I never saw them play.

Unlike the United States, where parks are primarily the sphere of the young, China's parks have largely become the domain of the elderly.[10] In part this is the result of the government's call for the elderly to keep active and an impressive use of state funds to make parks amenable to elderly exercise and socializing. Between 2001 and 2004 alone, the government devoted US$1.6 billion to establishing centers for the elderly to socialize and engage in activities ranging from playing cards to practicing calligraphy and dancing.[11] This marks a dramatic cultural shift in which elderly spend more time with peers than with family members.[12]

Although he did not play Weiqi at the park, Sun Yiguo, a forty-one-year-old career Weiqi player, also challenged my ideas of retirement and what it means to be elderly. At the age of forty-one, Sun Yiguo was semi-retired in that he continued to compete at Weiqi competitions but he no longer won enough prize money to maintain a viable income. As a result, his wife had become the primary breadwinner of his family. At this relatively young age he evoked a sense of the most important part of his life being behind him already.

Hong Feng is a Weiqi instructor at the Capital Sports Center in Beijing's Science and Engineering University. He did not play at the park either, but at the age of fifty his statements were particularly thoughtful about his changing stages of life and his anticipation of retirement. Young enough to radiate youthful vitality, he also voiced a decided appreciation for the calm of middle age in which the stressful decisions about his career and family had already been made. Unlike others I spoke with who saw their upcoming retirements with a certain sense of angst, Hong Feng seemed to look forward to it as but one part of an ongoing process. He used Weiqi to illustrate the pleasures of slowing down and enjoying his life:

> Foreigners' lives are too fast. When foreigners study Weiqi they have the flaw of speed (kuai de maobing). Because life is very busy, it is easy to speed through things. But Westerners are starting to learn how to slow down a little bit. When I was in England I found that they are beginning to appreciate their lives and embrace a very slow lifestyle. They don't like the fast life like in America with all

those tall buildings. They also emphasize slowing down and appreciating things in other parts of their lives as well.

Adults' lives are too busy—they need to focus on their careers. But maybe after they have become successful, after they have achieved their goals, they want to slow down a bit and they say, "I want to study Weiqi, that sounds nice." Then it is a very fulfilling life.[13]

Hong Feng used Weiqi as an emblem of leisure that linked to individual preferences but also to national identities. In his account, the luxury of playing Weiqi could be used to mark a more relaxed stage in the life course. It is important to note that his interpretation of Weiqi's significance differed markedly from that of university students, who usually use the game as a metaphor for relentless competition and the ways that one decision will continue to influence one's life years later. Weiqi's flexibility of cultural interpretation thereby demonstrates the ways in which it comes to be something of a Rorschach test in which one's own concerns emerge in vividly individualized images.

PARK CULTURE

In Weiqi-playing nations it is widely believed that the game can help to fight off senility.[14] While the parkgoers generally agreed that this was the case, they never brought up this sentiment as a rationale for why they played unless one of my questions had introduced the issue. Instead, the themes of the importance of keeping busy and enjoying one's later years were central to their discourse. This is part of a larger culture of aging in China, in which maintaining a positive attitude and keeping active is a cultural expectation.[15]

I stated that these Weiqi players were at a park, but to be precise they were a three-minute walk to the park entrance. While smaller parks usually had groups of people playing Chinese chess and cards, and some parks had Weiqi players, this particular park was a tourist attraction. For some reason the officials in charge decided that the presence of the game players would distract from tourists' pleasure of the pristine nature of the park.

The Weiqi players' little corner was a concrete area with several planted trees next to four lanes of road that were beleaguered by continual traffic. As such, the air and noise quality was closer to that of a contested freeway than that of a quiet park. They chose to meet at this locale because they lived nearby. In part it was also because they could play there at their leisure, without being harassed by storeowners who, in other areas, had forced them to leave for fear that they would clutter the walkway and scare away customers. Elder Liu told me the history of using that locale to play Weiqi: "I've been coming here for about ten years. We used to play over there [*he points East*] but everything has become privatized—everyone wants money. They said we couldn't play there anymore and we moved over here. For a while, the guy who runs that shop [*he points to the corner of their area*] said we couldn't play here anymore but then he died and it stopped being an issue so we came back. People have been playing together here for twenty years."[16]

At this park there were two to four Weiqi games taking place at any one time. The Weiqi players shared this space with a different group of elderly who surrounded two tables for card players. The people playing cards were by and large a much rowdier group, and there were frequently loud arguments that broke out over card games. I never saw money change hands, but the level of anger, which at times turned into ten-minute ranting sessions, suggested that money might have been lost. With the exception of my friend Mr. Yu, who occasionally took a break from the Weiqi corner to spend the day playing cards, I never saw the two groups interact beyond the occasional friendly greeting.

In many ways the park would be recognizable to anyone familiar with chess culture in U.S. parks, in that the Weiqi players made their moves quite rapidly compared to Weiqi games in other settings. Like chess in parks, one often sees a silent and intense Weiqi player paired off in a game with someone who spends much of the time displaying loud bravado.

For the most part, the park regulars were retired senior citizens. In addition to the age difference with the other groups I interviewed, there was also a marked class difference. Whereas one needs a middle-class income to be able to afford Weiqi lessons for one's children, and the students at Peking University were the future elite of their nation, the park regulars could not afford to go to indoor Weiqi clubs. Although a few of the people who visited the Weiqi corner were from white-collar backgrounds, all of the Weiqi-playing park regulars were from the working class. Many of them had been construction workers, and as they played it was hard not to notice that their hands, forearms, and legs were marked by an array of small scars incurred during years of hard physical labor.

In my first fieldwork period, my main opponent was Mr. Xu, a sixty-eight-year-old man with a quiet dignity common among his age group. Like many of the men at the park, Mr. Xu spoke little but radiated intelligence. With a mischievous glint in his eye he always greeted me with the overly formal appellation of "Professor Lin Feng" (my Chinese name). This would have been perfectly normal in other contexts, but at the park there was a working-class ethos of emphasizing equality among peers, and people were quick to use humor against anyone who seemed to be putting on airs. It was fairly clear that in teasing me about my status, Mr. Xu was reducing our differences with a gentle affection.

As with the other park regulars, Mr. Xu was a much better player than I was, with strokes of genius that were truly inspiring to watch, however painful to experience. Our odds evened out for two reasons, however. For one, he tended to play too aggressively and a bit carelessly. This was a common playing style at the park, where people made their moves relatively rapidly and the objective was not merely to win but to claim a decisive victory with dramatic flair. The weather also turned to my favor. When we first arrived at the park just after lunch he would beat me quite effortlessly. The blistering heat of the park usually took a toll on him, however, and it was not long before he began to make careless moves. This gave me a fighting chance. Because of this I tended to win more games than I lost, though there was little doubt that I was in fact the weaker player.

Mr. Xu and I had wild, dramatic, all-or-nothing games that were the prevalent style of play at the park, and I loved every minute of it. In the 2010 portion of my fieldwork, when I spent three weeks playing several games a day at the park, I don't think we ever had a close enough game to count—one side or the other was inevitably crushed by the victor. Win or lose, however, I was usually the one who was desperately trying to defend myself, and there was no doubt that Mr. Xu was in fact the stronger player.

Several of the regulars in 2010 were no longer at the park when I returned in 2011. Mr. Xu was one of the people who had stopped coming, much to my disappointment; no one seemed to know where he had gone. Because of the park regulars' relatively old ages, when people no longer showed up it took on a particularly ominous significance. Mr. Xu didn't seem to get along with some of the other park regulars, however, so it is quite possible that he decided to go to somewhere else to play instead. Each time I went to the park I held out a small bit of hope that I would see him there, but I never did.

In addition to Mr. Xu, several of the other people I had grown close to in 2010 were not there in 2011. In 2010 Mr. Zheng, at the age of forty-two, was one of the youngest members of the group. He was also unusual in that he was still employed, so he would only drop by when he didn't work in the afternoons. He did manual work at a hotel, but when he came to the park he always had a Weiqi book in hand. On my first day at the park Mr. Zheng had insisted on giving me one of the books he used to study Weiqi strategies. The book was faded and frayed at the edges. This was quite generous, because he clearly didn't have much money and at the time he didn't know he would ever see me again. I never saw Mr. Zheng play, but he clearly loved to watch other people's games.

Mr. Wang, a successful businessman from Shandong in his early fifties, also stopped coming in 2011. In 2010, he would drop by for approximately two hours every two or three days. He generally played one or two games, but on the whole he preferred to watch and give an occasional bit of advice.

When I returned in 2011, most of the regulars were still there. Elder Liu, though in his mid-fifties and therefore also younger than most of the others in the park, was older than a second Mr. Liu who I will call Little Liu. Elder Liu was short, stocky, and at times looked disheveled and a bit hung over. On good days he was exceptionally gregarious and something of a central personality in the park. He had been going there for ten years and was the one who brought the four boards and Weiqi stones, which solidified his role as an important part of their community. After lunch he rode up on his scooter every day like clockwork. He was the first to come, the last to leave, and he was the only one of the regulars who was there every day that I went to the park.

Most of the park regulars primarily interacted with the same few friends gathered around a Weiqi board. Though Elder Liu had his favorite opponents, he made a point of watching everyone's games at some point in the day and happily greeted everyone as he did so. When he played he would often provide a continual narration to the effect of "Oh, this guy [his opponent] is very tricky, yes very tricky. He is trying to surround my pieces. I didn't see that coming. But did he notice this area over here? [He plays a move.] I don't think so. I wonder what he's going to do now." Elder Liu's opponents were all friends of many years and they seemed to take his behavior in stride.

At the age of forty-six, Little Liu was the youngest member of the park who played, rather than just observing. Unlike the other regulars, he was too young to say that he had retired. With a certain bravado he simply proclaimed, "I'm free to do what I want." Unlike the older regulars who came to the park seven days a week, Little Liu dropped by to play approximately every other day. As one of the few extroverted regulars, Little Liu was also one of the larger personalities at the park. He always made an effort to greet and joke with members of each of the small groups that gathered around individual games. He often leaned over with a casually placed arm on a friend's shoulder or leg as he spoke.

Mr. Ma, a sixty-year-old with sharp birdlike movements, was quick to laugh and also one of the more popular players at the park, though unlike the two Lius he didn't make an effort to greet people on a daily basis. His most frequent opponent was Elder Liu, and by their happy banter one could immediately see that he was particularly close friends with the two Lius. Mr. Ma spoke exceptionally quickly, and with such a heavy Beijing accent that even native Chinese speakers had a hard time understanding all of what he had to say. Yet he radiated natural intelligence and often demonstrated a somewhat mischievous sense of humor. Like many of the park regulars, Mr. Ma didn't have one career but had taken jobs as they had presented themselves. In Mr. Ma's case, this ranged from being a delivery boy to a construction worker.

Mr. Zhang was a construction worker in his early sixties. He usually bore a perpetual scowl on his face and tended to yell his advice for other people's games with an intimidating angry tone, though he was in fact quite gentle if one spoke with him individually. Like the extroverted Lius, Mr. Zhang was in fact a personality type at the park, in that there were was another player who also expressed his criticism with surprising vehemence, though he too was quite pleasant to talk with in other instances. In 2011 Mr. Zhang tended to watch games more than play them. In 2010, when he played more frequently, he was one of the players who would verbally harangue his opponent throughout each game.

Mr. Zhang often watched my games with Mr. Xu. On one occasion I played an overly defensive stone and he angrily chastised me for being too timid. Mr. Wang, the businessman, agreed that I had wasted a move but tried to pacify Mr. Zhang by saying that it wasn't overly important since I had such a large lead in that particular game. Mr. Zhang angrily replied that I'd never get better if I couldn't count the sequence out in my head, after which he stormed off. We had a very nice conversation later that afternoon, however, and all evidence that he had been frustrated with me had disappeared. In fact, he took great interest in my games and often suggested moves as an act of friendship.

Although the park regulars rarely spoke about matters beyond commenting on the games that were being played, there was an exceptionally strong sense of camaraderie. Many of them had seen each other almost every day for ten years. Though admittedly more sedate, their interactions were not unlike the behavior of sports fans. There was of course no alcohol or shouting, but one witnessed the same enthusiasm of several people watching a masterful move. Inevitably, such moves were met with enthusiastic comments from several onlookers, and one could see their shared disappointment when someone missed an opportunity to deal his opponent a crushing blow.

FIGURE 11. The park in August.

FIGURE 12. The park in November.

At the park, Weiqi at times turned into a team sport in that there were so many people kibitzing that the people playing the game could do little other than choose between the various bits of advice being offered. Sometimes a whole crowd of onlookers would start commenting at the same time, each of them pointing a finger to the spot on the board that they felt the next stone should be placed. In other instances a stronger onlooker would all but take over a game for several moves in a row. Occasionally, players seemed frustrated by this, but more often than not they would take the advice because the people who made the suggestions were usually correct.

During my first fieldwork period in 2010 I refused to take advice, but this put me at a decided disadvantage. My reticence in this regard was born of Western chess etiquette that had been instilled in me as one of my earliest memories. In China, kibitzing and other disruptive behavior was also frowned on outside of the park setting. When I spoke with Sylvia, a senior at Peking University, I once mentioned that some of the people in the park slammed pieces on the board and tried to verbally intimidate their opponents throughout a game. She commented, "I don't like people who talk and insult as they play—there are rules of behavior—it's not just a game. There is a saying that those who watch should not speak—'A person who interferes with the game is not a true gentleman' (*guanqi bu yu zhen junzi*). There is also a rule that once you've put a stone on the board you cannot pick it up again (*luozi bu hui*)—this means you must think it out first. So it is not just a game but a set of behaviors that gives the game its meaning."[17] In spite of this, when I told her of my emotional struggle about making a move if someone kibitzed she surprised me by saying that I should take the advice. She was quick to emphasize that she did not approve of the behavior, however: "If an onlooker suggests a good idea, it is okay to make that move because you recognize that this is the best move. Giving advice means you care about someone. With Weiqi those who give advice are not well behaved, but as a player we can consider that advice, whether one wants to make that move or not. I have to say, though, that's why I never play in public like at a park—it's just no fun. It's great if people want to review a game and give advice after a game—after a game that's good."[18]

Outside of the park context it is very common to review games with one's opponent after the game has concluded. In doing so, the opponents would replay their games from memory. It may be that at the park kibitzing was in part in the result of the fact that, like mine, the parkgoers' memories weren't what they once were. For us, replaying a game from memory was just not feasible. It might also have been an indication that at that stage in life people were less willing to study the game as an investment for future improvement and preferred instead to play and analyze at the same time. This approach was certainly more dynamic.

Weiqi players at the park had never been able to afford lessons. Most of them did not study the game with books, though one or two of them had done so when they were younger. Mr. Rui went to the park infrequently but had been going there to watch Weiqi games for ten years. He pointed out that unlike younger people who received instruction on the game, the people at the park were for the most part self-taught: "People here are soldiers fighting in the wild (*yezhanpai*). In other words, we haven't received any formal training. We aren't playing based on set opening patterns (*dingshi*). We depend on our own thoughts—if we want to make a certain move we just do it. We couldn't really compete in a formal context."[19]

Based on Little Liu, who was the only player in the park who claimed to have an official rating, and judging people's strength against my own, I estimate that most of the players were between 1- and 3-*duan* amateur players. This is unusually strong for a player with no formal training.[20] How did they attain this impressive level? I would suggest that it is precisely because of the pervasive kibitzing at the park, when stronger players pointed out how to improve and entire groups might discuss the best strategy during a game. Though the players sometimes expressed a sense of feeling harassed by what often amounted to a barrage of kibitzing, more often than not they would take the advice unless they could explain why they were selecting another option. This meant that the players often had to outline their overall strategy in front of their opponent. This was something of a handicap for the game, but it also meant that these meetings of minds became centers for instruction. It was no wonder, then, that these players with no formal training had become so good.

Weiqi also allowed for camaraderie without social risk. Many people who lived through the Cultural Revolution have adopted a life strategy of avoiding conflict and withdrawing emotionally.[21] Most of the park regulars had come of age during the Cultural Revolution. Kibitzing, and talking about the game more generally, was an emotionally safe topic of conversation for a generation of people who had learned to guard their thoughts from even their closest friends.

In my second fieldwork period I decided that I should overcome my cultural bias against kibitzing and accept people's advice. On one occasion, however, four or five of the park regulars were enthusiastically giving me advice on how to beat Mr. Gao, a quiet but cheerful man in his late sixties who always came to the park in his pajamas. Because Mr. Gao had already been singled out as one of the weakest players when several of the park regulars insisted he play me, I felt a twinge of guilt when one of the kibitzers pointed out that Mr. Gao had overlooked a decisive move that would lead to my certain victory. For the first time that year I replied, "That is a great move but it would be unfair for me to make it since I didn't think of it myself." Everyone laughed and expressed their good-natured disbelief that I would miss out on the opportunity to deal my opponent a crushing blow when I had the chance.

The usually grumpy Mr. Zhang had frequently watched my games with a friendly interest, giving me a range of advice concerning my worst moves. Because he had seen me refuse advice several times the year before, he was not surprised by my behavior. To explain my reticence to the others he smiled and simply stated, "He's a professor," as if that explained everything. In China, professors are treated with extremely high regard, with none of the stereotypes of not understanding the "real world" or other ambivalent views that one might encounter in the United States. In fact, professors are often thought not only to possess greater knowledge but also to be more moral. Without using the word *suzhi,* therefore, Mr. Zhang seemed to be referencing the concept, predicated on Confucian precedents, by succinctly noting my status as a man of learning. By extension, the statement implicitly acknowledged that their practice of kibitzing was not *suzhi.* In another setting this could have been seen as self-critical. Yet here it seemed to point to the unnatural constraints, even pretentions, of the more educated while simultaneously emphasizing their bonds by publically reminding each other of their shared values and practices. Watching the men in the park, I have to say that they seemed happiest when kibitzing. It was a time when they would laugh and marvel at each other's insights. In sharing an appreciation for certain moves they were demonstrating their solidarity, and they never seemed more emotionally close than when huddled in a group commenting on a game.

LIVED HISTORIES

Though I have not heard the phrase used in China, I have often heard people in the United States refer to the "Chinese" curse: "May you live in interesting times." Few people alive today have lived in more interesting times than the age cohort at the park. Using 2011, when I was conducting my second period of research; as a reference point, we should remember that a sixty-year-old was born in 1951, two years after a brutal civil war that ended in the establishment of the People's Republic of China (PRC). He was seven at the beginning of the two-year-long Great Leap Forward (1958–60), when millions of people starved to death because of poorly thought out government planning. He was fifteen at the beginning of the ten-year-long Cultural Revolution (1966–76), when urban youth were sent to the countryside for political reeducation. During this time, neighbor testified against neighbor and family member against family member in political purges that have continued to leave psychological scars to this day. Public beatings and a mindless cruelty that took a certain amount of inventiveness were also a continual threat. This was all led by teenagers of his own age, against his peers, and everyone else for that matter. He was thirty-eight when the government ordered its troops to shoot student protesters at the 1989 Tiananmen protests. He witnessed China's transformation from a rabidly communist state to a nation that gave lip service to socialist ideals while pursuing free market capitalism. China's economy today is reminiscent of America in the 1920s, before laws to protect workers and ensure quality of goods and food were implemented.[22] Like me, he watched as the dull greys and blues of people's garb were slowly replaced by global fashion trends inspired by Taiwan and the United States.

Most Chinese men I've spoken with in their sixties and over are reserved, and many of them radiate a quiet melancholy. They survived these tumultuous times because they learned not to be the proverbial nail that sticks out lest it get smashed. Yet many of the park regulars had also come to appreciate the contemporary age, and their retirement, precisely because the misery of the early years of the communist era provided a low point with which to contrast the rest of their lives.

Somewhat paradoxically, given the Weiqi's elite associations, it was arguably the Cultural Revolution that broadened the game's class access. Though Teacher Wang, my first Weiqi teacher at the Wenbo School, did not frequent the park, his case is worth noting here. Teacher Wang had been a construction worker for most of his life, but, as with many of his generation, this occupation was chosen for him rather than because of any inclination on his part. He displayed none of the working-class bravado of his age cohort at the park. Instead, he was intensely shy and evinced a quiet dignity laced with a certain melancholy for a difficult life that had been lived in frightfully interesting times. In spite of being employed as a construction worker before he retired, he embodied the Confucian ideal in his quiet gentlemanly ways and his postretirement career as a Weiqi teacher. One got the sense that he had finally found his home. His clear adoration of children, who lived beyond the machinations of the adult world, was an important part of this as well. Teacher Wang was the first of many who told me of learning the game during the Cultural Revolution.

> WANG: I started playing Weiqi when I was thirteen or years old, during the Cultural Revolution.
>
> MOSKOWITZ: Did a lot of people play at that time?
>
> WANG: No, very few. Officially they didn't let people play. There were no teachers—you couldn't take classes. We taught ourselves with books from Shanghai. At that time we were living in the countryside. Later, we were playing in the park and there was an old man there who saw us playing and said, "You guys are terrible players, [he laughs] let me teach you."[23]

Several people told me that they learned to play Weiqi during the Cultural Revolution. Like Teacher Wang, most of them looked back fondly on playing Weiqi in parks, even if they no longer did so. In part, many people learned to play Weiqi in this era quite simply because they had nothing else to do. It was also because people ended up as laborers because of political destiny, although they might otherwise have chosen more intellectual pursuits. For many who had lived through this tumultuous time, and who had been assigned employment that had little to do with their interests or talents, Weiqi became a means of pursuing intellectual stimulation in a way that did not overtly threaten the status quo during the early communist reign.

There were many paradoxes that arose from discussions of this period. That many of the elderly people I spoke with had learned to play this elite game during the Cultural Revolution was perhaps the most striking. Also, for many, memories of that time were infused with nostalgia for their youth, which included many happy moments in spite of what was going on around them. The youngest person I interviewed who provided accounts of this period was the forty-one year old Sun Yiguo.

As a child, Sun Yiguo had a series of health issues that would plague him for the rest of his life. This included developing hemophilia and injuring his leg badly enough that he continues to walk with a limp to this day. This was one factor as to why he never succeeded in obtaining a professional rank in time to meet the age restrictions, although he has made his career playing

Weiqi in amateur competitions. Although his youth included battles with severe illness, and although the Cultural Revolution was arguably one of the most traumatic periods in China's history, for him it was also a time of youthful discovery that he looked back on with clear fondness. For Sun Yiguo, recollections of the Cultural Revolution were clearly mixed with nostalgia for his childhood and a time before the world had become quite so commodified. Part of these memories tied into the outdoor culture of the time: "When I was a kid my dad would tie a monthly train ticket to my neck and we would take a two-hour train to go play Weiqi. I have very vivid memories of that time—people would go play in a sports arena. We would get off the train and walk there." Sun went on to tell me of injuring his leg as a child. It was such a severe injury that he spent months confined to his apartment. He then described how one trained to be a professional player in the early 1970s.

> SUN: At first my mom would carry me to the Beijing Cultural Center. Beijing's best players all went there to play Weiqi. In the beginning I played outside—I couldn't go inside because I wasn't good enough. Because everyone inside was an expert. After a year I had gotten to know the people inside and sometimes they would let me in to study with them. Then my Weiqi improved faster and faster.
>
> MOSKOWITZ: Did you take regular classes or just study Weiqi?
>
> SUN: That had to do with the particular time in history. At that time we didn't have to pay tuition to study Weiqi. Because in those days people didn't like it if you charged others for your services. It was still rare to be able to play with experts but playing Weiqi depended on connections (*guanxi*) not on money. No one paid money.[24]

Sun Yiguo's account of playing Weiqi as a child spoke of a different political economy. Because of the early communist era's political climate, people were not allowed to charge money to teach Weiqi. Sun Yiguo used this to highlight the crass consumerism of the modern age.

Mr. Rui was one of the few educated people who frequented the Weiqi corner of the park. Though he no longer played, he told me that he continued to enjoy watching others play. He also spoke of learning to play Weiqi during the Cultural Revolution.

> RUI: I retired ten years ago. After I retired I started coming here pretty often. I've lived in this area for seventy years so it is convenient to come here. I started playing when I was twenty-four or twenty-five years old. Because at that time China was going through the Cultural Revolution. I

had just graduated from university in 1966 and I didn't dare get involved with the Cultural Revolution so I just stayed inside and studied Weiqi.

MOSKOWITZ: Weiqi has pretty high-class connotations—wasn't it a problem to play Weiqi during the Cultural Revolution?

RUI: No, it wasn't a problem. Weiqi is thought of as very upper class so they didn't really approve of it but they had more important things to worry about. No one had time to monitor if people were playing Weiqi or not. Many people started playing at that time. For instance, [China's most famous Weiqi player] Nie Weiping started playing at that time. He was a "sent-down youth"—the government sent him to the countryside in the North East. In that area the winters are too cold to go outside so he just stayed inside and played Weiqi. There was no one to teach us how to play but you could buy books on the game and learn from them—especially in used bookstores—you could find books on Weiqi. There were Weiqi books from before liberation [before 1949] or Japanese books on the game. But there were more Japanese books.[25]

Park Weiqi evoked a sense of lived history. Artistic depictions of gentry playing Weiqi on a veranda in bamboo forests were something of a constant in Imperial China. Many people suggested that this was also a continuing legacy from the early communist years when outdoor culture was even more common. Today, one can see China's parks filled with picnickers, young men photographing their girlfriends, husbands and wives playing badminton without a net, and of course Chinese chess, cards, and in some parks, Weiqi.

Given that Beijing's weather ranges from blistering hot summers to snow-filled winters, it is no surprise that those frequenting the parks are from an economic class that cannot afford the fees that Weiqi clubs (*julebu*) charge. Weiqi clubs are generally single rooms rented in buildings that protect the players from the elements, the noise of the street traffic, and the frequent comments of people passing by. Not having to sit on the ground or a concrete ledge with nothing but an old newspaper to protect one's pants is also a plus. The fee for such clubs varies. One of the better-known clubs charged US$.63 (4 RMB) an hour. While this was not a substantial fee for the middle class, it was prohibitively expensive for most of the park regulars.

In summers, the park regulars usually arrived just after lunch and would often play until dark. In winter months, when the weather went below freezing, many of them did not arrive until two or three in the afternoon, but there were usually still ten or fifteen people there on a daily basis. They bundled up in several layers of clothing and lit one cigarette from the last to distract themselves from the cold—but they were still there.

Though not a park player himself, the Weiqi instructor Hong Feng explained why some people continue to play Weiqi in parks in spite of the extremities of the weather.

> In olden days China had a lot of teashops. They wouldn't play on the ground in a park or on the road. In addition to playing Weiqi they paid a lot of attention to the entire environment. It was very comfortable. Playing Weiqi was a very elegant thing. You couldn't just play on the road in front of everyone else.
>
> In today's China a lot of things are in public. If you like Ping-Pong you might play right on the street. If you play pool you might do that right on the street. Or you might play Weiqi right on the street as well. If you want to play in a room it might be too much of a luxury. Why? Because today's apartments in China are very expensive. It might cost tens of thousands of yuan (reminbi) for a square meter (yi ping). So if you want to play Weiqi it's too expensive to open a teahouse [where people could play Weiqi]. It's all connected to economic development in China.[26]

Hu Tingmei wrote that Weiqi is a great equalizer in that when facing an opponent one is not concerned with his class background or anything other than his level of skill on the board.[27] Although Hu seems to overlook the fact that most people in China cannot afford to pay for Weiqi lessons, or that women are all but second-class citizens in the Weiqi sphere, there is an element of truth to his statement when applied to the parks. Though the park regulars were primarily from the working class, there were a handful of middle-class visitors such as Mr. Rui, Mr. Wang, or myself. We were not truly part of the inner circle, but we went often enough to be treated as part of the group. At the end of the day, however, we all went back to our homes, and everyone was very much aware of class difference as soon as the hypnotic trance of a game had worn off.

Yet if Weiqi was not a complete equalizer, it was indeed an activity that mediated our differences. A retired construction worker might play with a successful businessman, or a day laborer might play with an American professor. If I was from the United States, I had at least showed the good sense to have a love of the game. If my affiliation with Peking University marked me as a member of the elite in their eyes, the fact that they were so unequivocally better than I was at Weiqi leveled the difference in our relative status.

By virtue of my nationality, occupation, and relatively low playing skills I was an outsider to the park. I did play well enough to rival the weaker players, however. And if, at the age of forty-six I was a tad young compared to the park regulars, I was a few months older than Little Liu and a decade older than the two men in their mid-thirties who came to watch others play.[28] In some aspects I could relate to the park regulars in ways that went beyond their communication with China's younger generations, for the PRC's transformations during the past decades had created a generation gap that was arguably more dramatic than in any previous era. I was familiar with, and interested in, the history they had lived through that many in the younger generations dismissed as having little to do with their lives. Like the park regulars I too had a sense of being a part of two Chinas. The China that I witnessed on my first arrival in 1988 had barely left its early communist roots. It was visually grim, and one often felt the oppressive presence of the government. Yet people were also relatively equal by virtue of the fact that most citizens outside of the governmental bureaucracy had so little. In present-day China, foreign media, fashion, and music are seemingly omnipresent, and towering residence buildings cover urban centers. For Chinese youth this is all part of a taken-for-granted world that they have always known. On a daily basis I marveled at the changes in people's attitudes toward freedom, hard work, individual agency, and social relations. Everyone in China was aware of these transformations, but one had to be a certain age, to have lived through these events, to feel their full emotional impact.

On one occasion I was complimenting Elder Liu for bringing the Weiqi sets to the park every day. In response, one of the regulars joked, "Yes, he is our Lei Feng." Lei Feng was a person who died at a young age during the early communist era and was lauded in party propaganda for proper self-sacrificing behavior during the Mao Zedong years. I grinned and said, "Serve the people" (*wei renmin fuwu*), which was a political slogan from that era. Everyone laughed, and the man who had mentioned Lei Feng exclaimed, "Wow, you know who Lei Feng is. A lot of younger Chinese people don't even know who Lei Feng is anymore." Elder Liu sighed, "Yes, now young people are just like Americans. They only care about money. They don't care about the older values." He shook his head sadly for a minute, and then we all turned our attention back to the game we had been watching.

With one or two exceptions, the park regulars had little interest in waxing poetic about Weiqi's ancient roots or philosophical implications. They told me they liked the game because it kept them busy, because they found it interesting, and because they had nothing better to do. They said that their choice of playing Weiqi, as opposed to Chinese chess or cards, which were more popular in parks, was simply that they found the game to be more challenging and therefore more interesting. Many of them went to the park to play seven afternoons a week, from just after lunch until it was getting dark. That it was good to keep busy was taken as self-evident. To the degree that they tied the game in with larger cultural patterns, it was to celebrate the luxury of having a hobby—something that most Chinese people in China's long history did not have time for.

Though he did not frequent the park, Yu Rongxin, a member of Peking University's Weiqi team, also contrasted past hardships with the present day as being relatively carefree. To do so, he compared his father's childhood with his own: "China has changed a lot in the last decades. With my father this is very clear. Because my father was not born in a good background. He was born in a farmer's family. Because his family was poor, when he was young, in addition to going to school he had to work so that his family could get by. So if he played a game in secret and my grandfather found about it, my grandfather would take it away from him."[29]

In Yu Rongxin's account, having the luxury to play Weiqi was an emblem of the difference between his father's generation and his own. Though not a park player, Hong Feng, the Weiqi instructor at the Capital Sports Center in Peking Science and Engineering University, also provided insights worth mentioning here: "In ancient times it was only the aristocrats that had the time to play Weiqi. Everyone else was farming and working hard all day. Now our living standards have risen, so people should have more fulfilling lives. We don't have to worry or think, 'We don't have anything to eat today, what are we going to do, what will we do tomorrow?' Now we don't have to worry about this problem. Everyone says playing Weiqi makes one smarter and makes life a bit more fulfilling. That is very good."[30]

An interview I conducted with Mr. Ma and Little Liu echoed Hong Feng's sentiment when Mr. Ma stated that today is the best era in China's history, Little Liu readily agreed: "No one would play Weiqi if they were hungry, right? People need to find food and shelter first and it's only when they have a certain amount of security that they can turn to leisure activities. So the fact that you see people playing Weiqi and other games in the park is a sign that we are doing okay these days. We have enough to get by and that is enough, right?"[31] One should not forget that the elderly in Beijing have a much better standard of living than their rural counterparts. Even with this in mind, however, the prevalence of optimistic views such as this was surprising in that the people in the park had lived through some of the most traumatic moments in China's long history. Yet they had also been there when people's fears about the aftermath of the Tiananmen massacre had turned out to be exaggerated, and watched as each decade seemed to bring more economic prosperity and political freedom than the one preceding it.

China's government officials continue to be frustrated by their failed attempts to bring economic reform without cultural or political change. Today, however, people's fear of the state is noticeably less than it was three decades ago. It is tempting to suggest that by virtue of their class and age the park regulars were doubly left behind in China's economic reforms. They were quick to point out, however, that they too benefited from knowing they would not go hungry and that they no longer had to fear being politically purged. The relative benevolence of the current government means that state intervention just isn't a part of most people's everyday concerns the way it was on my first stay in 1988. Weiqi had become an emblem for the relative security and luxury of this new age. This was a very different discourse than commonly found among college-educated players who, more often than not, celebrated Weiqi's elite historical origins or used the game to illustrate the pressures of the modern age.

MASCULINITY AMONG THE WORKING CLASS AT THE PARK

Like most male residents of Beijing, the park regulars had surprisingly deep voices. Most seemed older than their actual ages, worn down by years of hard labor and having lived through some of the most tumultuous eras in China's long history. With the exception of one or two of the more extroverted personas, most of the park regulars tended to evince a quiet dignity. Having spent much of their youth living through the Cultural Revolution, at an early age they learned to keep their opinions to themselves. In a sense, the "hand conversation" that Weiqi provided, and the completely nonthreatening conversations that took place about the games, seemed to be a psychologically safe area that harbored their well-being.

Unlike their stoic countenance, however, their games were filled with flamboyant flair, strokes of genius, and acts of daring. Peking University students played far more conservatively in that if they were in the lead they would make cautious moves to protect that margin. Often they would point out that a one-point victory still meant they had won the game. At the park, winning or losing was less important than acts of brilliance, and players would continue in all-or-nothing battles regardless of who had the lead. This approach might lead to a dramatic victory or an equally spectacular turn of events because a person who was clearly ahead could lose everything by gambling on a different part of the board. At the park I only gained some modicum of respect as a player once I adopted this all-or-nothing blitzkrieg style.

Weiqi balances the cultured *wen* and the martial *wu*. Its elite associations ground it firmly in the world of *wen,* but *wu* can be seen in the emphasis on martial assertiveness as evinced in the Weiqi concept of seizing the initiative (*xianshou*). It is widely thought that if a player continues to make moves that his opponent has no choice but to respond to, he will win the game. At the park, seizing the initiative was not just a playing style. It was often interpreted as evidence of being a man of character—one who is not easily pushed around. It was believed that a man who could dominate his opponent in this way attested to his masculinity by asserting his strength of will over another.

In several of my games at the park I was confronted with the ways that one's playing style was seen to reflect gender-coded moral fiber. Because my opponents at the park were much stronger players than I was, I frequently focused on defending myself. On one such occasion a park regular who was watching my game commented on my playing style, stating "He is too *wenrou*."[32] *Wenrou* can be translated as "gentle" or "caring," and at times can be used to refer to what in the West might be called an effeminate man. He stated that my playing style was too *wenrou* with a gruff bluntness that was typical of the working-class ethos of the park regulars. His tone of impatience left little doubt that his comment was meant as a critique. I was intrigued, because although I had heard *wenrou* used quite often to describe a gentle and caring personality type, I had never heard it used to describe a style of play in Weiqi. To confirm that I had not misunderstood him, after the game I asked him about what he had meant by his earlier comment. He told me that my style "lacks strength" (*meiyou liqi*) with a clear expression of disapproval.[33]

While the game was still in progress I was spurred on by being accused of passivity and I made a very aggressive move. Mr. Yu, who had become something of a mentor to me, and who was also watching my game, smiled and proudly exclaimed, "Was that *wenrou*?" A few weeks earlier, when I was playing someone else, Mr. Yu also laughed with pleasure when I had ignored a move that seemingly gave my opponent the initiative. Instead, I forced my opponent to defend himself for six moves in a row before I went back to respond to his threat. At each of my moves Mr. Yu happily cheered, "He's not afraid of you! He's not afraid of you at all! Look at him go!"

In contrast to the park regulars, the university players were remarkably quiet and reserved. They rarely spoke during games, and when they had finished they would quietly review while instructing the loser with a gentle benevolence that was worthy of a Confucian master. At the park, winning was far less important than forcing one's opponent into submission or, at the least, avoiding being dominated by one's opponent. In this context, one's playing style is very much read as a display of masculine expression. In the park this also manifested itself with a rougher working-class form of masculine behavior, one in which spectators would enthusiastically congratulate players in response to their good moves and loudly chastise them for bad ones. This spectatorship bordered on the behavior one normally sees at a basketball game. It was decidedly more lively than the sedate styles of competition and spectatorship that took place in other Weiqi contexts. Weiqi's *wen* and *wu* thereby manifest themselves very differently in the contexts of age, economic class, and educational level. In addition to the etiquette demonstrated in particular Weiqi circles, one's very style of play is a vivid expression of what it means to be a man. It draws on differing conceptions of masculinity that are marked by age, economic standing, and locale.

SEVEN

Conclusion

LOOKING FORWARD TO A BYGONE AGE

[Games] *promise a temporary escape from the inescapability of history (whether personal or global) into a place where history is just a simulacrum built of rules, turns, strategies, and dice rolls, a weightless flow in which no outcome is so fatal that it can't be rewritten the next game around. After all these years, in other words, board games continue to show their religious roots, since even our simple, secular delight in these rough-hewn virtual worlds turns out to be, in a sense, just another way of wrapping our hearts and minds around religion's primal conundrum: the cosmic raw deal that gave us each just one life to live.*

JULIAN DIBBELL, My Tiny Life: Crime and Passion in a Virtual World, 1998[1]

Khasin lost his father to imprisonment and execution in 1932, lost both of his legs to a German aerial bomb outside Stalingrad in 1942, and lost full use of his hands to frostbite suffered during the war. Still, he rues a chess game lost fifty years before.

ROBERT DESJARLAIS, Counterplay: An Anthropologist at the Chessboard, 2011[2]

I have come for the usual reasons—the competition, the quest for experthood, the fact that I have no choice but to play.

STEFAN FATSIS, Word Freak: Heartbreak, Triumph, Genius, and Obsession in the World of Competitive Scrabble Players, 2001[3]

TOO OFTEN, WESTERN DEPICTIONS OF people who play games of logic hone in on the suffering of mad genius; of the toll of the game physically, psychologically, and economically; of ostracism from mainstream society ending in isolation, despair, and even death. In China's views of Weiqi this rhetoric is largely absent. In part this is because Chinese culture is less ambivalent about intellectual prowess and having a relentless work ethic. Characteristics that in the West might be labeled as "nerdy" (studying or working from morning to night, avoiding heavy physical activity, an exceptionally strong attachment to one's parents) are components of a highly idealized model of manhood in China. Though I have met a handful of Weiqi players in China who might have been deemed to be socially awkward by their peers, most of them were remarkably well adjusted. Many of the children I trained with, for example, were exceptionally charming and gave every indication of being some of the most popular kids in their neighborhoods.

Even if one accepts the premise that games of intellect can attract a certain compulsive personality type, one should also consider the insight of Bill Hartston, a former chess champion, who stated, "Chess is not something that drives people mad; chess is something that keeps mad people sane."[4] In other words, a less frequently told tale is that of the psychological benefits of finding one's passion, or the emotional trauma of leaving it behind. Most of the Weiqi players that I interviewed had stopped training in order to focus on their studies, which were also very demanding. Few of them felt that they had made the wrong choice, but their tone was unmistakably melancholy when they told me of these transitions.

Though I interviewed a range of people who expressed sorrow that they could not continue their Weiqi training, I have only met one person who felt that he had made the wrong choice in doing so, and this was in Taiwan. It is worthwhile to present his case study here, however, because it demonstrates that in leaving the arduous world of Weiqi training one is hardly free to lead a healthier or more carefree life.

Mr. Sun was a Weiqi prodigy as a child.[5] He grew up on the east coast of Taiwan, one of the poorer areas on the island, where skilled Weiqi players are few indeed. Using widespread stereotypes about people in poorer areas to his advantage, he and his childhood friend became Weiqi hustlers.

> SUN: I loved to play Weiqi as a child and my friend and I were surprisingly good. We used to work for the head of a Weiqi club who would back us gambling—especially with *waishengren* [people who had come to Taiwan in 1949 when they lost the war to the communist revolution in China]. Sometimes a schoolteacher would come to our club and lose half his month's salary playing us. Usually we won from skill but, I have to be honest with you, we also cheated sometimes.
>
> MOSKOWITZ: How can you cheat at Weiqi?

SUN: Well if you are playing fast you can move some pieces while you are putting down a new stone. You basically just brush it to another spot with your hand, but you do it very fast so your opponent doesn't see it. The manager of the club would set up the games and stake us so he took most of the money, but we made a pretty good income from this.

Rather than being ashamed of this past, Mr. Sun clearly relished this period of his life and longed for the relative freedom of his youth.

My friend went on to become a professional player and I really envy him. I wanted to become a professional as well but my father was dead set against it. One time I remember coming home with a trophy from a competition I had won and my father was really angry and said he'd put it up above the toilet. Basically he was saying it wasn't worth anything, that I wasn't worth anything if I wanted to pursue this career. So eventually I succumbed to my father's demands and quit playing Weiqi but my friend went on to be quite a success. I was just as good as my friend was as a child, maybe even a little bit better, so I think it's not unrealistic to think that I could have been a professional as well.

Mr. Sun was a government official, which is one of the most prestigious occupations in Taiwan. I tried to comfort him by pointing out that he had quite a successful career. He responded by saying, "I suppose so, but it has never been what I loved to do. As a father I try to support my children in their dreams. I always tell them to find something they love to do—that's what makes life worthwhile. But my father wasn't like that. He was much more concerned with what other people thought and with what was expected. I suppose I am successful in other people's eyes but I think I would have been happier following my heart."[6]

Mr. Sun's account is surprising on several levels. For the purposes of this book, the most salient point is that Weiqi is not the only way that children may be disciplined. Mr. Sun endured quite severe psychological disciplining in the form of a forceful insistence that he quit what his father saw to be a frivolous occupation in favor of a more practical and prestigious career.

By Chinese standards Mr. Sun's father was in fact behaving quite properly, in that patriarchs are expected to be strict and unwavering in their attempts to better their children. Part of Mr. Sun's interpretation of events is clearly informed by the values of today's generation, which has been far more influenced by Western mass media. Mr. Sun's account is important, then, because it reveals a surprising underbelly of the Weiqi realm, but also because it demonstrates that the disciplinary structure of Weiqi training is part of a larger worldview concerning the proper way to bring up sons.

For many, Weiqi is a fulfilling passion rather than a mere pastime. It is precisely for this reason that the sorrow of leaving it behind can be so devastating. Mr. Sun stated his regrets about discontinuing his training most directly, but he was hardly alone in this. Wang Wenbo, the owner and manager of the Wenbo School, had tears in his eyes when he spoke of his son failing to earn a professional rank. Peking University students Yu Rongxin and Sylvia were also at times visibly close to tears when they spoke of events that had occurred a decade earlier that led to their forsaking their Weiqi training. Their choices were informed by parental and societal expectations as much as by their own inclinations; by the rigid professional ranking system and its age limits; by the unfeasibility of making a suitable income even if one did achieve the coveted professional status. It had to do with gendered expectations as to who might succeed in the Weiqi realm, and with the fiercely competitive nature of China's economy and culture as a whole.

Even those who had abandoned their hopes of making a career playing Weiqi spoke of the profound ways that the game had changed their lives for the better. They told me that Weiqi had trained them in logic and good sportsmanship, and that it had given them insights into commerce and human relations. They spoke of the ways that, at a very young age, they learned from Weiqi the pleasures of reaping the rewards of having a strong work ethic and of using their intellectual abilities to face the challenges that they might encounter as an adult. They lauded the game for providing them with intellectual tools that helped them to find their place in the world, and of the ways that it shaped them into better people. They demonstrated the manner in which one might use this game to draw on previous iconic models of idealized cultural behavior that connected to China's long history of greatness.

When I first told people in the United States of this project, most were surprised at my attempt to connect a board game with male identity formation. Yet one should not ignore the fact that constructions of masculinity are not limited to sexuality, aggression, or patriarchal authority. Manhood is linked to a web of intersecting forces that include familial and social expectations, individual choice, and historical precedent. Weiqi might at first glance seem to be an odd choice in exploring Chinese masculinities, but clearly it sits on the intersection of a range of important cultural themes. In making Weiqi one of four requisites of being a cultured gentleman (along with learning calligraphy, music, and art) Imperial Chinese culture emphasized the importance of a board game to a degree that no other culture has done before or since. Weiqi's unique place in Chinese history as emblematic of a cultured gentleman lends players the prestige of a bygone age, when China was justifiably proud of its centrality in its known world.

The malleability of Weiqi's iconic significance is testament to the ways that historical images are adopted to fit the modern context. This begins with training boys to develop their intellect, to harness their natural aggression for productive ends, and to embody new visions of Confucian gentlemen for the modern age. In the university setting, Weiqi is an emblem of the kind of man one hopes to become and the struggles of making one's way in China's overwhelmingly competitive society. For the elderly, it represents the pleasures of leisure and a relative freedom from state intervention. It allows for the creation of a community of friends who are quickly being left behind in today's political economy. This is because of their economic status, but it is also because they came of age in an era that most people in China would prefer to leave as far behind as humanly possible.

It is hard to decide whether one should be more impressed by the versatility of Weiqi's metaphors or by their remarkable consistency in these different settings. In all three groups, Weiqi was seen as a way for a man to become a more moral person. The game was thought to teach him the proper balance between aggression and restraint. It was said to instruct him on how to control other men and, in turn, to avoid being dominated by them.

Contemporary China is rife with discussions about the need to promote heightened cultural aesthetics associated with the middle class, and the dangers of a society that many worry has lost its moral framework. The increasing centrality of the millennial generation in China's imaginary has been brought about by cultural values embedded in movies and popular music from the West, as well as from neighboring nations in East Asia. The "Little Emperor Syndrome," in which the One-Child Policy has seemingly created a nation of spoiled only children, marks a dramatic reversal of parent–child hierarchies. Today's political economy, in which parents no longer have absolute control over their adult offspring's residence and income, seems to heighten this anxiety.

Weiqi counteracts these fears in important ways. It is thought to help shape children's morality and intellect by training them to endure grueling training sessions. It provides them with historical models of Confucian gentlemen who were extolled for living life by a code of honor. Indeed, it is harder to think of a more stark contrast with the images of corrupt and immoral businessmen and politicians that one finds in China's popular imagination. Weiqi constructs manhood, it shapes citizenship, and it provides a tangible way of facing China's contemporary political economy with the cultural values extolled in a bygone age. It teaches boys to become men. It provides a topic that enables young adults to express their fears concerning the future, in which a casual misstep will seemingly dictate the outcome of the rest of their lives.

Although I made an effort to seek out female Weiqi players and include their voices here, there is little doubt that the Weiqi sphere is an overwhelmingly male domain. There were only three female players on the Peking University team, and the Weiqi club meetings often consisted of ten or fifteen men to one woman. The fact that China's national Weiqi team admitted women only in the year 2000 is further testament to the continued male dominance of this sphere.

Peking University's Weiqi players approached the contemporary moment by drawing on philosophies from Weiqi masters spanning millennia. They did so by evoking a nostalgic memory of a past that many sought to embrace in the contemporary era. It is important that the wisdom, behavior, and ideals that both male and female university students cited from this time were consistently drawn from these elite men in China's history. In large part this was because there were so few historical examples of Chinese women who served in the public domain. In most of Chinese history, women were evaluated by their ability to support their husbands and train their sons. As such, contemporary women seeking wisdom for how to succeed in the public sector often look to the examples provided by the learned men of history. Thus, both men and women draw on historical constructions of ideal personhood that were inspired by traditional forms of idealized masculinity.

In the Weiqi sphere, men are also the default identity. Both men and women assert that men's superiority at Weiqi is attributable to the innate masculine characteristics of logic and aggression, which can best be mastered through learning the game. These biases are also reflected in China's modern political economy in which women, if they are to succeed in business or politics, must learn to act more "like men." Because of women's recent successes in higher education and the workplace, one might predict a time when these characteristics are less gender coded. For now, however, men and women's roles are very clearly marked in China. This is not to claim that women will act, or be treated, exactly like men in their efforts to claim their place in China's modern political economy. As people in China begin to embrace traditional roles to explore cultural mores that were erased during the early communist years, there is arguably a clearer division between the behavior of men and women than in the preceding decades. Yet many believe that for women to become more successful in the public sphere they must learn to be more assertive and to rely on their wits—both of which are still male-coded attributes in contemporary China.

The retired park regulars also conceptually positioned Weiqi's cultural meanings with remarkable consistency. They spoke of the game's historical roots and its strong associations with morality, and they did so in decidedly male-coded cultural paradigms. Their comments were in remarkable alignment with the cultural frameworks presented at the children's schools and by the university players. Yet by virtue of the park players' relatively old age and low economic status, Weiqi had different meanings as well. Though the park regulars also employed a rhetoric that drew on Weiqi's associations with ancient Chinese thought, this was interspersed with the lived histories of the Cultural Revolution. Having experienced this history firsthand, rather than merely reading about it, they voiced a more cautious and introspective analysis of China's political economy, but they also showed a greater appreciation of the contemporary era.

For the park regulars, playing Weiqi evoked images of Confucian gentlemen and morality, but it also carried associations in which one's playing style celebrated being a rugged man. In marked contrast with the university students who often used Weiqi as a metaphor for the relentlessly competitive world that they found themselves in, the park regulars had decided to enjoy the last years of their lives by playing this game with their friends. For them, Weiqi represented a level of prosperity, leisure, and camaraderie that they would not have thought possible in their younger years.

Because they had already retired, the park regulars saw the game less as something that would shape them for a better future than a means of expressing who they had already become. In demonstrating their intellectual prowess and indomitable spirits, their playing styles also became a forceful means of rejecting the stigma that society might have placed on them by virtue of their age or economic strata. Their talent on the Weiqi board proclaimed that these working-class men possessed intelligence and moral fiber, in direct opposition to stereotypes that were leveled against them by those of more elite standing.

Weiqi is not only a skill but also an art. In offering cultural models for proper behavior, the game is an emblem of individual selves and national cultural formation. In this process, depictions of other nations' cultural identities bleed into portrayals of individual players. In these accounts, Japanese people are often seen to be controlled by tradition and to prefer the aesthetics of the game to winning competitions. In turn, Koreans are portrayed as discarding such concerns and aggressively prioritizing victory at any cost. Chinese Weiqi players claim to have found a balance between the two. Because these attributes are used to signify both individual and national identities, manhood and nation merge in modern manifestations of historical paradigms. Rather than trying to adopt, or resist, global culture, therefore, China is reclaiming and reinventing its own past to claim Weiqi dominance in East Asia. Not coincidentally, it does so in a manner that mirrors its economic and political efforts in this sphere.

Weiqi links to a shared memory of China's greatness. It draws on images of Confucian gentlemanly behavior in a rather willful disregard for Confucius' dismissal of the game. It evokes the male scholar of old but also draws on popular imaginaries of war and warriors—a world in which martial prowess and a touch of craftiness can never truly be separate. The central strategy of "seizing the initiative" calls on men to subdue their opponents and to avoid being dominated by other men. In this sense Sunzi's *Art of War* is as equally recognizable on the Weiqi board as it is in real-life conflict. The struggle between men might take place at school, in the business world, or on the battlefield, but the results are surprisingly consistent in that these ideals become part of what it means to be a man in this created nostalgic modernity.

The wealth of historical metaphors associated with the game is used in constructing masculine identities and speaks both to age-old ideals of the cultured *wen* and the martial *wu,* as well as new economies of transnational sharing. It is placed to represent men of iron wills and modern manifestations of Confucian gentlemen, warfare and restraint, conquest and intellectual detachment. The astonishing wealth of Weiqi's cultural meanings seems to speak less to its protean quality than its ability to be all things at once—to simultaneously occupy a range of historically and culturally nuanced fantasies and desires that revolve around what it means to be Chinese, a man, a person of greater worth.

NOTES

1. Hallman 2003:35.
2. Kawabata 1951:32.
3. Fatsis 2001:252.
4. Hewitt 2008:94.
5. Ibid.:98.
6. Ibid.:382.

7. Shank and Wasserstrom provide a very compelling argument for why government abuses have led to its loss of legitimacy for many of China's citizens (Shank and Wasserstrom 2012).

8. For more on this see Wasserstrom 2003; 2007. Wasserstrom points out that although this was a popular uprising, the government's control of news media exacerbated this issue by choosing not to cover certain facets of the event, such as President Bill Clinton's apology (Wasserstrom 2007:81–100).

9. The Shanghai interviews took place from June 16, 2006, to July 14, 2006. After that period I continued to live in Taipei until August 1999.

10. This occurred on the Firefox browser. Using the same Chinese input on the Google site with Internet Explorer did not have this problem.

CHAPTER 1

1. Ricci 1610:146. This quotation was taken from Paulo Zanon's translation (1996a:70–71).
2. Taken from Pinckard 2001b:20.
3. Hesse 1943:148.
4. *Qi* is also part of the Chinese name for Chinese chess (*xiangqi*) and Western/international chess (*guoji xiangqi* in the PRC, *xiangqi* in Taiwan).

5. For more on Chinese middle-class aspirations in connection with the piano, see Kraus 1989.

6. This is not to say that Weiqi is the only activity to do so. Calligraphy and mastering traditional Chinese instruments are but two other examples of this phenomenon. Yet, on the whole, Western symbology is far more salient in obtaining symbolic capital and class status in contemporary China.

7. Mahjong is also exceptionally popular. Yet, perhaps because it is a predominantly female pastime that often includes the illegal practice of gambling, one never sees it played outdoors.

8. See, for example, Aronofsky 1998; Gorris 2000; Edmonds and Eidinow 2004; Hallman 2003; Howard 2002; Waitzkin 1984; Weinreb 2007.

9. In 1992 Tim Casey released IGS, the first computer program to play Weiqi on the Internet. In 1996, IGS was purchased by a Japanese communications company that moved its server to Tokyo. The IGS server can be found at: www.pandanet-igs.com/communities/pandanet. The Tom server can be found at Tom.sport: http://weiqi.sports.tom.com.

10. The KGS server can be found at: www.gokgs.com.

11. Foster 2012.

12. In Japan and Korea there is also an 8-*duan* amateur rank that some Chinese people have earned by winning international competitions. Internet servers often have an 8- and 9-*duan* amateur rank.

13. Historically, on very rare occasions 10-*duan* pro ranks were given in Japan as an honorary rank. This practice does not exist in China.

14. Wiki.goratings. n.d.; Singapore Weiqi Association. n.d.

15. For a list of players and their relative ranking in competitions see Post.weiqi.com 2012.

16. GoBase.org n.d.: http://gobase.org/games/nn/.

17. Post.weiqi.com 2012.

18. F. Liu 2006:491.

19. For more on these issues, see Ibid.:498–99.

20. Ibid.:496.

21. Ibid.

22. X. Wang et al. 2008.

23. Ibid.:57.

24. Ibid.:70.

25. Ibid.:61.

26. Ibid.:60–61.

27. Ibid.

28. F. Liu 2006:497.

29. Jankowiak 2002:364; F. Liu 2006:500. This is arguably a modern continuation of trends that were established in the early years of the PRC. Honig and Hershatter have noted that Cultural Revolution images of the Iron Girls, in which women were expected to achieve parity with men in traditionally male occupations such as mining or machinery work, largely depended on women erasing their gender

and acting more like men rather than including attempts to reform men (Honig and Hershatter 1988). Susan Brownell explored the mixed reactions in the 1980s when the women's volleyball team outperformed male teams in international competitions and the ways in which women's identities were defeminized in emphasizing their Chineseness over their gender (Brownell 1999). Similarly, Nancy Chen explores the manner in which the public face of Qigong defaults to a generic male (N. Chen 2002).

30. Because some might find their assertions about women's incapacity for logic to be offensive I have not included the identity of the two men who made these statements.

31. Interview. Fang Weijing. October 22, 2011.

32. Ibid.

33. For more on this, see Moskowitz 2010, 2012.

34. 2,000 RMB. RMB (*reniminbi*) is China's currency.

35. For more on constructions of masculinity through sexual orientation see W. Chou 2000; Simon 2004. For more on womanizing see Boretz 2004; Festa 2004; T. Zheng 2007, 2009. For Chinese-style machismo, see Boretz 2004, 2010; Festa 2004; S. Liu 2011; Ownby 2004.

36. See M. Huang 2006; K. Louie 2002; X. Zhong 2000.

37. Margery Wolf is one of the rare and early exceptions in that she focuses on both masculinity and femininity in her book *The House of Lim* (1968). Susan Brownell and Jeffrey Wasserstrom's edited volume *Chinese Femininities/ Chinese Masculinities* (Brownell and Wasserstrom 2002a) is also notable for giving equal attention to men in a series of studies on gender issues in China. In framing the title as plural masculinities, they also subvert tropes of a unified patriarchal system and choose instead to explore a range of ways that establish male/female relations and power hierarchies.

38. For ritual, see Kipnis 1994. For the use of women as currencies of exchange, see Boretz 2004; Festa 2004, T. Zheng 2007.

39. Boretz 2004:183.

40. Interview. Guan Yang. July 16, 2010.

41. See K. Cheung 2002; Fitzgerald 1996; Harrist 2005; Z. Shen 2001; Tasker 1997; S. Zhao 2004.

CHAPTER 2

1. N. Zhang 1049–54:29.

2. Taken from Boorman 1969:6.

3. *A Beautiful Mind* (Howard 2002); *Pi* (Aronofsky 1998). For chess, see Gorris 2000; Hallman 2003; Nabokov 1964; Waitzkin 1993; Weinreb 2007; Zaillian 1993. For Scrabble, see Fatsis 2001. Weiqi also appears in Western literature and contemporary visual media on occasion. Ursula K. Le Guin's futuristic science fiction novel *The Left Hand of Darkness* (Le Guin 1969:223) mentions the game in

passing. Herman Hesse's *The Glass Bead Game* (1943) uses Weiqi as the inspiration for a game that becomes the focus for the elite of his fictional quasi-religious utopian society. Neither author seems overly concerned with the rules of the game—Le Guin refers to it is as a "game played on squares with little stones" (1969:223). Unlike Hesse, Le Guin refers to the game by name (using the term "*Go*"). Hesse adds a musical component, which is clearly an intentional deviation from the real game. Instead, both novels use Weiqi as a metaphor for something that is futuristic in its complexity and exotic in its otherness.

4. One exception to this is Taiwan's novelist Zhang Xiguo's *The Chess King*, about a child prodigy of the game Five in a Row (X. Zhang 1978). For admiring depictions of eccentric gamesters see A. Cheng 1984; S. Hong 1999; Kawabata 1951.

5. For example, for Chinese chess, see A. Cheng 1984. For Weiqi, see Kawabata 1951.

6. This included fictional and historical depictions of Chinese chess (A. Cheng 1984), Five in a Row (*wuziqi*) (X. Zhang 1978), and Weiqi (S. Hong 1999).

7. For Japanese anime and manga on Weiqi see Hotta and Takeshi 1998; 2001.

8. *First Kyu* (S. Hong 1999); *The Girl Who Played Go* (S. Shan 2001); *The Go Masters* (J. Duan 1982).

9. For the statement linking Weiqi to the genetic code, see Shirakawa 2005.

10. As but a few examples of this, see T. Huang 2006; X. Kong 1981; X. Ma 2003; Mizuguchi 2003.

11. Tkacik 2007.

12. F. Dong 2005.

13. *The Three Kingdoms* (G. Luo 1321).

14. Moskowitz. n.d.

15. This is an adoption of a Japanese Weiqi term. They are not called stones in Chinese.

16. "Killing groups" is the standard terminology in English. As with so many Weiqi terms this comes from Japanese. In China, one says "eat" (*chi*) a stone or group, though there are Chinese-language terms for dead (*si*) and living (*huo*) groups.

17. The hallway imagery is my own—it is not part of the usual discourse for Weiqi.

18. For more on this, see Deleuze and Guattari 1987:353.

19. The estimates vary on this. A *New York Times* article states that on average there are thirty-five possible moves in chess and two hundred in Weiqi (Johnson 1997). The computer programmer David Mechner suggests that there are on average twenty-five possible moves in chess and two hundred and fifty possible moves in Weiqi (Mechner 1998).

20. Johnson 1997.

21. Johnson 1997; Mechner 1998.

22. Johnson 1997; Mechner 1998.

23. J. Yue 2011.

24. Ibid.

25. For more on the ways that computers have changed the ways that people play, study, and conceptualize chess, see Desjarlais 2011:152–83, Hartman 2008.

26. Flanagan 2009:81–83.

27. Ibid.

28. *A Beautiful Mind* (Howard 2002).

29. As but a few examples of this are the American Go Association Web page (n.d.), which states that Weiqi originated twenty-five hundred to four thousand years ago. In Karl Baker's *The Way to Go,* he states that Weiqi "originated in China about 4,000 years ago." Goshawk Heron's YouTube Video Tutorial for the Game of Go—Part 1 (n.d.) states that Weiqi "is at least 3,000 years old." All of this inherits a tradition of taking mythology for fact in China, which seemingly arrived in the United States through Japan's books and instructors.

30. Interview. Fang Tianfeng. October 28, 2011.

31. Zuo Qiuming n.d.:774.

32. Needham 2002:321. Needham uses the word "chess" but is clearly referring to Weiqi in this context. For assertions on Weiqi's associations with divination see Flanagan 2009:69–70; T. Hu 2009:22–23; Shirakawa 2005:71; G. Xie 2006:3, 13–15; X. Yang 2007:9–12, 52; R. Zhang 1998:7. He Yunpo also asks if there is a link with Weiqi and divination but concludes that this is subjective (Y. He 2001:91).

33. Zhang Ni. 1049–54 A.D. Quoted in Shotwell 2001:43. In fact the 19 × 19 grid produces 361 intersections, not 360. Paolo Zanon suggests that this number was intended to correlate with the Chinese solar year of the time, which was 360 days (twelve 30-day months) (Zanon 1996b:12). Yet the traditional solar and lunar calendar alternated between 29-day and 30-day months. Another possibility is the excerpt excluded the 361st intersection to keep it at an even number (with an even number of black and white stones) or omitted the middle point. Zanon also notes that *The Classic of Weiqi* (*Dunhuan Qiqing*) (502–50 A.D.) makes the same comparison (Zanon 1996b:12).

34. Shirakawa 2005:1.

35. Ibid.:28.

36. Ibid.:133.

37. Ibid.:134; G. Xie 2006:3.

38. See G. Xie 2006:13–15, 22.

39. Ibid.:95.

40. Ibid.:98–99.

41. Ibid. For more on Weiqi's historical associations with Buddhism, see Y. He 2001:305–22. English-language explorations of the meanings of Weiqi have also incorporated many of the religious allegories that I have outlined above. Earnest Brown, for example, in writing an article for the *American Go Journal,* suggests that to win the game one must avoid "greed, desire, [and] attachment," which, he points out, align perfectly with Buddhist precepts (Brown 1990). William Pinckard also

draws on the game's religious associations, stating that the game teaches one to avoid "human weaknesses: greed, anger, and stupidity" (Pinckard 2001a:5).

42. This hand position also makes it more difficult to cheat because it minimizes the obstruction of the opponent's view of the board.

43. Interview. Fang Tianfeng. October 28, 2011.

44. Ibid.

45. Z. Chen 1997.

46. Ibid.

47. Chinese chess is sometimes linked with religious metaphors as well (see A. Cheng 1984:34, 82, 122).

48. For more on "The Axe Handle Story" see Y. He 2001:348–52; T. Hu 2009:17–18.

49. The stone in the title presumably refers to the stone bridge. I have translated this from J. Xu 1993:43. Ming Dynasty essayist Xu Jialiang also wrote a poem of this story entitled "Of Wang Zhi's Sketch of the Rotted Axe Handle (*Ti wangzhi lanketu*) (see J. Xu 1993:43–44). For more on poetry about Weiqi see T. Hu 2009:326–49.

50. Bo Juyi 772–846. This English translation is from Pinckard (2001b:17), who uses the romanization Po Chü-i.

51. Bo Juyi. 1997. Translation taken from Chen Zu-yan 1997.

52. Yang Xiong. *Exemplary Sayings* circa 5 A.D. Taken from Zanon 1996a:72. As with many of the other ancient quotes, it is hard to know if this was indeed written at the time it is credited to, or if it was added to the text years later.

53. Interview. Sylvia. July 16, 2010.

54. Examples of religious imagery in other board games includes the Taiwan novel *The Chess King* (*Qiwang*) as to whether a child prodigy of the game Five in a Row (*wuziqi*) could also predict the future (X. Zhang 1978). A PRC novel bearing the same Chinese name also includes a discussion of a Buddhist style of play in Chinese chess (A. Cheng 1984).

55. For examples of such assertions, see Potter 2001:8; G. Xie 2006:24.

56. *The Confucian Analects*. Book 17, verse 22. I have translated this from Li Zehou's edition (2000).

57. Mencius. Book 11, verse 9. I have translated this from Fu Peirong's 2004 edition of Mencius.

58. Mencius. Book 8, verse 30.

59. See P. Fu 2004:227–28, for example.

60. Shirakawa 2005:12; Shotwell 2003:133.

61. Potter 2001:7; Shotwell 2001:44. For fictional accounts of betting money on Weiqi games see S. Hong 1999; Kawabata 1951.

62. For more on early Confucian condemnations of the game, see G. Xie 2006 and Zanon 1996a.

63. G. Xie 2006:88. Fox spirits were thought to be able to take human form, appearing as irresistibly beautiful women. They would then seduce men to sap their yang essence though sexual intercourse. For more on this, see Moskowitz 2004.

64. For more on this, see J. Xu 1993:45.

65. Z. Chen 1997. According to Chen Zu-yan, Weiqi poems could roughly be broken up into three groups: war metaphors, symbols of political machinations, and emblems of man's place in the "cosmic game" (Z. Chen 1997). The poet Du Fu just dabbled in the game, but Bo Juyi was reputed to be an excellent player (Z. Chen 1997).

66. Zanon 1996a.

67. For more on this, see Mizuguchi 2003:165 and J. Xu 1993:56.

68. Interview. Hong Feng. September 21, 2011.

69. For specific mention of *The Art of War* within Zhang Ni's tract, see N. Zhang 1049–54:14.

70. N. Zhang 1049–54:13.

71. Ibid.:15.

72. Ibid.

73. Interview. Fang Tianfeng. October 28, 2011.

74. G. Xie 2006:8.

75. Ibid.

76. Ibid.:9.

77. Interview. Sylvia. July 16, 2010.

78. Boorman 1969.

79. D. Lai 2004.

80. Kissinger 2012.

81. A. Lee 2000.

82. For more on the similarities between Chinese martial arts dramas and American westerns, see Moskowitz 2004.

83. S. Shan 2001:3–4.

84. *The Three Kingdoms* (G. Luo 1321).

85. Ah Cheng's novel *The Chess Master* employs a similar technique in the description of Chinese chess (1984:128).

86. Kawabata 1951. One sees a similar theme in the Chinese novel *The Chess Master* (A. Cheng 1984), in which Chinese chess is a higher calling in that the hero is uninterested in financial success or status. This is another link to tales of wandering swordsman and American westerns.

87. *Hikaru no Go* (Hotta and Obata 1998; 2001).

CHAPTER 3

1. This was taken from Ralph Sawyer's translation of Sunzi's *The Art of War,* chapter 6 (1994).

2. This excerpt was taken from Shirakawa 2005:47.

3. M. Huang 2006:17.

4. Ibid.:14.

5. Ibid.

6. Ibid.:185.

7. Louie 2002:4.

8. Ibid.:8.

9. Ibid.:11.

10. For more on this in the West, see Bordo 1993, 2000.

11. Louie 2002:16–18.

12. Song Geng suggests that talented scholars are a southern creation (G. Song 2004:3).

13. W. Chou 2000:34–35.

14. M. Huang 2006:21–22.

15. For more on this, see Moskowitz 2004.

16. W. Chou 2000:35.

17. Ibid.

18. Ibid.

19. M. Huang 2006:135.

20. Ibid.:139.

21. Ibid.:145.

22. Ibid.

23. G. Song 2004:ix, 14.

24. M. Huang 2006:91.

25. Ibid.:106.

26. Ownby 2002:228. In turn, bandits characterized themselves as Robin Hood figures who fought those in power in order to bring greater prosperity to the people (Ownby 2002:228).

27. Van Gulik 1961:296.

28. Dikötter 1998:64. For more on Chinese racist views of Westerners, see Dikötter 1995, 1997.

29. Dikötter 1998:52.

30. Watson 1998:178.

31. For Nazi imagery, see Farrer 2002:32. For stereotypes of African American males, see Morris 2004a. For references to perceived Caucasian American brute strength, see Brownell 1995:186.

32. Morris 2004a. For similar stereotypes in Japan, see Cornyetz 1994:127; Kelsky 2001.

33. Harrist 2005:182.

34. Ibid.

35. Ibid.:181.

36. Ibid.:175.

37. Ibid.:180. Significantly, in 1872, when the Japanese switched their official dress from Chinese scholars' gowns to Western garb, the Meiji emperor cited his desire to distance Japan from the traditional effeminate Chinese style of clothing (Harrist 2005:182).

38. Louie 2002:19.

39. G. Song 2004:8–9.

40. X. Zhong 2000:3–4, 88.

41. Ibid.:5.

42. Ibid.:88–89.

43. Ibid.:5.

44. Ibid.:43.

45. Ibid.:5.

46. Baranovitch 2003; de Kloet 2010; Jones 1992; Moskowitz 2010.

47. G. Song 2004:9. Again, it should be remembered that traditionally the talented scholar represented the ideal masculine form of physicality in that it was associated with being civilized (G. Song 2004:16).

48. N. Chen 2002:317.

49. Brownell 2008:58.

50. Morris 2004b: 193, 240.

51. Ibid.:22.

52. Ibid.:30.

53. Ibid.:59, 78, 83, 193.

54. Boretz 2010; N. Chen 2002:321.

55. See Tasker 1997.

56. Barmé 1995; Davis 2002; S. Lu 2000.

57. K. Cheung 2002:182.

58. M. Huang 2006:200.

59. Ibid.

60. Baranovitch 2003; de Kloet 2010; Farrer 2002; Moskowitz 2010.

61. M. Huang 2006:3, 73, 80.

62. Ibid.:4. It has also been suggested that women at times represent the Chinese state. See Barlow 1994, 2004; L. Liu 1994.

63. For more on these issues, see Moskowitz 2010.

64. M. Huang 2006:7.

65. Louie 2002.

66. For more on performing masculinity in the context of womanizing, see Boretz 2004; Festa 2004; L.. Liu 2010; T. Zheng 2007.

67. Jankowiak 2002:364.

68. For more on machismo in religious circles, see Boretz 2010.

69. X. Zhong 2000:44–45.

70. Brownell 1995:180.

71. Ibid.:181–83.

72. Farrer 2002.

73. Louie 2002:99–118; Moskowitz 2004; 2010.

74. See Hughes 2006; Schrecker. 1971; P. Wang 2001; Wei and Liu 2001.

75. Harrison 2003:85; Townsend 1996:14; G. Xu 2001.

76. Kirby 2001:ix-x.

77. Z. Shen 2001.

78. Ibid.

79. G. Xu 2001.

80. For more on this, see Wasserstrom 2003.

81. For more on the ways that the Taiwan issue intersects with PRC nationalism, see Croizier 1977; Hughes 1997.

82. Gries 2004; Hays 2004:36–38.

83. Dirlik 1993:78.

84. Hughes 2006:147.

85. Ibid.:153.

86. W. Xu 2007:78.

87. Ibid.:80.

88. Ibid.:84–86.

89. Gries 2004:93.

90. Gries 2004.

91. Ibid.:96–97.

92. Ibid.:93.

93. Ibid.

94. Ibid.:96.

95. Dirlik 1993:71.

96. For an example of this, see X. Xie 2006:111.

97. Interview. Teacher Wang. July 19, 2011.

98. Go4Gonet n.d.

99. For a telling account of the problems of such patronage, see X. Zhou n.d.

100. Taken from Power 2001:122.

101. For more on Weiqi schools that stayed open during the Cultural Revolution, see J. Guo 2000:36–37.

102. Ibid.:34, 36, 118.

103. Ibid.:129.

104. Ibid.:v.

105. The only other person to be mentioned consistently was Wu Qingyuan, although his name arose less frequently than Nie Weiping.

106. I refer to him as a career Weiqi player rather than as a professional player because he does not have an official professional rank.

107. Interview. Sun Yiguo. October 20, 2011.

108. W. Xu 2007:1.

109. Interview. Guan Yang. July 16, 2010.

110. Ibid.

111. Interview. Sylvia. July 16, 2010.

112. Interview. Teacher Zhuang. August 25, 2011.

113. Interview. Teacher Wang. July 10, 2010.

114. Interview. Liu Xiaoguan. July 29, 2011.

115. For more on Weiqi as indicating innate cultural differences between China and the West see Y. He 2001:25–50.

116. Interview. Liu Xiaoguan. July 29, 2011.

117. Interview. Hong Feng. September 21, 2011.

118. The literal translation is "to bless a blade with a ghost." The idea is that one sharpens a new blade by using it to kill someone for the first time.

119. Z. Huang 2004.

120. *The Go Masters* (Duan, Satô, and Liu 1982). As Arif Dirlik points out, this film also frames Japanese militarism in terms of a populace that is deceived by its government (Dirlik 1993:73).

121. Hotta and Takeshi 1998.

CHAPTER 4

1. Waitzkin 1984:8.

2. Woronov 2009:576–77.

3. Ibid.:571.

4. For more on this, see Donald 2002; Gerth 2010; Woronov 2009:581–82.

5. The strongest student at each school was a 5-*duan* amateur.

6. Interview. Hong Po. September 27, 2011.

7. Ibid.

8. Interview. Hong Po. August 25, 2011.

9. Ibid.

10. School X charged US$14.39 (100 RMB) for Saturday lessons, which lasted from 1:30 to 5:00 P.M., as opposed to US$7.86 (55 RMB) for an equivalent class at the Wenbo School.

11. In part this was because they received a sticker for each game that they won—an easy and tangible recording system to monitor their process.

12. Interview. Sylvia. July 16, 2010.

13. Interview. Sylvia. July 22, 2011.

14. B. Lee et al. 2010.

15. Ibid.:9.

16. Ibid.:10.

17. Ibid.

18. Ibid.

19. B. Lee et al. 2010.

20. Ibid.

21. For example, Ban Gu, a Han Dynasty historian, suggested that Weiqi could teach a king to rule, to control power, and to fight a war (G. Xie 2006:90).

22. G. Xie 2006:81.

23. T. Hu 2009:248.

24. Pan and Chen 2007:138.

25. Ibid.:150–57.

26. Ibid.:165.

27. X. Ma 2003:17.

28. This topic was broached in the preface of a biography of Zhang Xu, Taiwan's best contemporary player, for example (X. Ma 2003:18). See also, T. Hu 2009:248.

29. Interview. Sylvia. July 16, 2010.

30. Interview. Liu Xiaoguan. July 29, 2011.

31. Interview. Teacher Zhuang. August 25, 2011.

32. Stuart Rachels was at one time the youngest chess grandmaster in American history and is now a philosophy professor. Rachels finds attempts to label chess a sport dispiriting. He suggests, correctly I think, that those attempting to do so are striving, unsuccessfully, to popularize the game with those who would otherwise take no interest in it (Rachels 2008:220–21). He succinctly outlines why chess does not fit U.S. definitions of a sport (Rachels 2008:220–21).

33. Teacher Zhuang. August 25, 2011.

34. *The Masters of Go* (Kawabata 1951). For fictional portrayals of child exploitation or the pressure put on youth in relation to Chinese chess, see A. Cheng 1984. For similar themes in the game of Five in a Row (*wuziqi*) see X. Zhang 1978. For Western chess see Gorris 2000; Nabokov 1964; Waitzkin 1993; Weinreb 2007; Zaillian 1993.

35. hooks 1997:74.

36. hooks 1997.

37. For more on Foucaultian disciplinary structures in sports training, see Brownell 1995:12, 166. The Weiqi analogy is my own.

38. For more on the conceptual links in China concerning middle-class training and the strength of the nation, see Woronov 2009:570, 573–74, 581–82. The Weiqi analogy is my own.

39. Interview. Guan Yang. July 16, 2010.

40. Interview. Mother 1. September 18, 2011.

41. Interview. Mother 2. September 18, 2011.

42. Interview. Sun Yiguo. October 20, 2011.

43. Allison 2000.

44. Ibid.

45. Ibid.

CHAPTER 5

1. Chapter 1. Taken from Ralph Sawyer's translation (1994).

2. N. Zhang 1049–54:31.

3. For more on class tensions in the PRC, see Gerth 2010; Y. Zhao 2002.

4. Oster 2009.

5. Weber 2011:33. Weber calculates this at a US$1: 7.23 RMB exchange rate.

6. Nationwide, in 1958 approximately 55 percent of college students were the children of workers and farmers (D. Yang 2010:60–61). By 1965 this had risen to 71 percent (D. Yang 2010:60–61).

7. D. Yang 2010:60–61.

8. Ibid.

9. Ibid.:76.

10. X. Wu 2008.

11. Ibid.

12. Ibid.:603.

13. D. Yang 2010:82.

14. X. Wu 2008:604.

15. D. Yang 2010:80.

16. Ibid.:81.

17. D. Yang 2010.

18. X. Wu 2008.

19. X. Wang 2008:60–61. The RMB to US$ amounts were taken directly from Wang's article—I did not convert the currency here.

20. CIA factbook 2012.

21. X. Wang 2008.

22. Ibid.:61.

23. For more on this, see Sigley 2009:556–57; Song and Lee 2010:167; Tomba 2009:592–93.

24. F. Liu 2008:197.

25. For more on this, see Jacka 2009:524–25; Kipnis 2007; Murphy 2004; Song and Lee 2010:166.

26. Song and Lee 2010:166.

27. Jacka 2009:523.

28. Ibid.

29. Ibid.:523–24.

30. Schak 2009.

31. See Anagnost 2004, 2008, Jacka 2009:524–25; Murphy 2004; Woronov 2009.

32. Kipnis 2007.

33. Ibid.

34. Ibid.

35. For those who explore the disciplinary nature of *suzhi* as a neoliberal discourse, see Anagnost, 2004, 2008, Jacka 2009; Murphy 2004; Woronov 2009.

36. Jacka 2009:529; Woronov 2009.

37. Murphy 2004:11.

38. Buddhism's long tradition of charity is a notable exception to this rule.

39. Brook 1997:20; Schak 2009; Weber 2011:30.

40. Weber 2011:30.

41. For more on this, see Moskowitz 2007.

42. Interview. Xue Lei. July 29, 2011.

43. Interview. Yu Rongxin. October 26, 2011.

44. This student was not a Weiqi player. Because this statement could be construed as critical of China's political economy I have not identified the speaker here.

45. Interview. Liu Xiaoguan. July 29, 2011.

46. Interview. Hong Feng. September 21, 2011.

47. Interview. Fang Tianfeng. October 28, 2011.

48. Interview. Mr. Ma and Little Liu. August 22, 2011.

49. Interview. Sun Yiguo was not a Peking University student.

50. Interview. Xue Lei. September 25, 2011.

51. Interview. Yu Rongxin. October 26, 2011.

52. Interview. Wang Wenbo. July 8, 2010.

53. Interview. Sylvia. July 16, 2010.

54. Interview. Wang Wenbo. July 19, 2011.

55. Ibid.

56. Interview. Yu Rongxin. October 26, 2011.

57. Interview. Fan Weijing. October 26, 2011.

58. Interview. Xue Lei. September 25, 2011.

59. Interview. Sylvia. July 22, 2011.

60. Interview. Sylvia. July 16, 2010.

61. Interview. Liu Rongying. October 12, 2011.

62. Interview. Xue Lei. September 25, 2011.

CHAPTER 6

1. Murasaki 1008:329.

2. S. Hong 1999:16.

3. Editorial Board of Population Research 2002:65; Flaherty et al. 2007:1296.

4. Flaherty et al. 2007:1296. Estimates also suggest that by the year 2036 the percentage of sixty-five-year-olds and older will have risen from 7 percent of China's population to 14 percent (Gallagher-Thompson 2010:157).

5. Boermel 2006:404.

6. Flaherty et al. 2007:1296.

7. Jackson 2011:33.

8. Savishinsky 2000:20.

9. Ibid.

10. H. Zhang 2009:211.

11. 13.5 RMB. H. Zhang 2009:212. I am using Zhang's currency conversion rate here.

12. H. Zhang 2009:210.

13. Interview. Hong Feng. September 21, 2011.

14. Kageyama (1978:34) and Traphagan (2000) have also documented this belief in Japan.

15. Boermel 2006:411.

16. Interview. Elder Liu. September 7, 2011.

17. Interview. Sylvia. July 16, 2010.

18. Ibid.

19. Interview. Mr. Rui. August 11, 2011.

20. Little Liu told me that he had a 3-*duan* amateur rank.

21. Boermel 2006:408.

22. For more on this, see Shank and Wasserstrom 2012:6.

23. Interview. Teacher Wang. July 19, 2011.

24. Interview. Sun Yiguo. October 20, 2011.

25. Interview. Mr. Rui. August 11, 2011.

26. Interview. Hong Feng. September 21, 2011.

27. T. Hu 2009:246.

28. I never saw either of the thirty-year-old men play, though they frequently came to watch for a few hours.

29. Interview. Yu Rongxin. October 26, 2011.

30. Interview. Hong Feng. September 21, 2011.

31. Interview. Little Liu. August 22, 2011.

32. September 7, 2011. Given this interaction it would be difficulty to fully express my satisfaction in beating him in a game the next time we met.

33. September 7, 2011.

CHAPTER 7

1. Dibbell 1998:53.

2. Desjarlais 2011:57.

3. Fatsis 2001:309.

4. Quoted in Desjarlais 2011:148.

5. Because of the sensitive nature of this account I have used a pseudonym here.

6. Interview. Mr. Sun. July 2, 2007. Taipei.

GLOSSARY OF TERMS

ATARI See *dachi*.

CHEN YI (1901–72) Chen Yi was a military commander during the communist revolution. He served as vice premier of the People's Republic of China from 1954 to 1972 and as a foreign minister from 1958 to 1972. Most people attribute China's current strength in Weiqi to Chen Yi's organization of Weiqi as a national sport. He is also thought to be primarily responsible for the game's ability to survive the Cultural Revolution relatively unscathed.

DACHI (JAPANESE: ATARI) A Weiqi term indicating that a stone or a group of stones is in danger. This is the equivalent of being in check in chess.

DAN See *ranks*.

DINGSHI (JAPANESE: JOSEKI) A Weiqi term that refers to set opening patterns. It is thought that Japanese people put more faith in these set openings.

DUAN See *ranks*.

GO SEIGEN See *Wu Qingyuan*.

JI See *ranks*.

JOSEKI See *dingshi*.

KILL A GROUP A Weiqi term referring to the act of ensuring that an opponent's group of stones can be taken off the board. Like so many English Weiqi terms, this is from Japan. The Chinese refer to "eating" (*chi*) a group.

KYU See *ranks*.

LIBERTIES (QI) A Weiqi term indicating the number of unblocked spaces one has for any given group.

NIE WEIPING (1952-PRESENT) Nie Weiping was the first Weiqi player to defeat Japanese Weiqi professionals at an international tournament. When he did so he became a hero in China in ways that are reminiscent of American Bobby Fischer after his defeat of Russian opponent Boris Spassky during the Cold War. Nie Weiping's victory is largely responsible for the popularity of Weiqi in China today.

QI See *liberties*.

RANKS There are three categories of Weiqi ranks: *ji* (Japanese: *kyu*), amateur *duan* (Japanese: *dan*), and professional *duan* (*dan* professional). *Ji* is weaker than amateur *duan,* which is weaker than professional *duan*.

RENMINBI See *RMB*

RMB (renminbi) The PRC's currency.

SEIZING THE INITIATIVE (Chinese: *xianshou*, Japanese: *sente*) A Weiqi term that emphasizes that keeping the initiative is essential to winning the game.

SENTE See *seizing the initiative*.

STONES The English term for Weiqi pieces.

SUZHI Usually defined in English as "quality," this term is part of a state-endorsed movement to encourage citizens to act in a refined manner. Heavily laden with associations of the educated middle class, Western scholars associate the term with civil society, neoliberalism, and class stratification.

WEN AND WU *Wen* (the refined and cultured) and *wu* (the martial). In Imperial China, *wen*-style manhood was the ideal, and the more physical orientation of *wu* was stigmatized. Somewhat paradoxically, Weiqi can represent both *wen* and *wu*.

WENROU Sensitive and caring. In the United States, *wenrou* males might be stigmatized as androgynous. In contrast, in China's mass media the *wenrou* male is a highly idealized form of manhood.

WU QINGYUAN (1914-present) Wu Qingyuan (a.k.a. Go Seigen) was born in China but moved to Japan when he was seven years old. He transformed the conceptualization of the game to emphasize the importance of the middle of the board. This overturned centuries-long understandings of the game.

XIANSHOU See *seizing the initiative*.

BIBLIOGRAPHY

Allison, Anne. 2000. *Permitted and Prohibited Desires: Mothers, Comics, and Censorship in Japan.* Berkeley: University of California Press.

American Go Association Web Page. n.d. "A Brief History of Go." www.usgo.org/brief-history-go

Anagnost, Ann. 2004. "The Corporeal Politics of Quality (*Suzhi*)." *Public Culture* 16(2):189–208.

———. 2008. "From 'Class' to 'Social Strata': Grasping the Social Totality in Reform-Era China." *Third World Quarterly* 29(3):497–519.

Aronofsky, Darren, dir. 1998. *Pi.* Los Angeles: Lions Gate.

Baker, Karl. [1986] 2008. "The Way to Go." www.usgo.org/files/pdf/W2Go4E-book.pdf

Baranovitch, Nimrod. 2003. *China's New Voices: Popular Music, Ethnicity, Gender, and Politics, 1978–1997.* Berkeley: University of California Press.

Barlow, Tani E. 1994. "Theorizing Woman: *Funu, Guojia, Jiating* (Chinese Woman, Chinese State, Chinese Family)." In *Body, Subject and Power in China,* eds. Angela Zito and Tani E. Barlow, 253–89. Chicago: University of Chicago Press.

———. 2004. *The Question of Women in Chinese Feminism.* Durham, NC: Duke University Press.

Barmé, Geremie. 1995. "To Screw Foreigners Is Patriotic: China's Avant-Garde Nationalists." In *Chinese Nationalism,* ed. Jonathan Unger, 183–208. Armonk, NY: M. E. Sharpe.

Boermel, Anna. 2006. "'No Wasting' and 'Empty Nesters': 'Old Age' in Beijing." *Oxford Development Studies* 34(4):401–18.

Boorman, Scott A. [1969] 1971. *The Protracted Game: A Wei-Ch'i Interpretation of Maoist Revolutionary Strategy.* New York: Oxford University Press.

Bordo, Susan. 1993. "Reading the Male Body." *Michigan Quarterly Review* 32: 696–737.

———. 2000. *The Male Body: A New Look at Men in Public and in Private.* New York: Farrar, Straus and Giroux.

Boretz, Avron. 2004. "Carousing and Masculinity: The Cultural Production of Gender in Taiwan." In *Gender Roles and Gender Consciousness in a Changing Society,* eds. Anru Lee, Catherine Farris, and Murray Rubinstein, 171–98. New York: M. E. Sharpe.

———. 2010. *Gods, Ghosts, and Gangsters: Ritual Violence, Martial Arts, and Masculinity on the Margins of Chinese Society.* Honolulu: University of Hawai'i Press.

Brook, Timothy. 1997. "Auto-Organization in Chinese Society." In *Civil Society in China,* eds. Timothy and B. Michael Frolic Brook, 19–45. Armonk, NY: M. E. Sharpe.

Brown, Earnest. 1990. "Go: The Study of Buddhist Ideals." *American Go Journal* 24:1.

Brownell, Susan. 1995. *Training the Body for China: Sports in the Moral Order of the People's Republic.* Chicago: University of Chicago Press.

———. 1999. "Strong Women and Impotent Men: Sports, Gender, and Nationalism in Chinese Public Culture." In *Spaces of Their Own: Women's Public Sphere in Transnational China,* ed. Mayfair Mei-hui Yang, 207–32. Minnesota: University of Minnesota Press.

———. 2008. *Beijing's Games: What the Olympics Mean to China.* New York: Rowman & Littlefield Publishers.

Brownell, Susan, and Jeffrey N. Wasserstrom, eds. 2002a. *Chinese Femininities/ Chinese Masculinities: A Reader.* Berkeley: University of California Press.

Brownell, Susan, and Jeffrey N. Wasserstrom. 2002b. "Theorizing Femininities and Masculinities." In *Chinese Femininities/ Chinese Masculinities,* eds. Susan Brownell and Jeffrey N. Wasserstrom, 1–41. Berkeley: University of California Press.

Chen, Nancy N. 2002. "Embodying *Qi* and Masculinities in Post-Mao China." In *Chinese Femininities/Chinese Masculinities: A Reader,* eds. Susan Brownell and Jeffrey N. Wasserstrom, 315–29. Berkeley: University of California Press.

Chen, Zu-yan. 1997. "The Art of Black and White: Wei-Ch'i in Chinese Poetry." *Journal of the American Oriental Society* 117(4):643–53.

Cheng, Ah (Trans. W. Jenner). [1984] 2005. *The Chess Master (Qi wang).* Hong Kong: Chinese University Press.

Cheung, King-Kok. 2002. "The Woman Warrior Versus the Chinaman Pacific: Must a Chinese American Critic Choose between Feminism and Heroism?" In *The Masculinity Studies Reader,* eds. Rachel Adams and David Savran, 175–87. New York: Blackwell.

Chou, Wah-shan. 2000. *Tongzhi: Politics of Same-Sex Eroticism in Chinese Societies.* Binghamton, NY: Haworth.

CIA factbook. 2012. "CIA Factbook: East and Southeast Asia: China." www.cia.gov/library/publications/the-world-factbook/geos/ch.html

Cornyetz, Nina. 1994. "Fetishized Blackness: Hip-Hop and Racial Desire in Contemporary Japan." *Social Text* 41:113–39.

Croizier, Ralph C. 1977. *Koxinga and Chinese Nationalism: History, Myth, and the Hero.* Cambridge, MA: Harvard University Asia Center.

Davis, Deborah. 2002. "When a House Becomes His Home." In *Popular China: Unofficial China in a Globalizing Society*, eds. Paul Pickowicz, Perry Link, and Richard Madsen, 231–50. New York: Rowman & Littlefield.

de Kloet, Jeroen. 2010. *China with a Cut: Globalization, Urban Youth and Popular Music*. Amsterdam: Amsterdam University Press.

Deleuze, Gilles, and Félix Guattari (Trans. Brian Massumi). 1987. *A Thousand Plateaus: Capitalism and Schizophrenia*. Minneapolis: University of Minnesota Press.

Desjarlais, Robert R. 2012. *Counterplay: An Anthropologist at the Chessboard*. Berkeley: University of California Press.

Dibbell, Julian. 1998. *My Tiny Life: Crime and Passion in a Virtual World*. New York: Holt Paperbacks.

Dikötter, Frank. 1995. *Sex, Culture, and Modernity in China: Medical Science and the Construction of Sexual Identities in the Early Republican Period*. London: Hurst & Company.

———. 1997. "Racial Discourse in China: Continuities and Permutations." In *The Construction of Racial Identities in China and Japan*, ed. Frank Dikötter, 12–33. Honolulu: University of Hawai'i Press.

———. 1998. "Hairy Barbarians, Furry Primates, and Wild Men: Medical Science and Cultural Representations of Hair in China." In *Hair: Its Power and Meaning in Asian Cultures*, eds. Alf Hiltebeitel and Barbara D. Miller, 51–74. Albany: State University of New York Press.

Dirlik, Arif. 1993. "'Past Experience, if Not Forgotten, Is a Guide to the Future'; or, What is in a Text? The Politics of History in Chinese-Japanese Relations." In *Japan in the World*, eds. Miyoshi Masao and H. D. Harootunian, 49–78. Durham, NC: Duke University Press.

Donald, Stephanie Hemelryk. 2002. "Crazy Rabbits! Children's Media Culture." In *Media in China: Consumption, Content and Crisis*, eds. Stephanie Hemelryk Donald, Michael Keane, and Yin Hong, 128–38. New York: Routledge.

Dong, Fangzhi. 2005. *Actually, Cao Cao Was a Management Genius* (*Qishi, cao cao shi ge guanli tiancai*). Taipei, Taiwan: National Library Publishing House.

Duan, Ji-shun, Jun'ya Satô, and Shu'an Liu, dirs. 1982. *The Go Masters*. Beijing, China: Beijing Film Studio.

Editorial Board of Population Research. 2002. "China's Aging Population in the Twenty-first Century: How Should We Respond?" *Chinese Sociology and Anthropology* 34(2):65–99.

Edmonds, David, and John Eidinow. [2004] 2005. *Bobby Fischer Goes to War: How a Lone American Star Defeated the Soviet Chess Machine*. New York: HarperCollins.

Farrer, James. 2002. *Opening Up: Youth Sex Culture and Market Reform in Shanghai*. Chicago: University of Chicago Press.

Fatsis, Stefan. 2001. *Word Freak: Heartbreak, Triumph, Genius, and Obsession in the World of Competitive Scrabble Players*. New York: Penguin Books.

Festa, Paul E. 2004. "The Blue Whirlwind Strikes Below the Belt: Male Sexuality, Gender Politics, and the Viagra Craze in Taiwan." In *Gender Roles and Gender*

Consciousness in a Changing Society, eds. Anru Lee, Catherine Farris, and Murray Rubinstein, 199–220. New York: M. E. Sharpe.

Fitzgerald, John. 1996. "The Nationless State: The Search for a Nation in Modern Chinese Nationalism." In *Chinese Nationalism,* ed. Jonathan Unger, 56–85. Armonk, NY: M. E. Sharpe.

Flaherty, Joseph, et al. 2007. "China: The Aging Giant." *International Health Affairs* 55:1295–300.

Flanagan, Mary. 2009. *Critical Play: Radical Game Design.* Cambridge, MA: MIT Press.

Foster, Angus. 2012. "China Confirms Leadership Change." *BBC News Asia.* www.bbc.co.uk/news/world-asia-20030681

Fu, Peirong. 2004. *Understanding Mengzi (Jiedou Mengzi).* Taipei, Taiwan: Lixu Cultural Business.

Gallagher-Thompson, Dolores, et al. 2010."Families Dealing with Dementia: Insights from Mainland China, Hong Kong, and Taiwan." In *Aging Asia: The Economic and Social Implications of Rapid Demographic Change in China, Japan, and South Korea,* eds. Karen Eggleston and Shipad Tuljapurkar, 157–76. Stanford, CA: Walter H. Shorenstein Asia-Pacific Research Center.

Gerth, Karl. 2010. *As China Goes, So Goes the World: How Chinese Consumers Are Transforming Everything.* New York: Hill and Wang.

Go4Gonet. n.d. www.go4go.net/v2/modules/news/article.php?storyid = 117

GoshawkHeron's YouTube Video Tutorial for the Game of Go—Part 1 (n.d.). www.youtube.com/watch?v = gECcsSeRcNo&feature = plc

Gorris, Marleen, dir. 2000. *The Luzhin Defense.* Los Angeles: Sony Pictures.

Gries, Peter Hays. 2004. *China's New Nationalism: Pride, Politics, and Diplomacy.* Berkeley: University of California Press.

Guo, Juan. 2000. *The World of Chinese Go: Some Stories about Chinese Go from 1970.* Santa Monica: Kiseido Publishing.

Hallman, J. C. 2003. *The Chess Artist: Genius, Obsession, and the World's Oldest Game.* New York: Thomas Dunne Books.

Harrison, Henrietta. 2003. "Newspapers and Nationalism in Rural China 1890–1929." In *Twentieth-Century China: New Approaches,* ed. Jeffrey Wasserstrom, 83–102. New York: Routledge.

Harrist Jr., Robert. 2005. "Clothes Make the Man: Dress, Modernity, and Masculinity in China Ca. 1912–1937." In *Body and Face in Chinese Visual Culture,* eds. Wu Hung and Katherine R. Tsiang, 171–93. Cambridge, MA: Harvard University Press.

Hartman, John. 2008. "Garry Kasparov Is a Cyborg, or What ChessBase Teaches Us about Technology." In *Philosophy Looks at Chess,* ed. Benjamin Hale, 39–64. Chicago: Open Court.

Hays, Peter. 2004. *China's New Nationalism: Pride, Politics, and Diplomacy.* Berkeley: University of California Press.

He, Yunpo. 2001. *Weiqi and Chinese Culture (Weiqi yu zhongguo wenhua).* Beijing: People's Publishing House.

Hesse, Hermann (Trans. Richard Winston and Clara Winston). [1943] 1990. *The Glass Bead Game*. New York: Picador.

Hewitt, Duncan. 2008. *China: Getting Rich First: A Modern Social History*. New York: Pegasus.

Hong, Sung-Hwa. [1999] 2003. *First Kyu*. Corte Madera, CA: Good Move Press.

Honig, Emily, and Gail Hershatter. 1988. *Personal Voices: Chinese Women in the 1980's*. Stanford, CA: Stanford University Press.

hooks, bell. 1997. "Eros, Eroticism, and the Pedagogical Process." In *Back to Reality? Social Experience and Cultural Studies,* ed. Angela McRobbie, 74–80. New York: Manchester University Press.

Hotta, Yumi, and Takeshi Obata (Chinese Trans. Xie Jiayun). [1998] 2005. *Hikaru no Go* (Chinese Trans: *Qihun*). Taipei: Dongli.

Hotta, Yumi, and Takeshi Obata. 2001. *Hikaru no Go Anime*. Tokyo, Japan: VIZ Media.

Howard, Ron, dir. 2002. *A Beautiful Mind*. Los Angeles: DreamWorks Pictures.

Hu, Tingmei. 2009. *The State of Black and White* (*Heibai zhi jing*). Shanghai: Shanghai Cultural Publishers.

Huang, Martin W. 2006. *Negotiating Masculinities in Late Imperial China*. Honolulu: University of Hawai'i Press.

Huang, Tiancai. 2006. *From Rebellious Teenager to Famous Honinbo: Lin Haifeng's Weiqi* (*Cong panni shaonian dao mingren ben yingfang: Lin Haifeng weiqi*). Taipei, Taiwan: Lingking Books.

Huang, Zichun. 2004. "The Sad Song of Japan's Weiqi (*Riben weiqi de beige*)." Weiqi Report Amateur Game World Section—Game Friends (*Weiqi bao yeyu qi jie*qiyou*).

Hughes, Christopher R. 1997. *Taiwan and Chinese Nationalism: National Identity and Status in International Society*. New York: Routledge.

———. 2006. *Chinese Nationalism in the Global Era*. New York: Routledge.

IGS Go Server. n.d. www.pandanet-igs.com/communities/pandanet

Jacka, Tamara. 2009. "Cultivating Citizens: *Suzhi* (Quality) Discourse in the PRC." *Positions* 17(3):523–35.

Jackson, Richard. 2011. "Can an Aging China be a Rising China?" *China Business Review* (April-June):32–58.

Jankowiak, William. 2002. "Proper Men and Proper Women: Parental Affection in the Chinese Family." In *Chinese Femininities/Chinese Masculinities: A Reader,* eds. Susan Brownell and Jeffrey N. Wasserstrom, 361–80. Berkeley: University of California Press.

Johnson, George. 1997. "To Test a Powerful Computer, Play an Ancient Game." *New York Times*. July 29:1.

Jones, Andrew F. 1992. *Like a Knife: Ideology and Genre in Contemporary Chinese Popular Music*. Ithaca, NY: Cornell University Press.

Kawabata, Yasunari (Trans. Edward G. Seidensticker). [1951] 1996. *The Master of Go*. New York: Vintage International.

Kelsky, Karen. 2001. *Women on the Verge: Japanese Women, Western Dreams*. Durham, NC: Duke University Press.

KGS Go Server. n.d. www.gokgs.com

Kipnis, Andrew. 1994. "(Re)Inventing *Li: Koutou* and Subjectification in Rural Shandong." In *Body, Subject and Power in China,* eds. Angela Zito and Tani E. Barlow, 201–23. Chicago: University of Chicago Press.

———. 2007. "Neoliberalism Reified: *Suzhi* Discourse and the Tropes of Neoliberalism in the People's Republic of China." *Journal of the Royal Anthropological Institute* 13:383–400.

Kirby, William C. 2001. "Foreword." In *Chinese Nationalism in Perspective: Historical and Recent Cases,* eds. C. X. George Wei and Xiaoyuan Liu, ix-x. Westport, CT: Greenwood.

Kissinger, Henry. 2012. *On China.* New York: Penguin Books.

Kong, Xiangming. 1981. *Everything I Know about Hideyuki Fujisawa (Wo suo renshi de tengzexiuxing).* Hsin-ju, Taiwan: Fanyi.

Kraus, Richard Curt. 1989. *Pianos and Politics in China: Middle-Class Ambitions and the Struggle over Western Music.* New York: Oxford University Press.

Lai, David. 2004. "Learning from the Stones: A Go Approach to Mastering China's Strategic Concept, *Shi." Strategic Studies Institute of the Us Army War College.* www.strategicstudiesinstitute.army.mil/pubs/display.cfm?PubID = 378

Le Guin, Ursula K. [1969] 1976. *The Left Hand of Darkness.* New York: Ace Books.

Lee, Ang, dir. 2000. *Crouching Tiger, Hidden Dragon.* Los Angeles: Sony Pictures.

Lee, Boreom, et al. 2010. "White Matter Neuroplastic Changes in Long-Term Trained Players of the Game of "Baduk" (Go): A Voxel-Based Diffusion-Tensor Imaging Study." *NeuroImage* 52:9–19.

Li, Zehou. 2000. *A Modern Reading of the Confucian Analects (Lunyu jindu).* Taipei, Taiwan: Yunchen Cultural Publishing Company.

Liu, Fengshu. 2006. "Boys as Only-Children and Girls as Only-Children—Parental Gendered Expectations of the Only-Child in the Nuclear Chinese Family in Present-Day China." *Gender and Education* 18(5):491–505.

———. 2008. "Constructing the Autonomous Middle-Class Self in Today's China: The Case of Young-Adult Only-Children University Students." *Journal of Youth Studies* 11(2):193–212.

Liu, Lydia H. 1994. "The Female Body and Nationalist Discourse: Manchuria in Xiao Hong's Field of Life and Death." In *Body, Subject and Power in China,* eds. Angela Zito and Tani E. Barlow, 157–77. Chicago: University of Chicago Press.

Liu, Lucia Huwy-Min. 2010. "Substance, Masculinity, and Class: Betel Nut Consumption and Embarrassing Modernity in Taiwan." In *Popular Culture in Taiwan: Charismatic Modernity,* ed. Marc L. Moskowitz, 131–48. New York: Routledge.

Liu, Shao-hua. 2011. *Passage to Manhood: Youth, Migration, Heroin, and AIDS in Southwest China.* Stanford, CA: Stanford University Press.

Louie, Kam. 2002. *Theorizing Chinese Masculinity: Society and Gender in China.* Cambridge: Cambridge University Press.

Luo Guanzhong (Trans. Moss Roberts). [1321] 2005. *The Three Kingdoms.* Beijing: Foreign Languages Press.

Ma, Xiping. 2003. *Chess Prodigy—Zhang Xu's Story (Tiansheng qicai—zhang xu de gushi)*. Taipei, Taiwan: Peace Culture Company.

Mechner, David. A. 1998. "All Systems Go." *The Sciences* 38:32–37.

Mizuguchi, Fujio (Trans. from Japanese to Chinese by Lu Zhenfang). [2003] 2006. *Weiqi Saint Go Seigen (Qisheng wu qingyuan)*. Taipei, Taiwan: Metropolitan Culture Enterprise Company.

Morris, Andrew D. 2004a."Baseball, History, the Local and the Global in Taiwan." In *The Minor Arts of Daily Life: Popular Culture in Taiwan,* eds. Andrew D. Morris, David K. Jordan, and Marc L. Moskowitz, 176–203. Honolulu: University of Hawai'i Press.

———. 2004b. *Marrow of the Nation: A History of Sport and Physical Culture in Republican China*. Berkeley: University of California Press.

Moskowitz, Marc L. 2004. "Yang-Sucking She-Demons: Penetration, Fear of Castration, and Other Freudian Angst in Modern Chinese Cinema." In *The Minor Arts of Daily Life: Popular Culture in Modern Taiwan,* eds. David K. Jordan, Andrew D. Morris, Marc L. Moskowitz, 204–17. Honolulu: University of Hawai'i Press.

———. 2007. "Failed Families and Quiet Individualism: Women's Strategies of Resistance in Urban Taiwan." *Journal of Archaeology and Anthropology,* 67:157–84.

———. 2010. *Cries of Joy, Songs of Sorrow: Chinese Pop Music and Its Cultural Connotations*. Honolulu: University of Hawai'i Press.

———. n.d. Weiqi Links. http://people.cas.sc.edu/moskowitz/weiqi/weiqilinks.htm

Murasaki, Shikibu (Trans. Royall Tyler). [1008] 2002. *The Tale of Genji*. New York: Penguin.

Murphy, Rachel. 2004. "Turning Peasants into Modern Chinese Citizens: 'Population Quality' Discourse, Demographic Transition and Primary Education." *China Quarterly* 177:1–20.

Nabokov, Vladimir. [1964] 1990. *The Defense*. New York: Vintage Books.

Needham, Joseph, et al. 2000. *Science and Civilisation in China*. Cambridge: Cambridge University Press.

Oster, Shai. 2009. "China's Rich Youth Spark Bitter Divide." *Wall Street Journal* (Eastern edition), September 22, p. A.1.

Ownby, David. 2002. "Approximations of Chinese Bandits: Perverse Rebels, Romantic Heroes, or Frustrated Bachelors?" In *Chinese Femininities/Chinese Masculinities: A Reader,* eds. Susan Brownell and Jeffrey N. Wasserstrom, 226–50. Berkeley: University of California Press.

Pan, Ning, and Chen Caiyun. 2007. *Magical Weiqi Girl (Weiqi xiaomonü)*. Taipei, Taiwan: Forest of Game Cultures Publishing.

Pinckard, William. 2001a. "Go and the Three Games." In *The Go Player's Almanac,* ed. Richard Bozulich, 4–5. Los Angeles: Kiseido.

———. 2001b. "The History and Philosophy of Go." In *The Go Player's Almanac,* ed. Richard Bozulich, 15–25. Los Angeles: Kiseido.

Post.weiqi.com. 2012. http://post.weiqi.tom.com/s/34000AB36211.html

Potter, Donald. 2001."Go in the Classics." In *The Go Player's Almanac,* ed. Richard Bozulich, 6–11. Los Angeles: Kiseido.

Power, John. 2001. "A Brief History of Modern Go: From 1868 to the Present." In *The Go Player's Almanac,* ed. Richard Bozulich, 84–127. Los Angeles: Kiseido.

Rachels, Stuart. 2008. "The Reviled Art." In *Philosophy Looks at Chess,* ed. Benjamin Hale, 209–25. Chicago: Open Court.

Schak, David. 2009. "The Development of Civility in Taiwan." *Pacific Affairs* 82(3):447–65.

Schrecker, John E. 1971. *Imperialism and Chinese Nationalism.* Cambridge, MA: Harvard University Press.

Shan, Sa (Trans. Adriana Hunter). [2001] 2003. *The Girl Who Played Go.* New York: Vintage Books.

Shank, Megan and Jeffrey Wasserstrom. 2012. "Anxious Times in a Rising China: Lurching Toward a New Social Compact." *Dissent* (Winter):5–11.

Shen, Zhijia. 2001. "Nationalism in the Context of Survival: The Sino-Japanese War Fought in a Local Arena, Zouping, 1937–1945." In *Chinese Nationalism in Perspective: Historical and Recent Cases,* eds. C. X. George Wei and Xiaoyuan Liu, 75–97. Westport, CT: Greenwood.

Shirakawa, Masayoshi. 2005. *A Journey in Search of the Origins of Go.* Santa Monica, CA: Yutopian Enterprises.

Shotwell, Peter. 2001. "Speculations on the Origins of Go." In *The Go Player's Almanac,* ed. Richard Bozulich, 43–63. Los Angeles: Kiseido.

———. 2003. *More Than a Game.* Tokyo: Tuttle.

Sigley, Gary. 2009. "*Suzhi,* the Body, and the Fortunes of Technoscientific Reasoning in Contemporary China." *Positions* 17(3): 537–66.

Simon, Scott. 2004. "From Hidden Kingdom to Rainbow Community: The Making of Gay and Lesbian Identity in Taiwan." In *The Minor Arts of Daily Life: Popular Culture in Modern Taiwan,* eds. David K. Jordan, Andrew D. Morris, and Marc L. Moskowitz, 67–88. Honolulu: University of Hawai'i Press.

Singapore Weiqi Association. n.d. "Weiqi Rank." www.weiqi.org.sg/WeiqiRank.aspx

Song, Geng. 2004. *The Fragile Scholar: Power and Masculinity in Chinese Culture.* Hong Kong: Hong Kong University Press.

Song, Geng, and Tracy K. Lee. 2010. "Consumption, Class Formation and Sexuality: Reading Men's Lifestyle Magazines in China." *China Journal* 64:159–77.

Sunzi (Trans. Ralph D. Sawyer). [722–481 B.C.] 1994. *The Art of War.* Taipei: SMC.

Tasker, Yvonne. 1997. "Fists of Fury: Discourses of Race and Masculinity in Martial Arts Cinema." In *Race and the Subject of Masculinities,* eds. Michael Uebel and Harry Stecopoulos, 315–36. Durham, NC: Duke University Press.

Tkacik, John J. 2007. *Reshaping the Taiwan Strait.* New York: Heritage Books.

Tom.sport. n.d. http://weiqi.sports.tom.com

Tomba, Luigi. 2009. "Of Quality, Harmony, and Community: Civilization and the Middle Class in Urban China." *Positions* 17(3):591–616.

Kageyama, Toshiro (trans. James Davies). [1978] 1996. *Lessons in the Fundamentals of Go.* Tokyo, Japan: Kiseido.

Townsend, James. 1996. "Chinese Nationalism." In *Chinese Nationalism,* ed. Jonathan Unger, 1–30. Armonk, NY: M. E. Sharpe.

Traphagan, John. 2000. *Taming Oblivion: Aging Bodies and the Fear of Senility in Japan.* Albany: State University of New York Press.

Van Gulik, Robert. 1961. *Sexual Life in Ancient China: A Preliminary Survey of Chinese Sex and Society from ca. 1500 B.C. until 1644 A.D.* Leiden, Netherlands: E. J. Brill.

Waitzkin, Fred. [1984] 1993. *Searching for Bobby Fischer: The Father of a Prodigy Observes the World of Chess.* New York: Penguin.

Wang, Peter Chen-Main. 2001. "A Patriotic Christian Leader in Changing China— Yu Rizhang in the Turbulent 1920s." In *Chinese Nationalism in Perspective: Historical and Recent Cases,* eds. C. X. George Wei and Xiaoyuan Liu, 33–51. Westport, CT: Greenwood.

Wang, Xing. 2008. "Divergent Identities, Convergent Interests: The Rising Middle-Income Stratum in China and its Civic Awareness." *Journal of Contemporary China* 17(54):53–69.

Wang, Xiao-lei, Ronan Bernas, and Philippe Eberhard. 2008. "Responding to Children's Everyday Transgressions in Chinese Working-Class Families." *Journal of Moral Education* 37(1):55–79.

Wasserstrom, Jeffrey. 2003. "The Year of Living Anxiously: China's 1999." In *Twentieth-Century China: New Approaches,* ed. Jeffrey Wasserstrom, 256–65. New York: Routledge.

———. 2007. *China's Brave New World and Other Tales for Global Times.* Bloomington: Indiana University Press.

Watson, James L. 1998. "Living Ghosts: Long-Haired Destitutes in Colonial Hong Kong." In *Hair: Its Power and Meaning in Asian Cultures,* eds. Alf Hiltebeitel and Barbara D. Miller, 177–94. Albany: State University of New York Press.

Weber, Ian. 2011. "Mobile, Online and Angry: The Rise of China's Middle-Class Civil Society?" *Critical Arts: A South-North Journal of Cultural & Media Studies* 25(1):25–45.

Wei, C. X. George, and Xiaoyuan Liu. 2001. "Introduction." In *Chinese Nationalism in Perspective: Historical and Recent Cases,* eds. C. X. George Wei and Xiaoyuan Liu, 1–11. Westport, CT: Greenwood.

Weinreb, Michael. 2007. *The Kings of New York: A Year among the Geeks, Oddballs, and Geniuses Who Make Up America's Top High School Chess Team.* New York: Gotham Books.

Wiki.goratings. n.d. "Go Ranks and Ratings." http://en.wikipedia.org/wiki/Go_ranks_and_ratings

Wolf, Margery. 1968. *The House of Lim: A Study of a Chinese Farm Family.* Englewood Cliffs, NJ: Prentice Hall.

Woronov, Terry. 2009. "Governing China's Children: Governmentality and 'Education for Quality.'" *Positions* 17(3): 567–89.

Wu, Xiaoxin. 2008. "The Power of Positional Competition and Market Mechanism: A Case Study of Recent Parental Choice Development in China." *Journal of Education Policy* 23(6): 595–614.

Xie, Guofang. 2006. *The Sky Is Round and the Space Is Square—the Language and Culture of Weiqi (Tianyuan difang—qiyu wenhua)*. Hubei, PRC: Hubei People's Publishing.

Xu, Guoqi. 2001. "Internationalism, Nationalism, National Identity: China from 1895 to 1919." In *Chinese Nationalism in Perspective: Historical and Recent Cases*, eds. George Wei and Xiaoyuan Liu, 101–220. Westport, CT: Greenwood Press.

Xu, Jialiang.1993. *Ancient China's Games of Skill (Zhongguo gudai qiyi)*. Taipei: Taiwan Commercial Books.

Xu, Wu. 2007. *Chinese Cyber Nationalism: Evolution, Characteristics, and Implications*. New York: Lexington Books.

Yang, Xiaoguo. 2007. *Weiqi's Origins (Weiqi suoyuan)*. Shanxi, PRC: Shanxi.

Yang, Dongping. 2010. "An Empirical Study of Higher Education Admissions Opportunities in China." *Chinese Education and Society* 43(6):59–85.

Yue, Jin. 2011. "Human Weiqi Players' Battle, [Professional Weiqi Player] Yu Bing Suffers Defeat *(Weiqi Ren Jizhan, Yubin Liangdu Baibei)*." *SZ News (Jingbao)*, September 17. http://jb.sznews.com/html/2011–09/17/content_1750892.htm

Zaillian, Steven, dir. 1993. *Searching for Bobby Fischer*. Los Angeles: Mirage Entertainment.

Zanon, Paulo. 1996a. "The Opposition of the Literati to the Game of Weiqi in Ancient China." *Asian and African Studies* 5(1):70–82.

Zanon, Paulo. 1996b. "Weiqi in Thirteen Chapters *(Qijing Shisanpian)*." In "*Qijing Shisanpian* (The Classic of Weiqi in Thirteen Chapters) Its History and Translation," 1–37. www.figg.org/areafile/qijing.html

Zhang, Hong. 2009. "The New Realities of Aging in Contemporary China: Coping with the Decline in Family Care." In *The Cultural Context of Aging: Worldwide Perspectives,* 3rd ed., ed. Jay Sokolovsky, 196–215. Westport, CT: Praeger.

Zhang, Ni (Trans. Paulo Zanon). [1049–54] 1996." Weiqi in Thirteen Chapters *(Qijing Shisanpian)*." In "*Qijing Shisanpian* (the Classic of Weiqi in Thirteen Chapters) Its History and Translation," 1–37. www.figg.org/areafile/qijing.html

Zhang Ruan. 1998. *China's Weiqi History (Zhongguo weiqi shi)*. Beijing: Tuanjie.

Zhang, Xiguo (Shi-kuo Chang). 1978. *Chess King (Qiwang)*. Taipei, Taiwan: Hong Fang Books.

Zhao, Suisheng. 2004. *A Nation-State by Construction: Dynamics of Modern Chinese Nationalism*. Stanford, CA: Stanford University Press.

Zhao, Yuezhi. 2002. "The Rich, the Laid-Off, and the Criminal in Tabloid Tales: Read All about It!" In *Popular China: Unofficial China in a Globalizing Society*, eds. Paul Pickowicz, Perry Link, and Richard Madsen, 111–36. New York: Rowman & Littlefield.

Zheng, Tientien. 2007. "Performing Media-Constructed Images for First-Class Citizenship: Political Struggles of Rural Migrant Hostesses in Dalian." *Critical Asian Studies* 39(1):89–120.

———. 2009. *Ethnographies of Prostitution in Contemporary China: Gender Relations, HIV/Aids, and Nationalism.* New York: Palgrave MacMillan.

Zhong, Xueping. 2000. *Masculinity Besieged? Issues of Modernity and Male Subjectivity in Chinese Literature of the Late Twentieth Century.* Durham, NC: Duke University Press.

Zhou, Xianfa (Trans. Roy Schmidt). n.d. "The Politics of Go in Old Shanghai." *The Bob High Memorial Library.* usgo.orgbobhighlibrary

Zuo Qiuming. n.d. "The Chronicles of Zuo" (*Zuo zhuan*). In *The Four Books and Five Classics* (*Si shu wu jing*). (Zhang, Caimei, 2009 version editor). Beijing: Zhonghua Books.

INDEX

age limits, 10–11, 108–111, 144
aggression: and gender, 11–14, 20–21,
    44–50, 89, 124, 139, 144–147; nationally
    bound cultural identities, 63–64, 67,
    70, 147–148; national rivalries, 30,
    58–59. *See also* Seizing the Initiative
Allison, Anne, 95–96, 160n43
American Go Association, 9, 153n29
Anagnost, Ann, 101, 161n31, 161n35
appropriation of the past, xviii, 4, 10, 22–23,
    35, 44–45, 72, 77, 105–106, 146, 148
Aronofsky, Darren, 150n8, 151n3
Art of War. *See* Sunzi
astronomy and divination (associations
    with Weiqi), 25, 36–37, 153n32
Axe-Handle Story, 38, 154n49

Baker, Karl, 153n29
Baranovitch, Nimrod, 157n46, 157n60
Barlow, Tani, 157n62
Barmé, Geremie, 157n56
Boermel, Anna, 162n5, 162n15, 162n21
Boorman, Scott, 45, 151n2, 155n78
Bordo, Susan, 156n10
Boretz, Avron, 151n35, 151n38, 151n39,
    157n54, 157n66, 157n68
boys: as innately aggressive, 11, 14, 145; as
    innately different from girls 11–13; as
    innately intelligent or logical 12, 14;
    relatively strict disciplining compared
    to girls, 12, 86; as rowdy, 12–14, 85–86;
    training to become men, xviii, xix,
    20–21, 71, 90, 96, 145–146

Brook, Timothy, 161n39
Brown, Earnest, 153n41
Brownell, Susan, 93, 151n29, 151n37, 156,n31,
    157n49, 157n70, 160n37
Buddhism, 1, 25, 37–38, 47, 153n41, 154n54,
    161n38

candor as a disciplinary mechanism, 14,
    90–91, 139
career amateur players, 10, 107–113. *See also*
    Sun Yiguo
cheating, 41, 79, 86, 142–143, 154n42
Chen, Caiyun, 159n24
Chen, Nancy, 151n30, 156n48, 156n54
Chen, Zu-yan, 38, 154n45, 154n51, 155n65
Chen Yi, 61–62, 165
Cheng, Ah, 152n4, 152n5, 152n6, 153n47,
    154n54, 155n85, 155n86, 160n34
Chess: Chinese chess, 4, 16, 106–107, 122,
    134, 136, 149n4, 152n5–6, 154n47,
    154n54, 155n85–86, 160n34; Western
    (International) chess, xiii, xviii, 8, 14,
    26–33, 44, 48–49, 71, 88, 91, 106, 109,
    123, 128, 141–142, 149n4, 151n3, 152n19,
    153n25, 160n32, 160n34, 165
Cheung, King-Kok, 151n41, 157n57
Chou, Wah-shan, 50, 151n35, 156n13, 156n16
Chronicles of Zuo (Zuo Zhuan), 34–35
cinema, xvii, 24–25, 43, 50–56, 99. *See also*
    films
civil society, 100–103, 166. *See also* suzhi
class tensions, xvii, 98, 100, 160n3
cognition, 7, 11, 13, 48, 87–89, 128–129

179

Four Houses, the, 60
Four Olds, 25, 47
fox spirits, 41, 154n63
Fu, Peirong, 154n57, 154n59

Gallagher-Thompson, Dolores, 162n4
gambling, 33, 40–41, 142, 150n7
Gao, Mr. 130
generation gap, 67, 69, 72, 93, 116–117, 136–137; 143, 145. *See also* Little Emperors
Gerth, Karl, xxi, 159n4, 160n3
globalization, xviii, 3, 16, 22, 54, 57–58, 72, 99, 100–101, 116, 131, 141, 148
Go Seigen. *See* Wu Qingyuan
Gorris, Marleen, 150n8, 151n3, 160n34
greed, 25, 41, 89, 153n41
Gries, Peter Hays, 158n82, 158n89–90
Guan Yang, xx, 21, 64, 93
Guangong (Guanyu), 25, 46, 56
Guo, Juan, 158n101, 158n107

Hallman, J, C, xiii, 149n1, 150n8, 151n3
hand conversation, 37, 106, 138
Harrison, Henrietta, 57, 157n75
Harrist Jr., Robert, 53, 151n41, 156n33, 156n37
Hartman, John, 153n25
Hays, Peter, 158n82
He, Yunpo, 153n32, 153n32, 153n41, 154n48, 158n115
Hershatter, Gail, 151n29
Hesse, Hermann, 149n3, 152n3
Hewitt, Duncan, 149n4
Hikaru no Go, 46, 70, 155n87. *See also* Hotta, Yumi
Hong, Sung-Hwa, 119, 152n4, 152n6, 152n8, 154n61, 162n2
Hong Feng, 42–43, 66, 106–107, 121–122, 135, 137
Hong Kong, 16, 52, 55, 56–57
Hong Po, xxii, 75–81
Honig, Emily, 150n29
hooks, bell, 92, 160n35
Hotta, Yumi, 152n7, 155n87, 159n121. *See also* Hikaru no Go
Howard, Ron, 150n8, 151n3, 153n28
Hsieh Yi-min, 18–19

Hu, Tingmei, 135,153n32, 154n48, 154n49, 159n23, 159n28, 163n27
Huang, Martin, 151n36, 155n3, 156n14, 156n19, 156n24, 157n58, 157n61, 157n64
Huang, Tiancai, 152n10
Huang, Zichun, 68–69, 159n119
Hughes, Christopher, 157n74, 158n81, 158n84

IGS (Internet Go Server, a.k.a. Pandanet), 5–6, 9, 150n9

Jacka, Tamara, 161n25, 161n27, 161n35–36
Jackson, Richard, 162n7
Jankowiak, William, 150n29, 157n67
Japan: anime and manga, 5, 46; conflicts with China, xviii, 49, 56–61, 67, 86; economy, 23; historical supremacy in Weiqi, xix, 3, 49, 60; influences on Weiqi in other areas of the world, xix-xx, 3, 28–30, 81, 134, 153n29; masculinity, 53–54; military aggression, 17, 21, 44–45, 49, 54, 57–61; playing style, 21, 64–67, 70, 148; ranks, 10; respect for, 67–70, 88, 106; religious associations with Weiqi, 36, 38; Weiqi competitions, 18, 49, 62–63. *See also* cinema; fiction; gambling; Four Houses; Hikaru no Go; Taiwan
Johnson, George, 152n19–22
Jones, Andrew, 157n46
Juqibuding, 34–35

Kageyama, Toshiro, 162n14
Kawabata, Yasunari, xiii, 46, 149n2, 152n4–5, 154n61, 155n86, 160n34
Kelsky, Karen, 156n32
KGS (Kiseido Go Server), 5–7, 9, 29, 150n10
kibitzing, 4, 87, 128–130
Kipnis, Andrew, 101, 151n38, 161n25, 161n32
Kirby, William, 57, 157n76
Kissinger, Henry, 45, 155n80
Kong, Xiangming, 152n10
Korea. *See* South Korea
Kraus, Richard Curt, 150n5

Lai, David, 45, 155n79
Le Guin, Ursula, 151n3

Lee, Ang, 155n81
Lee, Boreom, 159n14, 159n19
Lei Feng, 136
Li, Zehou, 154n56
Little Emperors, 72, 145. *See also* generation gap
Little Liu, 107, 125, 129, 137
Liu, Fengshu, 150n18, 150n28–29, 161n24
Liu, Lydia, 157n62, 157n66
Liu, Shao-hua, 151n35
Liu Rongxin, 117
Liu Xiaoguan, 65, 89, 105
logic, 3, 11–14, 20, 25, 30–32, 72, 88–90, 94, 141, 144, 146
Louie, Kam, 50, 151n36, 156n7, 156n11, 156n38, 157n65, 157n73
Luo Guanzhong, 152n13, 155n84

Ma, Mr., 107, 125–126, 137
Ma, Xiping, 152n10, 159n27–28
mahjong, 150n7
male/female ratio in Weiqi, 11, 15–16, 108, 135, 146
Mao Zedong, 24, 46–47, 56, 62, 136
martial arts, 9, 45–46, 51–56, 92,151n29, 155n82
masculinity: in comparison with others (a relative status), 56; constructing, xix, 19–23, 96, 138–140, 144–146, 151n35; differences in history, 55–56; differences in region, 55–56; differences in class, 55, 138–140; effeminate men as ideal, 50–53, 56–57, 139, 157n47, emasculinization, 22, 50, 52–55, 57, 63; eunuchs, 50–51; intellect, xix, 3–4, 20–21, 46, 73, 77, 79, 92, 96–97, 103, 105, 116, 132, 142, 144–145, 147–148; and nation, xv, 20–23, 49, 52–54, 57, 70; hero (yingxiong), 21, 46, 51–53; manly men (nanzihan), 53; performance of, 21, 107, 157n66; rugged men (haohan), 51–53, 55–56, 147; stigmatized machismo, 50–54, 166; talented scholars (caizi), 50–51, 54, 56, 156n12; sexual orientation, 19, 51, 66, 151n35; sexuality, womanizing xix, 56, 54, 144, 154n63; Western and Japanese masculinities, 52–55, 57, 66. *See also* aggres-sion; boys; Confucian gentlemen; fatherhood; male/female ratio in Weiqi; Seizing the Initiative; wen and wu; wenrou

mass media, xv-vi, 16, 18, 53–59, 69, 71, 143, 166. *See also* films; novels
math, 22, 24, 72, 89
Mechner, David, 152n19, 152n21–22
memory, 7, 58–59, 87–89, 128–129, 132–133, 146, 148
Missingham, Joanne, 18–19
Mizuguchi, Fujio, 152n10, 155n67
Monopoly, 33
Morris, Andrew, xxi, 156n31–32, 157n50
Moskowitz, Marc, 151n33, 152n14, 154n63, 155n82, 156n15, 157n46, 157n60, 157n63, 157n73, 161n41
motherhood, xvii, 12–15, 82–83, 85, 94–96
Murasaki, Shikibu, 162n1
Murphy, Rachel, 161n25, 161n31, 161n35, 161n37
mythology. *See* Axe-Handle Story; Emperor Yao; Guan Yu

Nabokov, Vladimir, 151n3, 160n34
national team, 15–16, 61–64, 91–92, 113–114, 146, 151
nationalism, xviii-xix, 22–23, 30, 47, 49–50, 52–58, 67–70, 93, 100–101. *See also* competitions; Japan; Korea; sports; the United States
Needham, Joseph, 36, 153n32
neoliberalism, 101, 161n35. *See also* suzhi
Nie Weiping, 62–63, 75, 134, 165, 158n105, 165
Nie Weiping Center of Learning, 75
Nie Weiping Classroom, xxii, 75–83, 90
nostalgia. *See* appropriation of the past
novels: The Chess Master, 152n6, 154n47, 154n54, 155n85–86, 160n34; Chronicles of Zuo (Zuo Zhuan), 34–35; The Defense, 151n3, 160n34; First Kyu, 25, 119, 152n4, 152n6, 152n8, 154n61, 162n2; The Girl Who Played Go, 25, 46, 152n8, 155n83; The Glass Bead Game, 1, 149n3, 152n3; The Left Hand of Darkness, 151n3; The Master of Go, xiii, 46, 92, 149n2, 152n4–5, 154n62, 155n86,

United States: Chinese emulation of, 102, 131; cultural difference from China, 4, 24, 90–91, 102–103, 105, 121–122, 130; global power, 57–58; masculinity in, 52–55, 156n31, 166; mutual distrust with China, xvi-xvii, 23, 57–58, 86; similarities with China, xvii, 23, 46, 70, 117, 131, 136, 155n82, 155n86, 165; stigma of game players, 4, 91; views of Weiqi, xx, 8–9, 28, 153n29, 153n41. *See also* chess, middle class

urbanization. *See* rural/urban divide

Van Gulik, Robert, 156n27

Waitzkin, Fred, 71, 150n8, 151n3, 159n1, 160n34
Wang, Mr., 126, 135
Wang, Peter Chen-Main, 157n74
Wang, Xiao-lei, 150n22
Wang, Xing, 161n19, 161n21
Wang Wenbo, xxii, 1, 111–113, 144
war, xix, 17, 19–22, 24, 30, 33, 42–49, 54, 56–61, 69–70, 79, 89, 97, 116, 131, 141, 148, 155n69, 159n21. *See also* Sunzi; wen and wu
Wasserstrom, Jeffrey, xxi, 149n7–8, 151n37, 157n80, 162n22
Watson, James, 52, 156n30
Weber, Ian, 160n5, 161n39–40
Weinreb, Michael, 150n8, 151n3, 160n34
wen and wu, 49–50, 53, 56, 139–140, 148, 166
Wenbo School, xviii, 1, 13, 73–77, 81–84, 92, 159n10
wenrou, 57, 139, 166
Wolf, Margery, 151n37
Women: as dangerous, 154n63; exploitation of, xv, 20, 59; idealized women, 51; Iron Girls, 16, 150n29; mothers, 12, 14, 16, 82–83, 85, 94–96; new opportunities for, 12, 15–16, 55–56, 146–147; perceived limitations of, 11–14, 100; professional Weiqi players, 11, 16–19,

108, 146; roles of, 15, 81, 118, 146–147, 150n29; retirement, 120. *See also* male/female ratio in Weiqi; motherhood
Woronov, Terry, 159n2, 159n4, 160n38, 161n31, 161n35–36
Wu, Xiaoxin, 160n10, 161n14, 161n18
Wu Qingyuan (Go Seigen), 60–62, 166

Xie, Guofang, 37, 44, 153n32, 153n37–38, 154n55, 154n62–63, 155n74, 158n96, 159n21–22
Xu, Guoqi, 157n75, 157n79
Xu, Jialiang, 154n49, 155n64, 155n67
Xu, Mr., 124, 126
Xu, Wu, 160n10, 161n14, 161n18
Xue Lei, 103, 110–114, 117

Yang, Dongping, 160n6–7, 161n13, 161n15, 161n17
Yang, Xiaoguo, 153n32, 154n52
yin and yang, 36, 38–39, 47–48, 53, 55
Yu, Mr., 119, 123, 139
Yu Rongxin, 104, 110–113, 137, 144
Yue, Jin, 153n23

Zaillian, Steven, 151n3, 160n34
Zanon, Paulo, 149n1, 153n33, 154n52, 154n62, 155n66
Zhang, Hong, 162n10–12
Zhang, Mr., 126, 130
Zhang, Ni, 14, 36, 42–43, 97, 151n1, 153n33, 155n69–70, 160n2
Zhang, Xiguo, 152n4, 152n6, 154n54, 160n34
Zhang Ruan, 153n32
Zhao, Suisheng, 151n41
Zhao, Yuezhi, 160n3
Zheng, Mr., 124–125
Zheng, Tientien, 151n35, 151n38, 157n66
Zhong, Xueping, 151n36, 156n40, 157n69
Zhou, Xianfa, 158n99
Zuo, Qiuming, 153n31
Zuo Zhuan. *See* Chronicles of Zuo